MOT

MOTORING

MOTORS AND MOTORING

Henry J. Spooner, C.E.

M.I.MECH.E., A.M.INST.C.E., M.INST. A.E., F.G.S.,
HON.M.J.INST.E. F.R.MET.S., M.AMER.SOC. FOR PROMOTION OF
ENGINEERING EDUCATION

DIRECTOR AND PROFESSOR OF ENGINEERING, AND CHIEF EXAMINER IN
MOTOR CAR ENGINEERING IN THE POLYTECHNIC, REGENT STREET, LONDON
AUTHOR OF "MACHINE DESIGN, CONSTRUCTION, AND DRAWING," "NOTES ON
AND DRAWINGS OF A 4-CYLINDER PETROL ENGINE," "MACHINE DRAWING
AND DESIGN FOR BEGINNERS," " ELEMENTS OF GEOMETRICAL DRAWING,"
"INDUSTRIAL DRAWING AND GEOMETRY," " ENGINEERING WORKSHOP
DRAWING."

ETC. ETC.

TWELFTH EDITION

REVISED, WITH ADDITIONAL MATTER, INCLUDING APPENDICES AND
AN EXTENSIVE INDEX

AMBERLEY

First published 2015
Amberley Publishing
The Hill, Stroud
Gloucestershire, GL5 4EP

www.amberley-books.com

British Library Cataloguing in Publication Data.
A catalogue record for this book is available from the British Library.

ISBN 978 1 4456 4455 4 (paperback)

Typeset in 9.5pt on 12.5pt New Century Schoolbook LT Std.
Typesetting and Origination by Amberley Publishing.
Printed in the UK.

PREFACE

WITH the object of assisting beginners to acquire useful information relating to motors and motoring, the author consented to write this little work, much of the matter consisting of what may be considered an introduction to the mechanics of motoring. He has endeavoured to explain things in non-technical language as far as practicable, and in such a way that those who have not the time, inclination, or opportunity to study any of the large books on the subject, may easily be able to get a general grasp of the principles which underlie the construction, assembling, and working of petrol cars.

The Petrol Engine System is first dealt with, and a careful examination of Fig. 1, with the assistance of the accompanying text, should enable the reader to understand the relationship and interdependence of its various parts; these parts being further dealt with in separate Articles, not the least important of which is No. 13, on the Float-Feed Carburettor, which is explained with the assistance of Fig. 6, specially devised to show, on a single drawing, the important features of the best-known carburettors, an expedient the author has found very useful for educational purposes.

Most of the figures are diagrammatic, and have been drawn in such a way as to give prominence to their important features, whilst, for simplicity's sake, minor details have been omitted, the leading parts being so shaped that their functions can be best understood by the novice, and these remarks particularly apply to Figs. 18 and 19.

In estimating the fuel efficiency of a car (Art. 56), the various efficiencies made use of are approximate ones only; indeed, very little appears to have been done to determine their actual values for the different types of transmission gear in use. So motor engineers are looking forward with interest to the Transmission Gear Efficiency Tests which are to be made in the testing laboratory of the Conservatoire des Arts et Metiers in Paris next January.

No attempt has been made to describe any particular car, as the details of construction of any one make necessarily differ in many respects from all others. But the author hopes that the contents of the following pages will help the novice to easily trace out the run of the various connections, pipes, leads, &c., on a given car, and to quickly understand its general arrangement and working, and also become acquainted with the methods of adjustment and lubrication peculiar to it. All this can be much facilitated by referring to the Instruction Books now supplied with most cars, and by reading week by week one or more of the admirable technical journals which so loyally and ably represent, promote, and encourage the pastime and industry. Although, due to the exigencies of space, the author has had to confine himself mainly to motor cars, it should not be overlooked that petrol motors, whether they be used to propel cars, boats, airships, flying-machines, cycles, or machinery, have much in common.

The author's best thanks are due to his friend and former pupil, Mr. Tyson Sewell, A.M.Inst.E.E., for his kindness in reading the proof sheets of the Articles on Ignition. And he acknowledges his indebtedness to the motor press.

H. J. S.

PREFACE TO TWELFTH EDITION

Some of the articles, &c., at the end of the book have been rearranged and some new matter added.

H. J. S.

March 1916.

PREFACE TO FOURTH EDITION

THE favourable way in which this little work has been received has encouraged the author, in thoroughly revising it, to include much additional matter, not a little of which relates

PREFACE

to the fuel question, both in regard to the economical use of motor spirit and to the use of possible substitutes.

The author's best thanks are due to his friend Veitch Wilson, the famous authority on matters relating to lubricants and lubrication, for his kindness in reading the proof sheets of Articles 12 to 50, and 116 to 126, and in making some useful and greatly appreciated suggestions. His thanks are also due to Mr. J. W. G. Brooker, F.I.C., for kindly contributing some helpful remarks.

The author is indebted to the technical press of England and America for information he has found useful, and whenever he has drawn from such sources or from technical works, or the proceedings of scientific and professional societies, he believes he has suitably acknowledged it.

For the guidance of the many young engineers and others who take a practical interest in the Annual Examination in Motor Car Engineering held by the Department of Technology of the City and Guilds of London Institute, the Syllabus of the subject, some recent Examination Papers set by the Department, and the Polytechnic papers for this year have been added. It will be found that many of the questions are of the type which interests the intelligent owner or driver of a car almost as much as they do the designer and constructor.

H. J. S.

June 1909.

PREFACE TO FIFTH EDITION

THE call for another edition has enabled the author to correct some slight errors which crept into the previous issue in re-writing some of the articles, slips that were not detected in time for correction before going to press. Any others that may be detected by the reader the author will be grateful to hear about.

The work has been generally revised for this Edition. It was in the Fourth Edition, published in June 1909, that the author first called attention to the advisability of examining the question of producing a home-made fuel, and he discussed the points in favour of alcohol and benzol as substitutes for petrol (pp. 216-241), which led to the matter being investigated in South Africa, where they have in second quality mealies an excellent raw material for the production of alcohol. Since that time the price of petrol has steadily advanced, and the fuel problem now is one of alarming economic importance to the whole Empire. Fortunately, some of our leading engineers, chemists, and economists are now engaged in tackling the general problem in all its bearings, and the time cannot be far off when alcohol (the ultimate fuel) will be extensively used as a motor spirit. Indeed, Mr. W. R. Ormandy, D.Sc., on November 12th, in a valuable paper he read before the Institution of Automobile Engineers, giving an account of his experiments, said that a conclusion he came to in conjunction with the best existing literature was "that the modern high-speed petrol engine will run on a half-and-half mixture of benzol and alcohol with as much power, flexibility, ease of starting, silence and economy in consumption, as with its ordinary petrol fuel; and this with merely slight modifications to existing types of carburettors." Further, "that the experiments bear out the contention that progress towards the final goal of using alcohol virtually as the sole fuel is to be sought by experimental work on mixtures containing gradually diminishing amounts of benzol."

H. J. S.

December 1913.

CONTENTS

MOTORS AND MOTORING

CONTENTS

CONTENTS

TABLES

CONTENTS

APPENDIX I

BRITISH AND METRICAL EQUIVALENTS RELATING TO THE
FOLLOWING

APPENDIX II

ILLUSTRATIONS

MOTORS AND MOTORING

INTRODUCTION

1. No one can fail to notice the growing interest the typical "man in the street" is taking in Motors[1] and Motoring. His eyes instinctively turn to critically view each passing car, and he knows that a peculiar ticking noise is a sure indication of the approach of an electric carriage, and light puffs of steam from underneath a car[2] a certain sign that it is a steam vehicle, whilst his ear is so delicately attuned to the wide range of detonations, due to the working of petrol motors, that he is rarely at fault in placing such cars in the right category; but, should he be in doubt, the offensive odour[3] of the exhaust gases from the cars too often gives his olfactory organ an opportunity of assisting in the matter, and he is generally able to differentiate between the various types of cars in use. Presumably he has not failed to notice that the electric car is used almost exclusively for town work, often in the form of a brougham. Its great weight for a comparatively small power, the limited distance it can run without recharging the batteries, to say nothing of its cost, and the

---

[1] Motor is a recognised abbreviation of "Motor Car"; strictly speaking, the *motor* is the *engine,* whilst a motor car, *autocar,* or *automobile,* as it is sometimes called, is the name for the complete vehicle.

[2] It should be mentioned that some of the best makes seldom, if ever, show any exhaust.

[3] The obnoxious odour of the exhaust gases that so often offend is largely due to the condensation of petrol vapour, which occurs before the engine, &c., is properly warmed up, and to the volatilisation of unsuitable lubricating oil used in excess in the cylinders, or to its unsuitable quality, Refer to Articles 116 to 125.

cost of running, precludes this otherwise almost perfect car from use for touring purposes, so that for long distances only petrol and steam cars are at present available; and, for reasons which will be explained later, comparatively few of the latter are now running. Thus the petrol engine is used in the great majority of cars now running, to say nothing of the enormous and rapidly increasing number of motor cabs, buses and bicycles now in use, in which the motive power is the petrol engine. This doubtless accounts for the kind of motor language that is heard at every turn by "the man in the street," and, if the truth must be known, by the boy in the school; for, strangely enough, the schoolboy's allegiance to the locomotive has been wavering in favour of the automobile for some time, and now his school locker generally contains a rare collection of pictures, plates, postcards, technical journals, and parts of models relating to autocars and motor bicycles, instead of such things concerning the various types of locomotives that were formerly so much in favour;[1] indeed, it is often astonishing to see what an amount of intelligent interest all kinds of people take in the arrangement and working of motor vehicles. This is particularly displayed whenever a car is stopped in a public street, and its bonnet is lifted for a moment or two;[2] the usual crowd, which seems to spring from the road itself, immediately surrounds the car, and much advice, more or less pertinent, is freely offered, and although the unhappy motorist may not profit much by it, he cannot fail to be impressed with the growing knowledge the "man in the street" has of autocar matters. Of course, this knowledge is in most cases very superficial and unsound, and requires to be organised and supplemented by a good grasp, or at least a rudimentary knowledge, of the principles which underlie and govern the construction and working of the motor, before it is of any practical use. So the author, in arranging the Articles

---

[1] In this connection there cannot be a doubt that the great progress we are making in automo bilism has had not a little to do with the astonishing increase in the number of boys whose greatest ambition is to become engineers.

[2] Since these lines wors writte (in 1904)' there har been a great improvement in the reliability of cars, and one now rarely sees an involuntary stoppage in the streets.

in this little work, has endeavoured to explain in simple, and as far as possible in non-technical, language the principles of construction and working that every potential motorist and driver should be acquainted with[1] before he attempts to drive a car upon the King's highway.

VARIOUS TYPES OF STANDARD CARS

2. Some idea of the range of power, price, and kind of cars that have been more or less standardised[2] by English and foreign makers can be formed by a glance at the *Autocar* list of 1909 cars, published on November 7, 1908, in which particulars of 473 petrol cars, constructed by 132 different makers, are given. These vary in power and price, from the 6-horse-power[3] Rover at £150 complete, and the 6-horse-power Torpedo at £125 complete, to the 90- horse-power, 6-cylinder Napier at £1460 complete. And between these extremes it is reasonable to suggest that there is something to suit every one's requirements. It is instructive to notice that of the 473 petrol cars, 323 of them are arranged for the transmission of power from the engine to the road wheels by propeller shaft, 97 by chains,[4] 27 by either method, and 26 by worm or planetary gears, &c. The list also gives particulars of **10 steam cars,**[5] exhibited by five different makers.

In a return of the private motor cars, industrial vehicles, public service conveyances, and motor cycles in use in the British Isles, it appears that 154,391 machines of all these kinds (including 65,026 motor bicycles), were licensed by June 1909, as against a total of 74,038 in 1904–5.

It is also interesting to note that, in addition to the motor

---

[1] The Articles in small type and those on alcohol, &c., near the end of the book need not be read by beginners or by the general reader.

[2] In most cases the Standard Chassis can also be had with a longer wheel base for special coach work.

[3] The word *horse-power* is usually abreviated to H. P. in technical works.

[4] Showing the trend of design so far as transmission-gear is concerned, it is interesting to compare these figures with those referring to the cars exhibited in March 1904. The petrol ones numbered 349, and of these 197 were fitted with propeller shafts, 167 with chains, and 2 were driven by belts.

[5] In 1904, 13 steam cars were exhibited.

car registration marks A, LC, LN, LB, LD, LA, LE, IF, LH, LK, LL, LM, each representing 10,000 cars, assigned in succession to the London County Council, since the passing of the Motor Act of 1903, the Local Government Board has acceded to the Council's request for the index mark LO, which will be affixed to the thirteenth 10,000 cars.

ELEMENTS OF A MOTOR CAR

3. Every car, whether it be driven by electricity, steam, or petrol,- consists of two principal parts, namely, *the carriage body* and the *chassis*.[1] The former is practically complete in itself; the latter embodies the following principal elements, the frame, to which the motor proper and its accessories are attached—the transmission gear (including the chains in chain-driven cars), axles, springs, road wheels, steering gear, &c.

A complete car, with all its fittings and accessories, appears to most novices a very complicated vehicle, but when it is carefully examined, and the function of each element and fitting understood, it really is often a fairly simple machine—particularly is this so in cars that have not been overloaded with refinements and fittings of doubtful utility. It has frequently been remarked that the general appearance of a car (with the exception of an electric one) is often no sure indication of the arrangement of its component parts, or the type of its motor, as makers have, with very few exceptions, adopted the outward form that every one is familiar with, and to accomplish this have even, in some cases, put on

---

[1] This French word has become anglicised. In France, when strictly used, it formerly meant the *frame part* only, but now, as in this country, the word chassis is used to denote the engineer's part of the complete car; in fact, a motor car as it leaves the works, *i.e.* without coachwork. As some makers keep down the price of their chassis by omitting certain parts, the purchaser should be careful to see that the specification includes the following, or make allowance for their omission in comparing the prices of different cars.

The complete chassis should include tyres, full kit of tools, spares, dash- and tail-lamps, signal horn, petrol tank, dash-board, foot-board over the pedals, bonnet, under-casing of motor and gear and front wings or mud-guard's The chassis does not include rear wings and stays, outride foot-boards or outside foot-board stays, as these parts are supplied and fitted by the body-builder.

dummy fittings and accessories. This tendency is particularly noticeable where a characteristic feature of some famous car is so imitated that at first sight it is not easy even for an expert to name the maker. It is a practice much to be deprecated, more particularly as some of the designers who have thus sinned have produced cars of such excellence that they should well be able to hold their own without such adventitious assistance. On the other hand, for obvious reasons there is much to be said in favour of co-ordinating in new cars, as far as is practicable, the driving fittings and arrangements (more particularly the pedals and brake levers), with those which are considered best arranged on the leading cars.

It will now be convenient to give some detailed attention to the various *elements* of the petrol car, commencing with the motor.

THE PETROL MOTOR
Elements of the Complete Engine

4. We have explained in footnote 1 to page 1, that the word motor, when strictly used, refers to the engine which drives the car or cycle; but as the term is often very loosely used, even by experts, who of course know exactly what they are talking about and to what they refer, it will be well to make clear that for our purpose the **petrol motor** will be considered to be **the complete working engine,** one that could either be used to drive a car, a boat, or any machine, such as a lathe, where power is to be transmitted to some rotating part—that is to say, the motor must embody the engine proper, and such auxiliaries as the carburettor, ignition apparatus, silencer, **&c. The engine** proper, as we have called it, is diagrammatically represented by Figs. 2 to 5; but as it is often referred to as the *Motor*, to be clear on this point, before we further proceed, it must be understood that when we use the word **motor** the **complete system** is referred to. Needless to say, this explanation is given to prevent that confusion of thought and meaning which too often hampers the progress of the tyro who is studying the

THE PETROL MOTOR

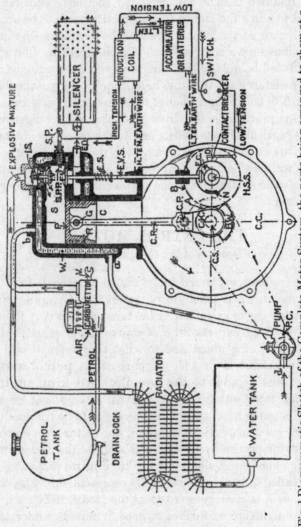

Fig. 1. Diagrammatic Sketch of the Complete Motor System, the parts being arranged to show at a glance their interdependence

THE PETROL MOTOR

DIAGRAMMATIC SKETCH OF THE COMPLETE SYSTEM, d.STORTED, AND PARTS ARRANGED
TO SHOW AT A GLANCE THEIR INTERDEPENDENCE

REFERENCE NOTES FOR FIG. 1

C. Cylinder

W. Water Cooling Jacket.

P. Piston.

R. Piston Rings.

I.V. Inlet Valve.

I.S. Inlet Valve Spring.

E.V. Exhaust Valve.

E.S. Spring to hold the Exhaust Valve down.

T.T. Supplementary Air Inlets.

V. Rod for control of Throttle.

E.O. Exhaust Outlook.

E.V.S. Exhaust Valve Spindle.

E.C. Exhaust Valve Cam.

A. and B. Two-to-Ono Gear Wheels.

C.C. Crank Case.

CK. Crank.

C.R. Connecting Rod

C.P. Crank-Pin.

B.W. Crank Balance-Weight

H.S.S. Half-Speed Shaft.

C.S. Crank-Shaft.

S. Combustion Chamber or Space.

G. Gudgeon or Piston-Pin.

S.P. Sparking Plug.

S.P.P. Sparking Plug Points.

I.S. Spring to hold Inlet Valve up

P.C. Circulating Pump

N. Brass Sector.

O. Contact Breaker

7

internal economy of the Motor Car. The first lesson in the art and pastime of motoring might very appropriately be a brief description of the petrol motor, and to facilitate this the author has made a **diagrammatic sketch** (Fig. 1) of what he has called the **complete system,** which shows the engine in relation to the subsidiary elements of the complete motor. Obviously, the component parts are arranged in such a way, in relation to one another, as to show at a glance their interdependence, and enable the beginner to get a grasp of the principles which govern the working of the machine; this means that all the parts must be arranged in the same plane, and some of them made to appear larger than they would be if they were drawn to scale. In other words, we have a **distorted sketch**, showing the **elements spread out for ready inspection**;[1] and a careful examination of the figure will enable the reader to become familiar with the technical names of the most important elements, details, &c., which will greatly assist him in understanding the description of the motor which is to follow.

DESCRIPTION OF THE PETROL MOTOR
Or "Internal-Combustion Engine"

5. As we have explained, the motor, although an element of the car, is a complete heat engine, consisting of a number of elements ingeniously arranged in relation to one another to form a whole working machine, in which the potential energy of the petrol is converted into moving energy at the crank-shaft (C.S., Fig. 1), All petrol engines in general use are reciprocating ones, that is to say, the straight line potion of the piston (P., Fig. 1) is converted into the circular motion of the crank-shaft by means of a connecting rod (C.R., Fig. 1) and crank (CK., Fig. 1). jfow, every single-cylinder reciprocating engine must be fitted with a fly-wheel,[2] fixed to the

---

[1] It should be hardly necessary to explain that for a fixed position of the engine on the frame of the car, the auxiliary elements of the motor can be fixed in an infinite number of positions in relation to one another, so long as they are connected up as shown in the figure.

[2] This wheel is not shown on the diagram; it generally also forms the outer shell of

crank-shaft, to carry the crank over the dead-centre;[1] but in the petrol or gas engine this wheel has also another function to perform, which can better be explained after we have made clear what goes on in the cylinder during the engine's complete cycle.

THE OTTO CYCLE

6. The petrol motor is an "internal-combustion engine," that is to say, one in which a mixture of petrol vapour and air, automatically made in an element called the carburettor (by the action of the engine), in such proportions as to form an explosive mixture, is drawn into the cylinder by the engine itself and electrically ignited, causing combustion to occur, and the piston to be pushed down with great force by the pressure of the burning and expanding gases, this pressure on the piston being transmitted through the connecting rod to the crank-shaft.

The series of operations which take place in the cylinder to form a complete cycle correspond to four strokes of the piston and two revolutions of the crank-shaft, and these operations make up what is called the "Otto cycle," after Dr Otto,[2] who introduced it in 1876 in his "Silent" gas engine.

THE FOUR STROKES

An examination of Figs. 2 to 5 (which have been drawn, with the positions of certain parts slightly altered, so that each essential detail can be seen quite distinctly, to conveniently

---

the friction clutch. In the engines of motor bicycles the liy-wheel and crank are usually combined.

[1] When the crank and connecting rod come into the same straight Hue, obviously no pressure on the piston, however great, could cause the crank-shaft to turn; but by fixing a fly-wheel to the crank-shaft, the momentum given to it during the explosion stroke of the piston carries the crank over the *dead-centre*, as it is called.

[2] The four-stroke cycle was first suggested by Beau de Rochas in 1862, but the gas engine invented by Dr. Otto, and made by Crossley Brothers, first established the economy and efficiency of internal-combustion engines working on this cycle. The invention was the subject of a patent granted in 1876, No. 2081, to C. D. Abel, for improvements in gas motor engines (a communication from abroad by N. A. Otto).

THE PETROL ENGINE

DIAGRAMMATIC DRAWINGS SHOWING THE FOUR STROKES
OF THE OTTO CYCLE

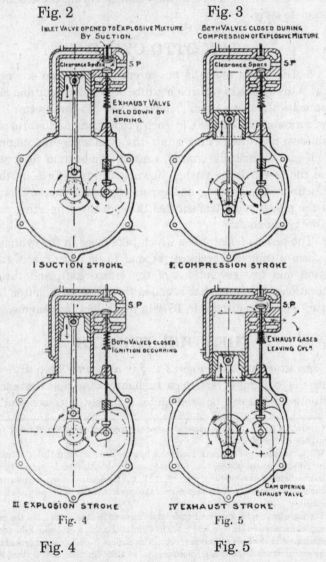

Fig. 2

INLET VALVE OPENED TO EXPLOSIVE MIXTURE
BY SUCTION

Clearance Space   S.P.

EXHAUST VALVE
HELD DOWN BY
SPRING

I SUCTION STROKE

Fig. 3

BOTH VALVES CLOSED DURING
COMPRESSION OF EXPLOSIVE MIXTURE

Clearance Space   S.P.

II COMPRESSION STROKE

S.P.

BOTH VALVES CLOSED
IGNITION OCCURRING

III EXPLOSION STROKE

Fig. 4

S.P.

EXHAUST GASES
LEAVING CYLʳ

CAM OPENING
EXHAUST VALVE

IV EXHAUST STROKE

Fig. 5

Fig. 4

Fig. 5

illustrate this description) will enable the reader to be clear about what occurs during each stroke.

1st. **The Suction or Charging Stroke** (Fig. 2).— During the first out-stroke of the piston a partial vacuum is formed, and, the piston acting as a pump, the explosive mixture is drawn into the cylinder through the inlet valve, the spring of which is only sufficiently strong to hold up the valve on its seat.

2nd. **The Compression Stroke** (Fig. 3).— During the return or in-stroke both the inlet and exhaust valves are closed, and the explosive mixture, which was drawn in during the previous stroke, is compressed by the piston into the clearance space (or combustion chamber).

3rd. **The Explosion and Expansion Stroke** **(Fig. 4)**.—The compressed charge is ignited by an electric spark[1] after the crank has just passed the dead- centre; and the pressure, due to the heat energy developed by the combustion, so rapidly rises that, before the piston has appreciably moved on this second or *explosion* stroke, it reaches its maximum, and work is done on the piston by the expanding gases.

4th. **The Exhaust Stroke** (**Fig. 5**).—When the piston has travelled about four-fifths of its explosion stroke, the *exhaust valve* is opened[2] by the cam on the two-to-one shaft[3] to reduce the back pressure (or give *release)*; the exhaust taking place during this fourth stroke of the cycle, or second return or in-stroke; the products of combustion being discharged from the cylinder, the gases which remain in the clearance space (or combustion chamber) minglingwith the incoming explosive mixture of the next charge.

Thus it will be seen that the *clearance space* (Fig. 2) is filled with the products of combustion at about atmospheric

[1] Refer to Article 60.

[2] The time of opening the valve should vary with the piston speed, being earlier the higher the speed. Refer to Article 8.

[3] This shaft is shown in Fig. 1. It is connected with the crank-shaft by a system of tooth wheels, which make the cam-shaft rotate once, whilst the engine-shaft rotates twice; thus the exhaust valve opens once during every two rotations of the crank-shaft.

pressure when we commence to trace the working of the engine; and the piston, whilst it compresses the explosive mixture and makes the other strokes, with the exception of the explosion one (the third), is driven by the energy stored in the rotating fly-wheel.

Strangely enough, this method of working (the Otto cycle) has never been equalled in efficiency by any other the mechanical genius of the world has been able to devise. Up to the time of its introduction, gas engines were worked by drawing in the charge during the first portion of the stroke and then firing it, the work being performed during the remaining portion of the stroke;[1] but the real and fundamental improvement made by Otto was the compressing of the contents of the cylinder (the explosive mixture) into the clearance space at the end before the charge was fired. This cycle of operations was new and original, and was founded upon true mechanical principles. The mode of working is not only admirable when examined from a mechanical point of view, but there is also the positive and direct gain of dealing with a compressed charge, instead of one at atmospheric pressure[2] (the engine acting as its own compressing pump); for the advantage of being able to start at the instant of explosion with the compressed contents of a whole cylinder full of explosive mixture, instead of the uncompressed contents of half a cylinder, is evident to ordinary apprehension. Then it is also claimed that the residue of the products of combustion remaining in the cylinder (the contents of the clearance space) after an exhaust stroke may act as a cushion to moderate the effect of the explosion upon the piston[3] during the next working stroke.

[1] The Lenoir engine, patented 8th February 1860.

[2] In recent years there has been a marked increase in the pressure to which the charge is compressed in gas engines, with a corresponding increase in efficiency.

[3] There is much to be said for and against this theory. Indeed, Capt. Longridge holds that **higher pressures are recorded as residual gases take the place of an excess of air,** and designed an engine to give effect to this theory. And we have Grover's statement that "The maximum pressure obtained from a given quantity of coal gas rises as the excess of air is diminished by the addition of products of combustion; but this no longer holds good when the volume of air to coal gas approaches the pro-Sortion of 10 to 1." Apparently a fresh .Mixture of

If we are to maintain, in explaining matters, something approaching a sequence, it will be convenient to now give a little attention to the valves of the engines.

VALVES

7. In the previous Article we have explained how the *inlet* or induction valve (called **automatic inlet** valve, and abbreviated to **A.I.V.**) is automatically opened by the suction action of the piston in the first stroke, being just kept on its seat at other times by the action of a weak spring;[1] on the other hand, we have seen that the exhaust valve was mechanically operated or lifted by a cam fixed on the *half-speed* or **two-to-one** shaft, the valve being spring-closed. Now the automatic working of the inlet valve, although simple and, under ordinary conditions of working, very effective, is not scientifically sound, particularly for high speeds, as the clearance space at the commencement of the first stroke is full of the burnt gases above atmospheric pressure, (due to the back pressure from the silencer; therefore, when the piston begins its suction stroke, these gases have to expand before the fresh mixture can be drawn in by the piston, hence the sluggish action of the valve in opening, just when it should be promptly responding to the invitation to move given by the piston when it commences its stroke; indeed, to secure a full charge in high-speed motors the inlet valve should open at the same instant as the exhaust valve closes, that is, when

petrol vapour and air does not easily mix with the burnt gases; probably stratification more or less occurs.

[1] This **spring** must be perfectly **adjusted for correct working.** If too weak, the valve will not close rapidly enough to prevent the escape of explosive mixture on the commencement of the compression stroke, and will subsequently close with violent impact on its seat; with such a spring the motor might be run very slowly, but it would be quite useless for high speeds. On the other hand, **if** the spring be **too** strong, it does not allow the valve to open readily enough, or to its full extent, to allow a full charge of mixture to enter, and the power of the motor is therefore reduced. A common practice is to arrange the spring so that an air pressure of one lb. per square inch will open it, but to get the best results the tension of the spring should be made adjustable. Spare springs are usually supplied long enough to allow them to be cut away bit by bit till the valve closes with a light beat.

the piston reaches the top of its exhaust stroke. Moreover, the effect of the inertia of the valve becomes more pronounced as the speed of the engine increases, and the volume of intake suffers whilst the metallic noise of the valve beating on its seat is objectionable. So, primarily for these reasons, makers have for some years, in increasing numbers, been fitting motors with **mechanically operated inlet valves** (abbreviated to **M.O.I.V.**), worked in the same way as the exhaust valves from a half-speed shaft.[1] This enables the time of opening and **closing of the inlet valve** to be arranged with **mathematical precision**,[2] and (should it be thought desirable) the valve to remain open a shade after the piston commences the compression stroke,[3] so that the momentum of the entering mixture may slightly add to the charge, before the piston on its change of stroke has converted the slight vacuum in the cylinder to a pressure above atmospheric.

In strictly examining the **relative merits** of these two **arrangements**, we ought to take into account the efficiency of the carburettor that is used in conjunction with each; but for our present purpose it will suffice to point out that in the **M.O.I.V.** a continuous flow of mixture can be relied upon for a definite movement of the piston, if the carburettor is capable of satisfactorily carburetting a sufficient quantity of air to keep pace with the protracted draw upon it, due to the longer time the valve remains open, as compared with an automatic one, for the latter cannot leave its seat till the vacuum in the cylinder is good enough to cause the spring to extend; the valve then suddenly opens, when a considerable inrush of mixture occurs, but the valve does not remain unclosed during the completion of the suction stroke, but rapidly flutters or pulsates on and off the seat (in a way every one can understand who is familiar with the behaviour of springs) till

---

[1] In some motors the same shaft operates both valves, but the more general arrangement is a separate shaft each side of the engine.

[2] Of course, the wear of valve stem ends, and cams sooner or later affects this precision. Refer to Article 8.

[3] For further information relating to the timing of the valves refer to the next Article.

the end of the stroke is reached,[1] consequently the demand on the carburettor is intermittent, and therefore less exhausting than in the other case.

Makers have from time to time, in acceding to the demand for mechanically operated valves, met with a good deal of trouble before they have reached satisfactory results; but the conditions which must be satisfied are so well understood now, that there is no difficulty in producing engines fitted with mechanically operated valves that are highly efficient, and are connected to carburettors adapted to their peculiar needs. Such valves are made **interchangeable** with the exhaust valves; they can never stick nor become sluggish in working, through oil or other foreign matter clogging the valve or its stem, and with them the engine at slow speeds is more easily controlled, their use involving a mere repetition of the cam gear required for the exhaust valve.

Of course, this slight complication is not in their favour, but in the best cars the design and workmanship are so excellent that they give no trouble; indeed, this is a case where some sacrifice of simplicity can be safely made for increased efficiency and flexibility.[2]

8. **Timing the Valves.**—We have explained in a general way how the inlet and exhaust valves behave, but, strangely enough, there is no commonly accepted practice as to the exact moment when the valves should open and close in relation to the position of the piston, each designer deciding these points for himself. Of course, the exact moment at which the **exhaust valve** should open mainly depends upon the speed of the piston, but, **for average speeds, it opens** after the piston has completed about eight-tenths of its explosion stroke. The exact amount, by which the **closing of the exhaust valve** should be delayed in any given case, is best determined by experiment. **Generally at low speeds it closes exactly when the exhaust stroke of**

---

[1] This action causes the actual working area to be only about half what it would be if the opening remained constant, so that an A.I.V. is made larger than a M.O.I.V

[2] Some engineers, whose opinions are entitled to respect, prefer, on the whole, the A.I.V., particularly for high speeds.

the piston is completed, but in some well-known engines it closes a little later. In the Cadillac, for instance, it closes $\frac{1}{64}$" past top of exhaust stroke, and in the De Dion $\frac{3}{32}$".

As to the **inlet valve**, the usual practice is to open it **immediately the exhaust closes**, and to close it either at the **end of the suction stroke or** at some point **between the end and about I" from the bottom** of the compression stroke, depending upon the speed of the engine. **Generally, the higher the speed the later the closing.**

9. **Leaky Valves.**—A fruitful source of trouble and loss of efficiency in the petrol motor is leaky valves. The burning and erosive effect of the hot gases (particularly if an exhaust valve has been held off its seat by dirt), and hammering of valves on their seats, must sooner or later lead to a sensible amount of wear occurring, both on valves and seats, even when the materials are just as perfect as it is possible to make them; but this legitimate wear is greatly increased in cases where the materials are too soft, or are in some other respects unsuitable. Of course, if this wear took place with absolute uniformity, without the surface departing from its true form, there is no reason why leakage should occur, but in practice, after a certain amount of wear, all valves leak, it being only a matter of degree; indeed, should the power of the motor diminish, and there is reason to suppose that it is due to leaky valves, the valves should be examined, and if there is any doubt about an inlet one, the spare valve (which should always be carried as part of the equipment) should be put in to replace it, and the old one can be examined and reground, if necessary, at home. The effect of leaky valves is at once felt, as during the compression stroke the mixture is forced through them, so that there is a smaller charge, and a full pressure cannot be reached during either the compression or power stroke.

10. **Grinding in Valves** is an operation that had better be left to the trained mechanic to perform, but cases occasionally occur where one is not available, and many owners of cars like to be able to do these little jobs themselves,

or at any rate to know how they are done. So a few words relating to them will not be out of place. Now, if the valve is merely inclined to stick, it should be well washed out with petrol, which will clear it of any bad oil or dirt. If, on the other hand, it requires grinding, as exhaust valves generally do **every 1500 or 2000 miles**, it will be found that the conical or mushroom valve has a groove cut on its upper part to fit a screw-driver or screw-driver bit that can be worked with a drill brace.[1] The grinding material is a paste made of ordinary lubricating oil and fine sharp emery powder;[2] the seat of the valve should be smeared with this, and the valve twisted backwards and forwards on its seat (under considerable pressure), with the screw-driver or brace, being taken off occasionally, turned half-way round, and the face resmeared to prevent grooving. This tedious operation must be continued until both surfaces present a bright and even appearance, without inequalities past which gas could escape. A piece of cotton waste should be carefully placed to prevent any of the powder or dirt getting into the cylinder and causing serious trouble.

11. **Valve Lifter.**—To enable a motor bicycle to be freely pushed along or pedalled when the engine is not working, it is necessary to open the exhaust valve to prevent the motor being converted into an air-compressor, for, obviously, a good deal of work would have to be done by the cyclist on the machine in giving motion to the piston during the compression stroke.[3] So, to obviate this, motor bicycles are fitted with a device called a *Valve Lifter,* by means of which the exhaust valve may be kept permanently lifted at the driver's will. This fitting enables him to start the engine by walking the bicycle and suddenly letting go the lifter after the

[1] Of course, this necessitates **removing** the cotter-**pin from** the valve Stem. To do this, turn the crank so that the valve is fully lifted, then place a hard wood peg under opposite sides of the spring washer, and bearing on the crank chamber; turn the crank until the valve-lifter falls, and push the valve on to its seat. The cotter can then be pulled out and the valve withdrawn, the wooden legs supporting the spring and washer.

[2] Meteoric Knife Polish is a preparation of emery powder, and will do.

[3] Of course, the whole of this work is not lost, as some of it is recovered during expansion.

fly-wheel has had given to it enough momentum to perform the compression stroke. Skilful use of this lifter when on down grades will have a cooling effect on the cylinder (which often tends to become too hot for satisfactory working), cool air[1] being drawn into the cylinder through the exhaust pipe from the silencer each two revolutions of the engine. The only objection to this convenient expedient is, that the air in passing through the silencer tends to carry with it any dirt *or* dust that may be in it.

When using the lifter care must be taken to cut out the spark, or explosions may occur in the silencer.

We may now proceed to describe the nature of the explosive mixture, and how it is produced ready for use in the cylinder.

CARBURATION AND CARBURETTORS

12. If the odour of escaping gas be detected in a house, it is proverbial that the ordinary householder will seek for the leak with a lighted candle, too often with a result that every one has heard of and no one seems to profit by. In such cases the escaping gas mingles with the air in the room and carburates[2] it, as it is called—that is to say, the carbon and hydrogen of the gas, of which it nearly wholly consists, become rapidly diffused in the air, the oxygen of which forms, or tends to form, with the hydrocarbon gas an explosive mixture which only requires igniting to cause an accident.[3]

Now the **explosive mixture** we use in the petrol motor

---

[1] After the engine has been running the silencer becomes very hot, and therefore the first few charges of air which pass into the cylinder when the lifter is used are warmer than the outside air.

[2] When air is impregnated with carbon, it is said to be carburetted or carburised.

[3] It is instructive to note that a mixture of this kind may be either too weak or too strong to explode, as for complete combustion about 6 3 *volumes* of air to 1 of gas are required; but the range of ignition appears to be about 1 of gas to 5 of air, to 1 of gas to 13 of air. And so, in the cylinder of the motor, we may have a charge which consists of too much air, or, the more usual case, one that has been super-carburetted (one that is too rich in petrol vapour). Between these extremes there is a particular or critical mixture that in any case will be more efficient than any other, as we shall directly see.

consists of **air carburetted by the vapour of petrol,**[1] and the apparatus used to prepare or form this mixture is called a **carburettor,** a fitting that appears in a great variety of forms; indeed, a month rarely passes without the pages of our admirable motor journals being adorned with some new device, which more or less differs from existing ones. There is nothing astonishing about this when it is understood how easily a mixture can be made, for every one has noticed how quickly a little Eau de Cologne vaporises when applied to the hands or face. The same thing occurs **with petrol**; it is an exceedingly volatile spirit, rapidly evaporating when exposed to the air, and this action is much increased by the application of heat, but it (light petrol) does not require any *preliminary* heating for use in even the smallest engines. It can be readily vaporised by the simplest and crudest form of carburettor, and this principally accounts for the wonderful flexibility of the petrol motor; indeed, it now appears difficult to make a motor that won't go, although years ago, when so many were commencing to experiment with motors who were unacquainted with matters relating to carburation and ignition, much trouble was experienced in coaxing them into motion.

If an explosive mixture can be readily produced, it is not such an easy matter to satisfy all the **important conditions, for a satisfactory carburettor** should be capable of regularly supplying a perfectly adjusted mixture of petrol vapour and air (in which the fuel is completely vaporised), to the motor cylinder under all conditions of speed, load, and temperature;[2] it should be self-adapting, and be able to automatically and definitely carburet the air to form a mixture of an exactly predetermined degree under all conditions of working. The very perfect speed control, over a wide range, of some of the best- known motors is largely due to

---

[1] Petrol is also a hydrocarbon. Refer to Article on the fuel, p. 43.

[2] Most carburettors on large cars are fitted with **hot jackets** for use in cold and damp weather, as will be explained, the heat of the engine itself sufficing in other cases to make up for the **refrigerative effect of** the evaporation of the petrol.

these conditions being more or less satisfied, and to a well-controlled throttle[1] and ignition.[2]

In designing carburettors it is a maxim that the explosive mixture must never be saturated at the minimum temperature of the carburettor. In practice this means that the carburettor must be heated, and the supply of air increased in the case of a fuel of low volatility, like heavy petrol or alcohol, as we shall see later.

13. **The Float-Feed Carburettor.**—The type of carburettor that has survived all others, owing to its simplicity and absolute automatic action, is the *float-feed* one or **spray or jet** kind, shown in Fig. 6, which shows the principal features of the class of carburettor to which it belongs. **An atomising nozzle N** (whose size should be calculated[3]) is supplied with petrol from a **float-chamber.**

FC, into which the spirit (petrol) flows by gravitation from its tank through the pipe X, and is kept at a *constant level* by a float FF, the needle valve V regulating its flow; thus the petrol is drawn from the float-chamber through an exceedingly fine orifice[4] in the nozzle N, in the form of a spray, into the mixing chamber MM (pulverisation being assisted by it impinging upon the roughened surface of the fixed cone K and becoming atomised), where, by mingling with the air from the inlet AV on its way to the cylinder, it carburises the air, the explosive mixture being drawn through the throttle valve **T** (as it passes to the inlet valve of the engine) by the suction stroke of the niston. Vaporisation of the atomised spray in the mixing chamber MM may (in cold or damp weather) be assisted by the hot jacket *j*, which is heated by passing

---

[1] When a motor is governed by the governor, *throttling or reducing the quantity of the charge* of the explosive mixture, without altering the proportions of air and vapour, it is said to be governed on the throttle. But when the throttle valve is manipulated by hand the engine is said to be controlled. Refer to Article on Governing and Controlling by Throttling the Mixture.

[2] Refer to Article on Advancing and Retarding Ignition.

[3] It is by no means easy to satisfactorily do this. Usually the most efficient size is determined by the system of trial and error.

[4] The correct and economical working of the carburettor very much depends upon the size of the orifice being properly proportioned to the power of the engine. In cleaning the orifice great care should be taken not to iucreasa its size.

FLOAT-FEED CARBURETTOR

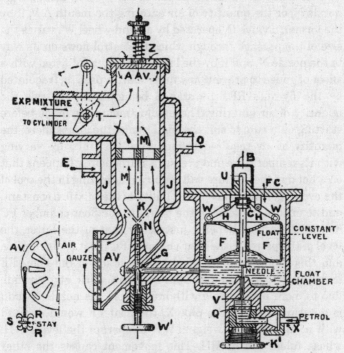

Fig. 6.—Float-Feed or Jet Carburettor. Arranged to show tlie principal features

through it (entering at E and passing out at O) either hot water from the cylinder jacket or exhaust gases.[1]

---

[1] The well-known **Longuemare carburettor** is heated **by** the exhaust gas. In either case the flow of fluid through the jacket should be regulated by a cock or plug, as when too cold the petrol does not volatilise sufficiently, and when too hot it does so to excess. As a matter of fact, with light petrol it is only when the atmosphere is heavily charged with moisture, or when running through keen frosty air, that a heating jacket is required; if such means for regulating the temperature of the jacket are not provided, the resultant cylinder charge is often much richer than is necessary or good for the engine, causing the plugs and valves to become sooty. **When a hot jacket is not used** on a carburettor, it is usual to so fix the latter that the air mouth is near enough the cylinder for the air entering the carburettor to **bo** previously warmed; indeed, **long cold pipes** should never be used to convey the mixture from the carburettor to **the** cylinders, as **the petrol vapour** in the mixture is apt to **condense** when reduced in

14. **The richness of the mixture is** regulated either
by controlling the quantity of the petrol passing through the
nozzle N, or the quantity of air entering the mouth A V; if by
the former, a valve G, operated by a hand-wheel W', varies the
size of the passage through which the petrol flows on its way
to the nozzle N; and if by the latter, a shutter AV, fitted with a
sheet of gauze to prevent any fluffy matter passing (regulated
by the fly-nuts RR, the stay S being fixed), controls the
quantity of air entering. These adjustments are made before
starting on a run, to suit the condition of the atmosphere; the
quantity of air required to make the best mixture varying
with its temperature and pressure, it frequently happens that
on a hot day the mixture will require readjusting in the cool of
the evening. Now to keep the quality of the mixture constant,
and to ensure the level of the petrol in the float-chamber FC
and in the orifice N being just below that of the latter, the
level of the petrol in the float-chamber FC must be unvarying,
and this condition is satisfied by the action of the float[1] FF
and needle, for should the level of the spirit slightly fall,
due to more petrol being withdrawn from the nozzle N than
is entering through the pipe X, the float FF would descend
with it, allowing the weights WW to operate the levers WH,
whose fulcra are at HH. This movement causes the other
ends of the levers to move upwards and carry with them the
grooved collar on the needle, into which they fit; this lifts the
needle point off its seat and allows more petrol to pass from
the tank to the float-chamber; this in its turn lifts the float
and depresses the needle closing the valve, so that the float
automatically maintains the level of the petrol. Great care
must be taken to **pass the spirit through a strainer in
filling the tank.** In the best arrangements a screen of fine

---

temperature; and, **of** course, **the longer** the pipe **the greater the frictional
resistance** the flowing mixture has **to** overcome.

[1] If great care is not taken to make the float perfectly fluid tight, the petrol will
penetrate it and cause it to bo "water-logged," as it is called; it then, of course,
ceases to act as a float. The remedy then is to locate the leak by placing the float
in boiling water, when petrol vapour and air will bubble out of the part that
requires repairing. If the leakage is due to a number of porosities in the drum
metal, the whole float should be treated with a coat of nickelplating.

gauze is placed, as at Q, to exclude any dirt which may be in the petrol, which, if allowed to enter, would tend to stop up the small passages, and prevent the flow of petrol; indeed, such stoppages are a fruitful source of trouble, particularly at the nozzle, where dust, carried in by the air, is apt to give trouble.[1]

Should the **screwed bung** which is generally used to stop the filling-hole in the **petrol tank** get lost, it **should never be replaced by a cork one**, as cork-dust sooner or later will find its way into the carburettor, and cause endless trouble by blocking the small passages.

The spray type of carburettor, largely owing to its compactness and the small amount of room it takes up, has practically **superseded** the **surface type** for **motor cycles**, although it has the disadvantage of being easily flooded when the machine is run over a rough road, the jolting allowing the petrol to escape into the reservoir or float-chamber each time the needle is bumped off its seat; as a result, the petrol supply-pipe has to be fitted with a small cock or valve, so that the quantity flowing can be regulated by hand when necessary.

In starting, it is sometimes necessary (owing to the nozzle becoming more or less closed by dirt, and the **petrol** in it becoming **stale**[2] by standing) to **flood** the **carburettor** and to assist in forming a rich mixture by spraying the spirit by hand; to do this, the thimble B (Fig. 6) is taken off (if one is fitted) and the end U of the valve spindle moved up and down, an upward movement allowing the petrol to enter the float-chamber from the tank, and, the float descending, raises the spirit level in the chamber and causes the petrol to freely flow through the nozzle.

15. **Auxiliary Air.—It** would be interesting and instructive to go into all the points which must be considered

---

[1] The usual expedient in this case, if time will not admit of the carburettor being properly cleaned, is to push a piece of fine wire through the hole and twirl it round; this invariably answers the purpose, but tends to enlarge the hole and make the mixture too rich; so, to be on the safe side, carburettors should be periodically taken apart and thoroughly cleaned.

[2] Petrol, when allowed to stand exposed to the air, rapidly evaporates, the most volatile part passing off first, the portion remaining being impoverished or stale.

in deciding how the degree of carburation should vary with different -temperatures, atmospheric pressures, speeds and other conditions of running, but space will not admit of this, and it must suffice to point out that the practice, which is found to give excellent results with this type of carburettor in maintaining a *uniform mixture*, is to admit what is called *auxiliary air* to the mixing chamber (to mingle with the mixture and reduce its richness), when the engine is running fast and the vacuum is good. The air is admitted through the auxiliary air-valve AAV, which is fitted with an adjustable spring Z (so that its strength may be adjusted to give the best results), and when the suction is strong enough, this valve is forced open by the air outside, against the action of the spring, and extra air flows in and mingles with the mixture. Now, let us try and be clear why this extra air is required.[1] To do this, we must realise that during a rapid suction stroke, air and petrol are being drawn through the openings AV and nozzle N respectively, at a high velocity; at the end of the stroke the inlet valve of the engine cylinder suddenly closes, and no further mixture can enter. This means that the flow of air through AV almost immediately stops; but not so the petrol, as, due to its much greater density and inertia, it continues to flow into the mixing chamber M, and would make the mixture much too rich to give a good result in the cylinder were it not for the extra air entering by the auxiliary valve. Again, as the engine slows down, let us say, due to throttling (partly closing the throttle valve T), there is a greatly reduced suction (not enough to open the auxiliary air-valve), and although air may be freely entering at AV, the petrol will be passing out of nozzle N in a very sluggish way, and there will be an abundance of air in the chamber to form a proper mixture, until at a critical speed of the engine the suction will not be strong enough to draw petrol out of the nozzle, as the normal level of the spirit in the nozzle must always be a little

---

[1] In some carburettors, instead of admitting air by an auxiliary valve, it ia passed into the mixing chamber by increasing the opening of the air inlet at AV by a control arrangement.

below the orifice;[1] but this speed, of course, the motorist soon becomes familiar with, and he is careful to avoid touching it if he wishes to keep the motor running.

Formerly (in the days of the old cut-out governor) it was not practicable to vary the speed of the engine very much, but with the introduction of the **throttle control**,[2] which has been so generally adopted, a great amount of elasticity or flexibility in running became possible, and now most engines have a range from about 200, or even 150 revolutions per minute when throttled, to 1500 or 1600 in some cases when the throttle is fully open, the amount of mixture used being almost in proportion to the speed.

In many of the carburettors in use (notably Kreb's), great ingenuity has been displayed in endeavouring to devise them, so that the fundamental condition for perfect working may be automatically satisfied, namely, *the production of a constant degree of carburation at all speeds, so that the 'power of the motor may be, as nearly as possible, directly proportional to its speed.* In those carburettors that are not fitted with such an automatic arrangement, the mixture is made by controlling the quantity of air by hand, usually by a Bowden wire or through a system of levers and links whose operating handle is attached to the steering column. In any case, the adjustment should be made to enable the carburettor to take in as much air as it possibly can whilst producing a good mixture, as a faulty mixture is nearly always due to an extravagant and wasteful use of petrol, with all the evils attending it.[3]

16. **The essential conditions under which carburettors should most efficiently work are as follows :—**

(A) Throttle wide open and high engine speed, as when running fast on the level or climbing hill.

---

[1] About $\frac{1}{16}$ inch.

[2] The amount of mixture entering the cylinder is controlled by hand or governed by a governor when one is used.

[3] Generation of steam in the Cylinder Jacket, Sooty Plugs, loss of power, and waste of fuel.

(B) Throttle wide open and slow engine speed, as when accelerating from standstill or travelling slowly on the high gear.

(C) Throttle partly closed and high engine speed, as when running fast downhill or on a low gear.

(D) Throttle nearly closed and low engine speed, as with engine running idle when the car is standing.

17. **Surface Carburettors.**[1]—The carburettors that were first generally adopted, and are still used on some motor cycles, were of the surface type, an example of which, of the pattern used on motor tricycles,[2] namely, the De Dion, is shown in Fig. 7. Outwardly it consists of a triangular brass or copper box or reservoir, shaped to fit between the tricycle frame tubes and the rider's seat. In the figure one side has been removed to show the arrangement of the interior; a flat metal baffle plate D, fixed to the air-tube or chimney AT, divides the whole box into two parts, the lower forming a reservoir for the petrol, a further quantity of which is generally carried in a cylindrical tank attached to the rear frame of the machine, and placed just above and connected to the carburettor by a pipe. The plate D is used to prevent the spirit splashing into the upper chamber X in the form of spray, instead of passing into it as vapour. The air enters through the air-tube AT at its perforated upper end, and passes down and between the plate D and the petrol surface (which in starting is just below the plate) as shown, licking the surface, and carrying with it a charge of spirit vapour to the upper part of the reservoir on its way to the **mixing chamber or twin tap, MC**. The function of the tube AT is

---

[1] The general reader need not trouble about studying this carburettor, as it has long been discarded for car work; but it is described here, as students should be acquainted with all the typical carburettors that have been used. These remarks also more or less apply to wick carburettors, described in the next Article, No. 18.

[2] The **principle of the surface carburettor** can be best understood by examining this pattern. Those used on bicycles are very much alike in principle and general construction. In a type that was largely used (called **bubbling carburettors**, a variation of the one shown) the air-tube AT is carried down nearly to the bottom of the reservoir R, and its lower part perforated or zig-zagged, so that **the air bubbles up through the spirit instead of skimming** its surface, as it does in the arrangement shown; then almost the last drop can be used, even if it is a little stale.

THE DE DION SURFACE CARBURETTOR

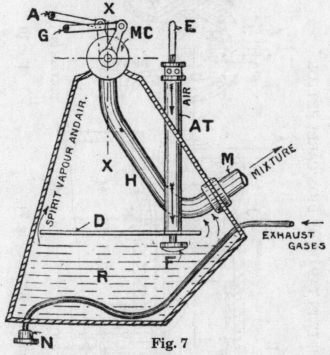

Fig. 7

to admit air below the plate D during the suction stroke of the engine,[1] so that it may be diffused in the petrol vapour, as explained, and be drawn through the twin tap MC, which is arranged to admit an adjustable quantity of additional air to form a suitable mixture to enter the cylinder of the engine from the carburettor through the pipe M. A bent pipe from the engine exhaust passes through the lower part of the reservoir (terminating at N) to warm the petrol, and to accelerate its vaporisation, as evaporation of the spirit lowers its temperature.[2] F is a float fixed to a wire EF, which

---

[1] The cap on top of AT forms an adjustable shutter, used to regulate the quantity of air entering, and the air-pipe AT is made to slide snugly through the hole in the side of the reservoir, so that the attached plate D can be lowered as the level of the petrol falls.

[2] It is well known that when a liquid is vaporised a certain amount of heat (called

MIXING CHAMBER OR TWIN TAP OF DE DION CARBURETTOR.

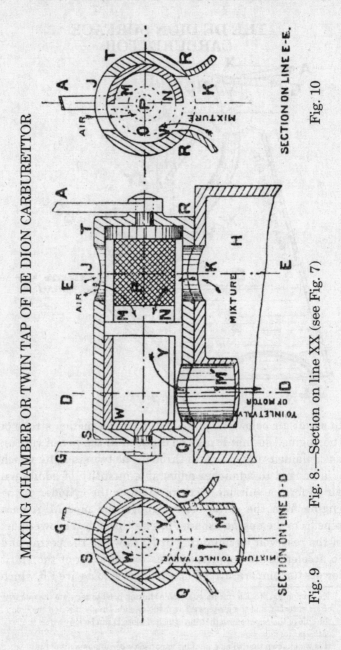

Fig. 9

SECTION ON LINE D-D.

Fig. 8.—Section on line XX (see Fig. 7)

SECTION ON LINE E-E.

Fig. 10

passes through the air- tube AT, and rises and falls, the length of wire at E projecting above AT indicating the level of the petrol in the reservoir.

The most interesting and important feature of this type of carburettor is the **twin tap MC**, shown in detail in Figs. 8, 9, and 10, the Fig. 8 showing a vertical longitudinal section on line XX (Fig. 7), and Figs. 9 and 10 being transverse sections taken through the vertical lines DD and EE (Fig. 8) respectively. These show how the air lever A is connected to a hollow cylindrical part; a half of it, **MON,** being made of wire gauze, in such a way that a movement of lever A controls the quantity of rich mixture entering below at K from the chamber H, and the amount of auxiliary air passing in from above at J, the two streams mingling in the chamber P to form the perfected mixture, which passes into the pipe M on its way to the cylinder: a movement of the lever A (Fig. 10) to the right increasing the opening for air, and decreasing the opening VN for the rich mixture, so that the quality of the mixture can be regulated when starting to give the best results for the petrol used, and the temperature, pressure, and condition of the atmosphere.

Figs. 8 and 9 show how the gas lever G moves the hollow cylinder WY, which is free to revolve in the outer cylindrical case, so that it acts as a throttle valve, giving the rider control over the quantity of mixture which passes into pipe M from the mixing chamber P on its way to the cylinder.

One of the drawbacks of this carburettor is that it takes up more room than the spray one, and it cannot be used with such heavy petrol as the latter can. On the other hand, it has some advantages (which perhaps have not always been appreciated as they should be) for small engines, particularly for motor bicycles. Not the least of these is, it has no very small petrol holes to get clogged with dirt, and throttling does not affect the carburation, as it does in many of the simplified spray carburettors, leading to excessive petrol consumption. But both the **skimming**

latent heat of the vapour) is required to prevent a sensible fall in temperature, or the possible formation of snow on the outside of the reservoir in damp weather.

and bubbling types of carburettors, as at present arranged, fail when a rapid alteration of mixture is required, and on account of this they have long been discarded for car work.

Another very interesting form of surface apparatus is the **wick carburettor**, and although this type is also practically obsolete for car purposes, it should interest the student, and therefore we will briefly describe it.

18. **Wick Carburettors.—In** this type of surface carburettor the capillary action of a wick is utilised. The best-known example is the **Lanchester,** used in connection with the famous engine of that name. In this ingenious carburettor a large circular bundle of wicks, threaded out at their lower ends, is so arranged that these lower ends are immersed in petrol contained in a tank, which tank is fixed within the main-supply petrol tank. Air, warmed in passing the cylinders of the engine, is drawn through the upper part of the bundle of wicks, and it volatilises the petrol drawn up the wicks by capillary attraction, carburating the air and forming the explosive mixture; the admission of **additional air** for **proportioning the mixture** (on its way from the wicks to the engine) when necessary being admitted and regulated by an **air-tap or regulator.** After running some 10 miles, petrol is pumped from the main tank, by a few strokes of a **hand-pump** fixed in the centre of the apparatus, to the wick tank, the handle of the pump being conveniently near the driver's right hand. Among other carburettors in which wicks were used may be mentioned Balbi's, Pappillon's, W. G. Buck's, and Ader's. The Friedman carburettor (an American make) was arranged with perforated plates, which were made to act much in the same way as wicks in the wick carburettors.

It is claimed for wick carburettors that the wicks do not discriminate between spirits of different density, and that therefore they give a particularly **constant mixture,** and that it is not possible for the tank after a time to be partly full of a **spirit residue** of too great density for ordinary use.

It is further claimed that, should water get into the petrol tank, it will not be raised by the wick, owing to the antagonism between the oil and water.

Mainly for reasons given at the end of the previous Article, this type has so far failed to make any headway, although it is conceivable that the last word has not yet been said in their development.

19. Blow-Backs or Popping in the Carburettor.— This trouble is caused by a portion of the still-burning exhaust gases finding its way through the inlet valve and igniting the **in-coming charge**, and it may be primarily brought about by either a very **weak mixture,** a very **rich mixture**, or by an **improperly timed or broken inlet valve**. In most cases there is not more than sufficient **pressure** to produce the familiar **popping noise**, but in extreme cases, owing to the mixture being too poor or too rich, very slow burning occurs and **flames** issue from the carburettor, the mixture being still on fire, not only after the completion of the power stroke, but after its discharge into the air. If it is found that the inlet valve is properly timed and is in working order, free from pitting or grit, and that the pipe connecting the petrol tank to carburettor is not too long, too bent, or too small, the **remedy** is to change the **adjustment** (or size) of the **spray nozzle** so as to give more or less petrol as may be required. But occasional blow-backs or **coughings**, as they are sometimes called, are more often due to weak mixtures alone; then a decrease of the air-supply or an increase of the petrol removes the cause of the trouble.

20. Pressure- *v*. Gravity-Feed for Carburettors.— The petrol tank of most cars is fixed under the driver's seat or on the upper part of the dashboard, with a copper pipe, fitted with a tap, connecting the tank to the carburettor, the petrol flowing by gravity from the former to the latter, as shown in Fig. 1. With this arrangement the carburettor is said to be **gravity-fed**, but the quantity of petrol required to be carried by very high-powered cars is so great that there is a difficulty in finding a suitable place above the chassis for the large tank without encroaching too much upon the room required for baggage, &c. So a way out of the difficulty has been devised by slinging the tank under the chassis itself, generally at or near the back end and below the level of the carburettor, and utilising the exhaust gases to create a pressure in the petrol tank great enough to force the fuel into the carburettor, which is then said to be **pressure-fed**. This arrangement necessitates the use of a **regulating** or non-return **blow-off valve** (sometimes fitted with a gauze diaphragm) in the branch pipe from the exhaust to the tank, to prevent the pressure in the latter exceeding some 2 lbs. per square inch, a gauge on the dash-board to indicate the pressure, also of a **stronger tank**, with a **bung** fitted to be air-tight under pressure, and of a **hand-pump** to create air pressure in the tank for **starting purposes**. The pressure-feed arrangement has **one** undoubted **advantage**, for it makes it possible to fix the **carburettor** in a **high get**-at-able **position** near the inlet valves, and, no matter how **steep** the **hill** climbed, there will be no falling off in the supply of fuel, whilst the tank can be placed in any convenient position. On the other hand, the **disadvantages** are not a few, for with the extra parts and **long pipe** the possibilities of **trouble** are **increased**, and the loss of petrol due to any leakage is greater. The **low position** of the **tank** increases the **dust nuisance**, and there is the danger of the **tank** being **pierced** by a flying stone thrown up by the wheels, or by a collision, unless it is properly protected.

In bus work forced feed is the rule, and it is not easy to see how, as the chassis is at present arranged, the position of the tank can be improved upon; but being placed under the platform, **as** it usually is, a fire at that part would be a terrible thing for the imprisoned occupants of the vehicle.

20A. **Water in the Carburettor.**—One of the most obscure causes of trouble with the carburettor is the presence of water, either in the float-chamber or in the fuel passages, and perhaps parts below the jet. Too often the carburettor is fixed in such a way that it is very un-get-at-able, perhaps necessitating the removal of the under-screen to reach the unions. When this is the case, that periodical cleansing of all the parts, which is so necessary to keep it in working order, is sure to be neglected in most cases until trouble occurs. Doubtless some of this water is due to **hygroscopic action**[1] in the petrol tank, caused by the presence there, in gravity-feed arrangements, of aqueous vapour in the air. Then we have the quite small proportion of water which, through one cause or another, may be admitted to the tank with the petrol, no matter how carefully the latter is strained and filtered.

Of course, the loss of heat, due to the vaporisation of the spirit in the jet chamber, is a **contributory cause of the presence** of water in any part of the latter where it can lodge.

THE FUEL

21. **Petrol and its Properties.**—The fuel that is almost exclusively used by motorists in this country is the light hydrocarbon petroleum spirit, called **petrol spirit**[2] (abbreviated to **petrol**). It possesses valuable properties,

---

[1] The air is at all times more or less moist, and the **degree of moisture** is spoken of as its **hygroscopicity,** and this is measured by instruments called **hygrometers**. The amount of water which can exist as vapour in a given volume of air is dependent upon its temperature; accordingly, on lowering the latter sufficiently, the moisture which existed as invisible vapour is rendered visible in the form of **dew**. **The greater the amount** of water **vapour** in the air, the **less is the amount of cooling required** to form a deposit of dew, or the higher is the dew point.

It should be understood that the **dryness** (or moisture) of the air is **related** to the **degree of its saturation** with water vapour, and not to **the actual amount** of water vapour that is present in it. Thus we may have air holding much vapour, but, from its warm temperature, capable of holding much more. Such air feels and is drier, or more drying, than air holding far less vapour, but, due to its coldness, is more nearly saturated with all the vapour it is capable of holding at its low temperature.

[2] The name petrol was given to this spirit by Messrs. Carless, Capel and Leonard about 1896, when the lighter fractions distilled from petroleum came into commercial use as a fuel in this country. Petrol has also the following synonyms—*gasoline, mineral spirit, motor naphtha, motor spirit, benzoline*, and *motor essence*, but under whatever name it is sold it is, chemically speaking, approximately the same; indeed, in no other branch of industry has such confusion existed in its terminology, refiners putting on the market the same products under all kinds of names, and all kinds of products under the same name. However, at the present time it is generally marketed in England as petrol and in America as gasoline.

which, notwithstanding its drawbacks, make it at present considered the most suitable fuel for motor purposes. **It is a distillate of crude petroleum,** the various products of which (called fractions or cuts) are obtained by what is known as **fractional distillation.**[1] The first spirit which comes over from the still, when, say, crude American petroleum oil of about 0.824 specific gravity is being distilled, is petroleum ether[2] (keroseline or rhigolene), with boiling point 104° to 158° F., and density 0.650 to 0.660. The second fraction is gasoline[3] (canadol), boiling point 158° to 176° F., and density 0.640 to 0.667. The following fractions comprised in the cut from density or specific gravity[4] 0.667 to 0.737 and boiling point 176° to 302° F. are known as **petroleum spirit**. Thus these fractions embrace what is a **light petrol at one end** of the scale and a **very heavy one** at the other, each being made up of several hydrocarbons of various densities, some being below and others above the average density.[5] The spirit when it leaves the still is crude, and before it is ready for use in the motor it has to be **re-distilled and refined** to free it from all deleterious matter, as it is essential for motor purposes that the spirit should have **no residue**; the other requisite qualities being that it should have the correct specific gravity, and that it should vaporise at the right temperature.

The next fraction gives us illuminating oil[6] (the

---

[1] The process of boiling off, condensing, and again collecting is known as "distillation."

[2] Used as a solvent for resins, caoutchouc, &c., for the production of cold, and as a local anasstlietic in surgical operations.

[3] Used for the extraction of oils from acids, &c., and as an illuminant in lamps of special construction.

[4] **Specific gravity** is the gravity or weight peculiar to the liquid compared with the weight of an equal volume of pure distilled water at 60° F. whose specific gravity is unity. Thus the 0 667 spirit is lighter than water in the proportion of 667 to 1000.

[5] In the American method of refining, the crude oil is very slowly distilled, and, instead of allowing the volatile portion to pass over and condense in another retort, they fall back into heated oil, and, by being subjected to a heat above their boiling point, they become broken up into their components. This process is called **cracking, or destructive distillation,** and it enables a larger yield of kerosene to be obtained, as much as 65 or 70 per cent.

[6] This is the oil (called **heavy oil**) which is used with so much success in a type of engine invented by Mr. Priestman, who has developed the oil engine as Messrs.

kerosene or **paraffin** of commerce), with a density of
0.753 to 0.830. And if the distillation is continued, **heavier
oils** pass over, the range of their density being from about
0.840 of the **solar or intermediate oils** to the **0.900** of
the **heavy cylinder oil**; intermediate cuts giving **Spindle
oil, lubricating oil** and **light cylinder oil.** But to make
these heavier oils for the market, they are, ordinarily, treated
with sulphuric acid and soda, a primitive treatment which
is acknowledged to be barbarous, generally leaving in the
oil impurities more or less of a gummy nature[1],compared
with the beautiful refining process invented by Macalpine,
in which all the impurities can be neutralised and made
innocuous by salining and oxidising, without subjecting the
oil, either before or after distillation, to the destructive and
deleterious action of the strong sulphuric acid with which
it is universally treated at present.[2] Indeed, if we are to
rely upon the heavier spirit for use in our motors, when the
demand for that which is at present used cannot be met
(for reasons explained later on), and if the problem is not
solved in another way, more attention will probably have
to be given to producing a spirit of, say, 0730, or even up to

---

Crossley did the gas engine. The most important part of this engine is the vaporiser, for unless almost perfect combustion is obtained, there is much more deposit than in gas engines. It is claimed for the **Cremorne carburettor** that it can be used with either petrol or kerosene; with the latter it is first started with petrol, and it is jacketed with the exhaust gases.

[1] Heavy petrol should be tested for these. A very simple and rough test for such **impurities in illuminating** oils is to burn the oil in a lamp and examine the amount of char on the wick, which is a sure indication of the amount of this kind of impurity in the oil. The author, in carrying out an exhaustive series of these wick experiments, found that with the best kerosene he could buy there was a sensible retrogression of the flame after burning for a short time, with considerable charring of the **wick** in three or four hours, the **gummy matter affecting the capillarity**, the minute canals of the wick being obstructed by impurities whereby the ascending power of the oil is decreased, thus causing **the** char. But with oil that had been refined by Dr. Macalpine's process, the wick was much less charred after burning over one hundred hours; indeed, so pure was the oil that it is doubtful whether any char would have been formed if the air entering the burner had been filtered. In **wick** carburettors any **gummy** matter present in the petrol sooner or later affects the capillarity of the wicks in a similar way.

[2] Unfortunately, owing to the death of Dr. Macalpine, the process invented by him has not so far been further developed.

0.760, of a great degree of purity[1] and high calorific value. In this connection, attention may be called to a paragraph in Professor Perry's well-known book on "Steam and Heat Engines," in which the following sagacious remarks appear: "If I were devoting my attention to the invention or improvement of an oil engine, I would make a careful experimental study of the physical and chemical properties of oils." Now, these judicious words should sink deep into the minds of those who are anxious to improve the efficiency of the petrol motor, as much remains to be discovered relating to the **maximum explosive pressures of mixtures** varying in their **degree of carburation;** and apparently not much is known about the **times taken** in reaching **maximum pressure** after ignition, nor the **rates of cooling** during expansion, &c.

The best quality English petrol used to have a density of 0.680 at the standard temperature 60° F. ($15\frac{5^0}{9}$ C.), but, owing to the enormous and ever- increasing demand for it, and the practical limit to its production,[2] there has been a growing tendency on the part of the refiners to put on the market spirits of increasing density, and a specific gravity of 0.700 to 0.720 may be looked upon as the lightest high-quality petrol commercially procurable; indeed, the British Petroleum Co. Ltd. market a 0.760 spirit, which is **practically kerosene** at **petrol prices**, for ordinary kerosene varies in specific gravity from 0.760 to 0.820, exceptionally light kerosene, such as a Pennsylvania light oil, having a specific gravity below 0.760. But as the denser spirit

---

[1] To use spirit of this density many **carburettors** would have to be slightly modified and the **floats readjusted**, and special precautions taken to keep the valves and sparking plugs clean. Some of our motor buses are already running on the 0.760 spirit.

[2] Before the advent of the motor car there was commercially little or no use for petrol, and it was practically run to waste, as large quantities of heavy Borneo spirit were up to recent times when a market was created for the heavier spirit. The amount now produced depends upon the world's demand for kerosene (illuminating oil), as, owing to the small percentage of the 0.680 to 0.720 spirit in crude oil, it can never pay to handle the crude for the production of petrol alone. Of course, the quantity of 0.720 spirit available is very considerably larger than that of 0.680.

does not so readily evaporate, and, as at present refined, does not appear to be so pure,[1] it behoves the motorist to test its density if in doubt. This may be done with the instrument called a densimeter,[2] or hydrometer used by motorists, the readings on which give the density of the spirit for a temperature of 15° C. or 59° F. But should the temperature be higher, the following simple rule gives a very near reading: Deduct from the density indicated 0.8 times the number of degrees above 15° C. Thus, let us wish to ascertain what the density reading should be for 0.680 spirit, if the thermometer stood at 20° C. (68° F.). Now 20-15 = 5 and 5x.8 = 4, so 680—4 = 676, and this reading means s.g. = 0.676, and if the reading be above this, we should know that the spirit was heavier than the normal, 0.680. Of course, should the temperature of the atmosphere be below 15° C., we should have to add the amount instead of deduct. Thus for 10° C. (50° F.), 15-10 = 5, and 5x.8 = 4, then 680 + 4 = 684, and this reading means s.g. = 0.680.

When a Fahr. thermometer is used in correcting the specific gravity measured at any temperature, subtract from or add to the reading of the densimeter[3] 0.48 for every 1° F. below or above the standard temperature 60° F. Thus suppose when the thermometer is at 50° F. and the petrol is really 0.680 specific gravity, the reading of the densimeter should be 680 + (10 x 0.48) = 6848, and this means that the s.g. is 0.685 nearly.

But no motorist really troubles about measuring the

---

[1] **Good petrol** ought **to evaporate** from white blotting-paper at **normal temperatures** without leaving a stain. Of course, any **spirit up to 0.735** can be made to vaporise sufficiently well in a petrol engine under favourable running conditions, but the difficulty is in **starting from cold** with the **heavy spirit.** And there is the further disadvantage, that when the engine is reduced in speed till it runs very slowly it does not **pick up** so quickly or with as much certainty as with the lighter petrol. With **very heavy spirit** it must be remembered that **the float** is less immersed, therefore, the **needle valve closes earlier,** with a lower level in the **float** chamber and the nozzle. But the difficulty has been overcome **by packing the needle valve** to **raise the** shutting-off level **about** 0.02", **and** allowing more air **to flow round** the **jet than above it by** altering the air **inlet position.**

[2] A simple inexpensive instrument sold at most accessories shops.

[3] The 0.48 corresponds to a co-efficient of expansion of 0.00048.

density of petrol now for ordinary use when it is a well-known brand. Further, it may have the right density but still be unsatisfactory, as may be seen in the following Article. Of course, when petrol is supplied in large quantities to a specification for a public company, the density is an important factor, and proper tests are made. See Article 28.

22. Mixing Spirits of different Densities.—Spirits have been made of standard specific gravity by mixing a heavy spirit with an exceptionally light one, but these are useless for motor purposes, for, when used in the carburettor, the lighter part rapidly vaporises, leaving a heavy spirit that can only be efficiently vaporised at a much higher temperature than usually obtains in the carburettor. This should make clear the fact that a motor spirit may have the right density and still be of little use. Indeed, the **unreliability of specific gravity as a test for commercial petrol** has been strikingly brought out by the following fractional distillation tests Veitch Wilson made (and kindly sent to the author) on different motor spirits, some white rose kerosene, and mixtures of heavy and light fuels to give a specific gravity of 0.680.

FRACTIONAL MIXTURES

TABLE I.—FRACTIONAL DISTILLATION OF PETROL,
KEROSENE, &C. J. VEITCH WILSON

Pratt's Motor Spirit	100					
" Gasolene		100			35 } =100	73 } =100
" Benzoleno			100			
White Rose Kerosene				100	65 }	27 }
Specific gravity of fuel tested	0.680	0.640	0.700	0.786	0.680	0.680
1st drop distilled	97° F.	74° F.	117° F	288° F.	80° F.	76° F.
5 per cent. distilled	119° F.	88° F.	152° F.	325° F.	111° F.	90° F.
20 " "	132° F.	97° F.	167° F.	355° F.	132° F.	104° F.
50 " "	156° F.	112° F.	189° F	412° F.	165° F.	136° F.
90 " "	220° F.	165°F.	248° F	532° F.	240° F.	459° F.
95 " "	282° F.	207°F.	282° F.	596° F.	295° F.	599° F.

Thus it will be seen that the first drop of Pratt's 0.680 motor spirit distilled at 97° F., and the boiling temperature, after 95 per cent. had come over, was 282° F.; the corresponding temperatures for gasolene of specific gravity 0.640 being 74° F. and 207° F. But a mixture of 73 per cent, of the latter and 27 per cent, of kerosene (whose specific gravity was 0.786) commenced to distil at 76° F., but required a temperature of 599° F. to bring over the gas after 95 per cent, of the mixture was distilled, showing how the presence of the heavy constituent impaired the volatility of the mixture. These figures should not astonish when it is remembered that we have in these fuels **mixtures of hydrocarbons** whose relative densities may vary within considerable limits without the fact becoming known to the consumer, for the spirits are graded for commercial purposes by the reading of a **densimeter** or hydrometer which merely **indicates** the **densities** of possible mixtures and **not their chemical character.**

23. Stale Petrol.—We have seen (in the two previous Articles) that petrol, when exposed to the atmosphere, quickly evaporates, the lighter part of the spirit passing off first, thereby increasing the average density of the remaining portion, and the temperature it must be raised to before it will readily vaporise. So when the density has been reduced to a point at which the spirit does not freely evaporate, the petrol is said to be **stale**. Now the tanks of all **gravity-fed cars** have an air inlet to maintain the atmosphere pressure acting on the surface of petrol, and this causes a certain amount of evaporation to take place (particularly when a car has been standing some time), and the consequent increase of density of the remaining part makes it much more difficult to ignite when it is drawn into the cylinder as part of the explosive mixture. So in starting from cold it usually happens that the first spirit drawn through the nozzle is from the residue of the petrol left in the carburettor the last time the car was out, and generally the spirit left in the tank at the end of the previous run will be heavier than fresh spirit. This being so there is often a difficulty in getting the engine to start. When this is the case, it is usual to run the stale spirit out of the carburettor[1], and, if necessary, out of the tank too, and fill up with fresh petrol. **The starting** is sometimes **facilitated** by **squirting** a little 0.680 **petrol** (from an oil-can of good make) through the compression cocks of the cylinders, if the latter are fitted with them, or, much better still, through a **priming-hole** made about half-way along the induction pipe, and fitted with a suitable plug. Of course, after running for a few minutes the cylinders begin to heat up, and hot air coming in contact with the carburettor, induction pipe, &c., improves the running of the engine by raising the temperature of the petrol and mixture.

---

[1] It is the practice of some motorists to store this stale spirit for cleaning purposes, as it is an excellent stuff for removing dirt and grease from the metal part of the car; but under the new regulations, dated 31st July 1907, there is an injunction that petrol shall not be used for cleaning purposes in larger quantities than a gill, and then only when every precaution has been taken.

SOME NOTES ON CRUDE PETROLEUM AND ITS DISTILLATES

24. Origin of Crude Petroleum, Division of its Distillates, &c.—Petroleum, as its name implies, is of geological origin. The crude oil is a hydrocarbon liquid which is found underground in most countries of the world, but, notwithstanding its wide geological distribution, it is only obtained in a few countries in sufficient quantities to supply the raw material of important industries. Among these countries may be mentioned the United States of America, Russia and Caucasus, Roumania, Galicia, Borneo, Sumatra and Burma.

We have referred in the previous Article to the various products of the crude oil which are obtained by fractional distillation, and may now explain somewhat more in detail a few matters many students will like to be acquainted with. **The usual process of refining petroleum** oils may be briefly summarised as follows:—

The stills, in which the crude oil is distilled, consist of cylindrical boilers grouped in series, and are worked on the principle of **continuous distillation**—that is to say, the crude oil, as it is derived from the wells, is pumped into the first still of the series, where it is heated in the usual way by fire below, the **benzine vapours** being first expelled and subsequently condensed, and run into tanks in the form of **crude benzine**. The oil left in the still flows by gravitation into the second still, and so on, oils of increasing density being distilled off during its progress, and collected into separate tanks for refining with acid and alkali; the successive stills being maintained at successively higher temperatures.

The **crude benzine** is afterwards redistilled in a rectifying still (usually a vacuum one, the residue being an oily paraffin) and refined, as we shall see later.

The **kerosene distillate** (paraffin or illuminating oil) is treated with concentrated sulphuric acid, and afterwards washed with water. It is then treated with a solution of caustic soda, and again washed with water.

The **solar oil**, which is next distilled over, is collected, but generally is not treated with acid or alkali.

The heavier oils (**lubricating and cylinder**) are next distilled in the same way, and treated with a considerably increased quantity of acid and alkali, and repeatedly washed with warm water.

In many cases it is customary not to carry the distillation very far, but to stop at a point when the residue is suitable **for fuel** oil. In the oil trade this residue is named **"Astatki."**

But there are few refineries which have the plant or facilities for treating, handling and putting on the market all these distillates of the crude petroleum in a refined form. Therefore we have refiners who confine themselves exclusively to the light products of petroleum, such as petrol, and others who refine only kerosene, whilst there are manufacturers who refine and put on the markets lubricating oils only. There are still others who manufacture mineral grease, vaseline, &c. Usually in distilling crude oil efforts are made to introduce into the illuminating oil (cut) as much as possible of the heavier constituents of the essences, and increase the gravity by making the cut include some heavier oil; then on redistillation what is **residuum** to the refiner of kerosene becomes **crude material** to the manufacturer of **lubricating oils,** and that which is in the nature of a **by-product,** such as **benzine,** is sold by the maker of illuminating oils to the manufacturer of petrol as the raw material. Of course, there are some large manufacturers who have separate departments for dealing with two or more of the above specialities,

25. The following table approximately gives the **commercial products yielded by crude American petroleum** of specific gravity 0.802.

CRUDE PETROLEUM

TABLE II.—COMMERCIAL DISTILLATES OF CRUDE
AMERICAN PETROLEUM

Name of Distillate.	Spacific Gravity	Average Percentage.	Boiling point, Fahr.
Petroleum ether	0.590 to 0.658	1 to 1.6	32 to 162
Petrol, motor spirit, petroleum spirit, gasoline or benzine	0.680 to 0.745	14 to 15	140 to 266
Kerosene (paraffin or burning oil)	0.780 to 0.810	50 to 65	300 to 680
Intermediate solar oil(for enriching gas and making oil gas)	0.840 to 0.860	9 to 12	
Soindle oil Engine oil } Lubricating Cylinder oil	0.870 to 0.920	16 to 18	500 upwards
Paraffin wax	0.908	2	
Loss and residuum		6 to 11	

Usually American crude oils yield a larger proportion of kerosene than Russian oils, whilst the latter yield a larger proportion of lubricating oils and a smaller proportion of kerosene.

26. **Manufacture of Petrol.**—The light product known under the **generic name benzine** obtained in distilling crude petroleum is generally subjected to redistillation and purification before it is fit for use. As we have seen (Article 21), it consists of a mixture of very volatile hydrocarbons, whose specific gravities range from about 0.630 to 0.745, and Fig. 10A shows one of the simplest **rectifying stills** used for the redistillation. The still S (which is surrounded by a steam jacket A, through which steam, having a temperature of 266°" to 284° F., passes from B to C, where it leaves with the water of condensation) receives the crude benzine from the pipe D, and the benzine vapours pass out of the still through the condensing pipe E, which is usually long enough to effect the condensation of the vapours, which, in the form of drops, falls into a cooling tank, from which it is run into barrels or into tanks placed underground. The **residuum** is discharged

43

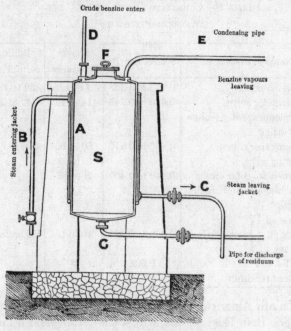

Fig. 10A.–Petrol-rectifying Still

through the pipe G into a tank containing the illuminating oil distillate, and F is a manhole for cleaning purposes. **To** assist the heating effect of the jacket a steam coil is sometimes placed in the interior of the still. In working the still the crude benzine is allowed to flow in through D till the still is three-quarters full, when steam' is admitted to the jacket and coil. This immediately causes drops of the most volatile portions to fall from the end of the vapour pipe E, as explained, and these are allowed to fall into the tank until the bulk density of the **petrol spirit** becomes, say, 0.680—what used to be the standard density of petrol—when the distillate from the pipe E is turned into other tanks, the cuts being made to give the heavier spirits their required densities. The distillation is carried on till the density of about 0.745 is reached, when, as we have seen, the residuum in the still, consisting of the constituents whose boiling points are higher, and the fractions of the illuminating oil carried over in the distillation of the benzine from the crude oil, is run into the kerosene tank.

If the petrol I.C. produced from a crude oil of great purity, such as is found in some parts of America, it usually requires no further treatment, but the benzine from some kinds of crude oil requires to be treated with sulphuric acid and caustic soda before distillation, and, if the odour is bad, to further treatment after distillation, or perhaps to a redistillation in a still of the Heckmann type.

The most troublesome constituent, indeed, the great enemy, of an oil or spirit is sulphur, and Texas oils in particular are remarkable for the amount they contain; probably, petrol from such oils, as ordinarily treated, always remains tainted, no matter how complete the treatment with acids to purify and deodorise it may be; for even if the sulphur be practically eliminated, there is the probability that some acid will remain to attack the cylinder and other parts it comes in contact with.

27. **Best-known Brands of Petrol.**—-The following are the seven best-known brands of petrol that are on the market, with their specific gravities, calorific values[1] in British thermal units per lb., and percentages of sulphur.

TABLE III.—DENSITIES, CALORIFIC VALUES, &C., OF THE BEST-KNOWN BRANDS OF PETROL

Name of Brand.	Spacific Gravity	Calorific Value B.T.U.'s.	Sulphur per Cent.
Carless Capel Standard	0.700	20.344	0.06
Carless Capel Moveril	0.718	20.160	
Russian Petrol	0.705	20.218	0.06
Pratt's Perfection	0.710		0.07
Pratt's Motor Spirit	0.711-0.717	20.212-20.268	Trace
P.G.R.	0.705	20.320	
P.G.R.	0.715	20.281	0.07
Carburine	0.717	20.137	0.07
Shell	0.716-0.719	20.254	0.06
Anglo "760"	0.736-0.739	20.092	0.03

[1] The calorific values and percentages of sulphur are due to tests made by Mr. Bertram Blount, F.I.C. A paper read before the Institute of Automobile Engineers on March 10, 1909.

28. **Typical Specification for Commercial Petrol.**—As we have remarked, the well-known brands of petrol have densities that are on the whole satisfactory, and no one troubles very much about testing the spirit for specific gravity when it is purchased for private use. However, there is much to be said in favour of makers labelling each can with the density of its contents. But when very large quantities of petrol are contracted for it is usual to specify the properties the spirit must have, and the following specification is suggested as a typical one for good commercial spirit; indeed, one that can be conformed to by at least some three or four producers.

TYPICAL SPECIFICATION FOR COMMERCIAL PETROL

Specific gravity at 60° F. not to exceed 0·717. The spirit to have the following **average fractional composition:**—

Distilling below 100° C. at least 65 per cent.

    „   „   100° to 120° C. at least 23·6 per cent.

    „   „   120° to 133° C. at least 5 per cent.

At least 95 per cent, of the spirit to be distilled when the temperature of 140° C. is reached.

The **percentage of sulphur** not to exceed 0·07.

The **calorific value** as tested by a bomb calorimeter, to be within 2 per cent, of 18,900 British Thermal Units.

29. **Petrol Gauges or Tank Indicators.**—Every motorist sooner or later becomes aware of the importance of knowing how much petrol remains in his car tank, especially on long trips or at night-time, when, if the petrol gives out, the position may be an exceedingly awkward one. This being so, every car should be fitted with a petrol gauge as part of its standard equipment. **A glass gauge,** similar to the ordinary water gauge of a boiler, is sometimes fitted, but for these to be reliable and free from the possibility of leaking they have to be

very carefully fitted; even then they may at some time register incorrectly owing to an accumulation of dirt in the passages. Some arrangement of **a float to indicate the petrol level**, several of which are in use on cars, is probably on the whole the best arrangement. But be the arrangement what it may the necessity of being able to **see at a glance** what **amount of petrol** remains in the tank should be obvious to the merest tyro. **As a makeshift a piece of glass thermometer tube**, open at both ends, is sometimes used to test the level of the spirit, the tube being graduated by dipping it into the tank when a known quantity is in it, say, a half-gallon; then, pressing a wet thumb on the upper end of the tube, and withdrawing it, file a notch on the tube corresponding to the height of the petrol in it. If this is repeated for a gallon, a gallon and a half, and two gallons, it serves as a handy rough gauge till a more satisfactory one is fitted.

30. Straining and Filtering Petrol.—Comparatively few motorists realise the necessity of carefully straining the petrol as it is poured into the supply- tank of the car. If they commence by using a strainer, sooner or later it will become mislaid, and the spirit is poured into the tank direct from the can; in doing this they risk getting an accumulation of dirt in the tank, which in due course finds its way into the carburettor, with the inevitable stoppage, for, even if the carburettor is fitted with a disc of gauze within the union below the float-chamber, as shown at Q in Fig. 6, it is only a matter of time for its minute interstices to become completely filled and the flow of petrol to be stopped; so, should the strainer become mislaid, one should be improvised. For instance, a clean handkerchief folded three or four times has been found to be an effective substitute. Many motorists have been troubled by a kind of short silky fluff getting into the union below the float-chamber; this stuff is much too fine to be arrested by the gauze, so something with a much finer mesh is required for the strainer. A good-sized piece of clean thin chamois-skin has been found to effectually filter the spirit without unduly delaying the filling of the tank. Of course, this necessitates the use of a funnel of large diameter, say some 8 or 9 inches at least.

PETROL: ITS DANGERS, AND THE PRECAUTIONS TO BE TAKEN IN USING IT

31. No one should be entrusted with a can of petrol who is unacquainted with its dangerous properties; every motorist should make a point of learning what liberties he may and may not take with it and of becoming acquainted with the Home Office regulations as to its storage, &c. (Art. 32). It being **a highly volatile spirit**, a **naked light** or ordinary lamp should never be taken into a place where it is stored, or into a motor-house, nor should **smoking** be allowed in such places, as a slight **leakage of the spirit** would probably lead to an accumulation of **petrol vapour,** which would be **highly dangerous** if ignited. On the other hand, leakage of petrol on a moving car would cause no more danger from explosion than a gas jet escaping for a few minutes in the open air; but a fairly **large quantity of petrol spilled** in the street or in a room would be a **cause of danger**, from its vapour mixing with the *air* and forming an **explosive mixture**, through which **a flame could leap several feet.** Petrol spirit itself merely ignites with a hot flame, and does not cause an explosion; indeed, a poker almost red-hot may be placed in petrol without its igniting, although a white-hot one would cause it to burn; but when petrol vapour mixes with about 8 to 10 times its volume of air, a rich gas is formed, which will burn without exploding; a larger proportion of air, about 17 or 20 of air to 1 of petrol vapour **forms an explosive mixture**. Finally, petrol is **dangerous for transport or storage** unless the precautions mentioned in this Article and in **Art. 32** are taken; and the risk is greatly increased in a **hot climate**, owing to its **low flash-point**, as any oil is dangerous when heated above its flashing-point, be that high or low. Of course, the **ideal light** for the **motor-house** is the electric one, but when this is not available a **Davy lamp**[1] should always be used when petrol is under cover, to avoid risks, as the conditions necessary for an explosion should be assumed to always exist. Should it be necessary to **empty a tank** in the dark and no electric light or Davy lamp be available, it should be done **out of doors**, and the light should be as high up as convenient and as far away from the car as possible. A **match** should never be struck or a **naked light** used in a garage or near a car when there is a **gassy odour** round it.

The gravity type petrol tank, placed under the driver's seat, should be fitted with a **screw-down valve**, so arranged that it can be actuated from outside the car, so that in **case of fire the petrol** can be **shut off from** the carburettor by the driver whilst standing quite clear. Many serious accidents have happened and valuable cars been destroyed through the absence of such a simple safeguard.

It is not so generally known as it should be that it is **dangerous to work a petrol engine in a garage** with the **doors and windows closed;** for the **engine consumes the oxygen** in the air, which is necessary to support life, and in time will cause death to any one in the house unless the supply of air from outside is renewed. The first symptom of **asphyxiation** is a drowsy sensation, followed by sleep, and possible death. Further, there is the very real danger of the **poisonous** gas carbon monoxide being given off at the exhaust due to imperfect combustion. This gas **is odourless**. In the Home Office Regulation No. 14 (Art. 32) reference is properly made to the prevention of the **escape of petroleum spirit into a sewer or drain.** Such escape or discharge represents a very **real danger** where suitable **interceptors** have not been fixed in the drainage system of the garage, and several cases of risk to

---

[1] This lamp is surrounded by wire gauze, so the explosive gases, though they pass freely through the meshes, are so cooled by contact with the comparatively cold metal, and by its high radiating powers, that though they may be burning on one side of the gauze, the combustion ceases as the gases pass through. **Note.—** **Petrol** vapour is three times heavier than air, and therefore lies on the ground; hence the danger from lighted matches, &c. struck or a **naked light** used in a garage or near a car when there is a **gassy odour** round it.

life and actual **damage to property** have occurred owing to negligence in these matters. A careful perusal of this Article should lead the reader to understand that so long as **petrol in bulk** is contained in a strong **fluid-tight enclosed case** or tank, it is **safer than in any other form**, notwithstanding its excessively inflammable character. For it is only inflammable or combustible in the presence of air, as we have seen, so that so long as there is **no escape** of petrol vapour to **mix with the outside air**, and no admittance of air to mix with the vapour in the case or tank, no conflagration can occur.[1] In considering the **petrol in the feed-tank**, we always have a certain amount of air present in the tanks of gravity- feed arrangements, but such air is sure to be so **overcharged** with petrol **vapour** that **no explosion** could take place, even if ignition were possible. This should explain away the **popular fallacy** that the petrol tank on a car, or, indeed, petrol properly stored anywhere, is liable to explode, but it should not cause a relaxation of ceaseless vigilance, and intelligent supervision wherever this dangerous stuff is being stored, used, or transported.

32. HOME OFFICE REGULATIONS AS TO THE STORAGE, &c., OF PETROL

Regulations dated July 31st, 1907, made by the Secretary of State under Section 5 of the Locomotives on Highways Act, 1896, as to the Keeping and Use of Petroleum for the purposes of light locomotives.

1.The following shall be exempt from licence under the petroleum Act, 1871, namely:—

(a) Petroleum spirit which is kept for the purpose of, or is being used on, light locomotives when kept or used in conformity with these regulations.

---

[1] One volume of petrol will give rather more than 164 volumes of vapour at ordinary temperatures, and one volume of petrol vapour becomes strongly explosive when mixed with 60 volumes of air, or inflammable in 113 volumes of air. So that one volume of the spirit would render about 10,000 volumes of air strongly explosive, and about 18,000 volumes inflammable. But perhaps the greatest danger is due to the extraordinary flame-carrying power of petrol vapour when mixed with air. Refer to pages 70, 71, and Appendix II.

(*b*) Petroleum spirit which is kept for the purpose of, or is being used on, light locomotives by, or by authority of, one of His Majesty's principal Secretaries of State, the Admiralty, or other department of the Government.

2. These regulations shall apply to petroleum spirit which is kept for the purpose of, or is being used on, light locomotives, and for which (save as hereinafter provided) no licence has been granted by the local authority under the Petroleum Act, 1871, and shall not apply to petroleum spirit which is kept for sale, or partly for sale and partly for use on light locomotives, and which must be kept in accordance with the provisions of the Petroleum Acts as heretofore, except that Regulations 13 and 14 shall apply to petroleum spirit which is kept partly for sale and partly for use on light locomotives.

These regulations shall not apply to the keeping or use of petroleum spirit by or under the control of any Government department. Such keeping or use may be the subject of regulations to be made by the department concerned.

3. Where for any special reason a person keeping petroleum spirit for the purpose of light locomotives applies for a licence under the Petroleum Act, 1871, and the local authority see fit to grant such licence, such petroleum spirit shall be subject only to Regulations 8 to 15 and the conditions of such licence, in so far as the said conditions are not contrary to the said Regulations 8 to 15.

4. Where a storehouse forms part of, or is attached to, another building, and where the intervening floor or partition is of an unsubstantial or highly inflammable character, or has an opening therein, the whole of such building shall be deemed to be the storehouse, and no portion of such storehouse shall be used as a dwelling or as a place where persons assemble. A **storehouse** shall have a **separate entrance** from the open air **distinct from that of any dwelling or building in which persons assemble.**

5. **The amount of petroleum spirit** to be kept in any one storehouse, whether or not upon light locomotives, **shall not exceed 60 gallons at any one time.**

6. Where two or more storehouses are in the same

occupation and are situated within 20 feet of one another, they shall for the purposes of these regulations be deemed to be one and the same storehouse, and the maximum amount of petroleum spirit prescribed in the foregoing regulation shall be the maximum to be kept in all such storehouses taken together. Where two or more storehouses in the same occupation are distant more than 20 feet from one another, the maximum amount shall apply to each storehouse.

7. Any person who keeps petroleum spirit in a **storehouse** which is situated within **20 feet** of any **other building** whether or not in his occupation, or of any timber stack or other inflammable goods not owned by him, shall give notice to the local authority under the Petroleum Acts for the district in which he is keeping such petroleum spirit, that he is so keeping petroleum spirit, and shall renew such notice in the month of January in each year during the continuance of such keeping, and shall permit any duly authorised officer of the local authority to inspect such petroleum spirit at any reasonable time. This regulation shall not apply to petroleum spirit kept in a tank forming part of a light locomotive.

8. **Every storehouse** shall be **thoroughly ventilated.**

9. **Petroleum spirit** shall not be **kept,** used or conveyed except **in metal vessels** so substantially constructed as not to be liable, except under circumstances of gross negligence or extraordinary accident, to be broken or become defective or insecure. Every such vessel shall be so constructed and maintained that **no leakage,** whether of liquid or vapour, can take place therefrom.

10. Every such vessel, not forming part of a light locomotive, when used for conveying or keeping petroleum spirit, shall bear the words "petroleum spirit highly inflammable" conspicuously and indelibly stamped or marked thereon, or on a metallic or enamelled label attached thereto, and shall be of a capacity not exceeding two gallons.

Provided that this limitation of capacity shall not apply in any place of storage which is licensed under the Petroleum Act, 1871, unless such limitation is required by the conditions of the licence.

11. Before **repairs** are done to any such **vessel,** that vessel shall, as far as practicable, be **cleaned** by the **removal of all petroleum spirit** and of all **dangerous vapours** derived from the same.

12. The **filling or replenishing** of a **vessel** with **petroleum spirit** shall not be carried on, nor shall the contents of any such vessel be exposed **in the presence of fire or artificial light,** except a light of such construction, position, or character, as not to be liable to ignite any inflammable vapour arising from such spirit, and **no fire or artificial light** capable of igniting inflammable vapour shall be brought within **dangerous proximity** of the place where any vessel containing petroleum spirit is being kept.

13. In the case of all petroleum spirit kept or conveyed for the purpose of, or in connection with, any light locomotive, (a) all due precautions shall be taken for the prevention of accidents by lire or explosion, and for the prevention of unauthorised persons having access to any petroleum spirit kept or conveyed, and to the vessels containing or intended to contain, or having actually contained the same; and (b) every person managing or employed on, or in connection with, any light locomotive shall abstain from every act whatever which tends to cause fire or explosion, and which is not reasonably necessary, and shall prevent any other person from committing such act.

14. In the storehouse or in any place where a light locomotive is kept or is present, **petroleum spirit shall not be used for the purpose of cleaning or lighting,** or as a **solvent** or for any purpose other than as fuel for the engine of a light locomotive.

Provided that where due precaution is taken to **prevent petroleum spirit from escaping into a sewer or drain** and provision made for disposing safely of any surplus petroleum spirit and where no fire or naked light is present, **quantities not exceeding one gill may be used for the cleaning of a light locomotive at a safe distance** from any building, place of storage of inflammable goods, or much frequented highway, or for the **repair of tyres,** under suitable precautions.

This regulation shall apply to premises on which petroleum spirit is kept for the purpose of, or is being used on, light locomotives, whether such premises are licensed or not, unless the **local authority** see fit, in the case of **licensed premises,** to **grant an exemption** by a special term of the licence.

15. **Petroleum** shall not be allowed to **escape into any inlet or drain** communicating with a **sewer.**

16. These regulations shall come into operation on August 15th 1907, from which date all previous regulations made under the Fifth Section of the said Act are hereby repealed.

> H. J. GLADSTONE,
> One of His Majesty's Principal
> Secretaries of State.

WHITEHALL, *July* 31*st,* 1907.

The author is responsible for putting some of the instructions above in heavy type, to arrest the attention of the reader. These regulations affect all motorists who use petrol or any other liquid fuel whose flash-point is under 73° F. A wilful breach of any of them may on summary conviction be punished by a fine of £10. Private owners who cannot see their way to comply with Regulations 4, 5, 6 and 7, may, on application to their local authority, get exemption, but they must comply with all the other regulations. The above **regulations** affect **private owners only**. Petrol kept partly for use and partly for sale, or entirely for sale, comes under the Petroleum Acts. For the purposes of these regulations **all automobiles are light locomotives.**

Points to be remembered.—(*a*) Keep your petrol in 2-gallon tins only. (*b*) Your storehouse must have a separate entrance. (*c*) Don't store more than 60 gallons. The quantity in your car tank counts if the car is kept in the storehouse, as it usually is; not otherwise.

Impending **Revision of Regulations**.—In December 1908 the Home Secretary informed Captain Faber, M.P., that he was about to appoint a Departmental Committee to inquire into the existing regulations relating to the storage, use, and conveyance of petroleum spirit.

(d) You may not refill petrol tins in your storehouse. (e) You can only have one gill of petrol loose about for cleaning purposes, (f) Be careful to comply with Regulation 7, if it affects you.

33. Objectionable Odour of the Exhaust Gases.—The offensive odour of the exhaust gases from most petrol cars causes a deal of unfavourable comment. It is bad enough for the perfume of the sweet-smelling brier in the country lane to be polluted by an occasional passing car, but in our streets and parks, with a succession of passing cars, the nuisance is more pronounced, although to most people less objectionable than the odour from animal excrescences, and probably more sanitary and wholesome; still, all who are interested in the future of the automobile should do their best to minimise it. It is mainly due to **exhausting unburned fuel**, and to the use of either an **unsuitable lubricating oil** in the cylinder, or one that may be very good for the purpose, but is being **used in excess.** The splashing of oil on the silencer, or on an air-cooled cylinder, or other hot part, will also cause this trouble. Briefly, the trouble is more likely to occur in engines (a) fitted with unjacketed carburettors; (b) with long and large pipes connecting the carburettor to the cylinder; (c) at slow speeds than at high speeds; (d) in small cylinders than in large ones; (e) when starting, due to condensation of the spirit vapour in the cylinder, &c., and it is bound to occur whenever an unclean cylinder lubricating oil of too low flashpoint is used.

CARBURATION, &c.

34. Air required for Combustion.—We have seen that when a charge of mixture, or petrol vapour and air, is exploded in the cylinder, rapid combustion or burning of the gas occurs, the evolution of heat occurring as it burns and expands, causing the piston to be pushed forward with great force. We must now be clear about the elementary chemical conditions which must subsist, if the **chemical combination** which causes the explosion is to be perfect. Now, by chemical analysis it is found that petrol (heptane, $C7H_{16}$),[1] of specific gravity 0.700, contains nearly 84 per cent, of carbon and 16 per cent, of hydrogen,[2] and by the aid of chemical equations we can deduce the proportion of air required to supply **oxygen** enough to mix with these gases, in order that when the mixture is ignited it may burn so rapidly[3] as to produce a sharp explosion, no gas remaining unburnt. Thus 1 lb. of hydrogen (H) requires 8 lbs. of oxygen (O) to burn it (the product of combustion being steam),[4] and 1 lb. of carbon (C) requires $2\frac{2}{3}$ lbs. of oxygen to burn it to carbonic acid[5] (carbonic dioxide, CO_2). But the **composition of air** by weight is 1 of oxygen to $3\frac{1}{2}$ of nitrogen (N) nearly, so, for each lb. of oxygen required, $4\frac{1}{2}$ lbs. of air must be provided. Then, to burn 1 lb. of petrol we must have 0.16 x 8 x $4\frac{1}{2}$ = 576 lbs. of air for the H, and 0.84 x $2\frac{2}{3}$ x $4\frac{1}{2}$ = 10.08 lbs. of air for the C, or 5.76+ 10.08 = 15.84 lbs. in all. But if we had taken the **exact ratio** of O to N in the air, which is 23 to 77 by weight, 1 lb. of O is given by $\frac{100}{23}$ = 4.35 lbs. of air, then we can more conveniently express the quantities thus :—

---

[1] This formula denotes that the spirit consists of 7 atoms of carbon (C) with 16 atoms of hydrogen (H). It is a peculiar fact that in all members of the petroleum series the number of atoms of **hydrogen is twice that of carbon plus 2**. Thus we have **hexane**, C_6H_{14} (s.*g.* 0.680), octane, C_8H_{18} (s.*g.* 0.719), and nonane, C_9H_{20} (s.*g.* 0.741).

[2] The more exact values are 83.72 per cent, of C and 16.28 per cent, of H.

[3] The rapidity depends upon the pressure reached during the compression stroke. This law applies to all explosives. Nobel found that a pebble of gunpowder, which took two seconds for its combustion in free air, was burned in about $\frac{1}{200}$th part of a second under pressure in the barrel of a gun.

[4] Or water, if the temperature be low enough for condensation.

[5] The carbon will only burn to carbonic acid (or carbon dioxide, CO_2) when it has time and opportunity to combine with a sufficient amount of oxygen. Any shortage of the latter means that the carbon burns to carbon monoxide (CO), giving out only about a third, the amount of heat, and therefore capable of doing only about a third the amount of work. Refer to Article 50.

35. Weight of Oxygen chemically required =

$$2\tfrac{2}{3}C+8H=8\big(\tfrac{C}{3}+H\big).$$

But since for each lb. of O we require 4-35 lbs. of air—

36. Weight of Air chemically required=

$$4.35 \times 8(\tfrac{C}{3}+H)=34.8(\tfrac{C}{3}+H).$$

Therefore weight of air chemically required per lb. of petrol[1] $=34.8\big(\tfrac{.84}{3}+.16\big)=15.312$ lbs.

But there are 13.14 cubic feet of air to the lb. at a temperature of 62° F., so we get the **Volume of air required per lb. of petrol = 15-312 x 13-14 = 201-12** cubic feet, say, 200 cubic feet, nearly.

37. Composition of Air by Volume.—It may be noted that the air consists of **oxygen** and **nitrogen** in the **ratio of 21 to 79 by volume**, or nearly 1 to 4.

38. Relative Volumes of Air and Petrol Spirit.—The volume in cubic feet of 1 lb. of 0.700

petrol$= \dfrac{1}{62.3\text{x}0\text{-}700}=0.02293$

and therefore

$$\frac{\text{Volume of air required for chemical combustion}}{\text{Volume of petrol spirit}} = \frac{200}{0.02293} = \frac{8722}{1}.$$

39. Extra Air.—But we must not forget that the hydrocarbon fuel is being burnt in the cylinder in presence of nitrogen and some of the products of the previous explosion. So it is necessary to allow from 20 to 40 per cent, more air than the theoretical quantity,[2] about 30 per cent, more giving the best result. So we require about $\tfrac{130}{100}$ x 200 = 260 cubic feet of air to completely oxidise 1 lb. of petrol. Then the above ratio of air to petrol spirit becomes

$$\frac{130 \text{ x}8722}{100} = \frac{130 \text{ x}8722}{100} \text{ Say } \frac{\text{Vol of air}}{\text{Vol. of spirit}} = \frac{11040}{1}$$

40. Relative Volumes of Air and Petrol Vapour.—It

---

[1] For alcohol and solid fuels which also contain oxygen the weight of air required per lb. of fuel=34.8 $\big(\tfrac{C}{3} + H - \tfrac{O}{8}\big)$ lbs.

[2] Refer to Articles 43–46, 70.

is found that 1 lb. of petrol (heptane, C_7H_{16}) at a pressure of 29-92 inches of mercury (760 mm.) and at 59° F. yields 3.78 cubic feet of vapour, and we know that 200 cubic feet of air are required to burn 1 lb. of petrol, so the ratio[1]—

$$\frac{\text{No. cu. ft. of air chemically required per lb. of petrol}}{\text{No. cu. ft, of vapour yielded per lb. of petrol}} = \frac{200}{3.78} = \frac{52.19.}{1.}$$

That is to say, the **percentage of petrol vapour** in the ideal or theoretical **mixture** $= \frac{100}{(52.19 + 1)} = 1.88$.

This squares very well with Sir Boverton Redwood's experiments, for he found that when using a 0.720 petrol, and firing the mixture in a closed vessel, without previous compression,[2] by means of a naked flame, the most explosive mixture consisted of 1.86 per cent, of petrol vapour. With the lighter 0.680 petrol this percentage was found to be 2.352. In this connection the following table, due to Redwood, will be instructive. (Also refer to Appendix II.)

TABLE IV.—EXPLOSION EXPERIMENTS ON 0'680 PETROL, GIVING 190 TO 260 TIMES ITS OWN VOLUME OF SATURATED VAPOUR

No ignition with	1.075	Per cent. by volume of petrol vapour in the mixture			
Silent burning with	1.345	„	„	„	„
Sharp explosion with	2.017	„	„	„	„
Violent explosion with	2.352	„	„	„	„
Less violent explosion with	3.362	„	„	„	„
Burning and roaring with	4.034	„	„	„	„
Burning silently	5.379	„	„	„	„

41. Relative Volumes of Petrol and Petrol Vapour.—It is found by calculation that one part of hexane[3] (C_6H_{14}) yields 276 volumes of vapour or gas, and the same weight of heptane (C_7H_{16}) 240 volumes, and that the theoretical quantities agree very closely with what has been obtained from commercial spirits.

---

[1] Also refer to the reaction given in Article 48.

[2] In all internal combustion engines it is chiefly owing to the compression that weak mixtures can be exploded.

[3] The specific gravity of hexane at 15° C. is about 0.674, and of heptane 0.688.

A gallon of 0.680 petrol (weighing 6.8 lbs.) yields about 29 cubic feet of **vapour,** the **weight of each cubic foot** being nearly 0.235 lb.—that is, about **2.9 to 3 times the weight of dry air**. This heavy petrol vapour **flows** by gravity **along pipes** or **vessels like water**—and this should be remembered when petrol is being used in buildings or under cover.

42. Evaporation of Petrol by Dry Air.—The quantity of petrol that can be evaporated and taken up by dry air depends upon the temperature[1] and density of the spirit. This is shown in a very interesting way by the following table, due to Sir Boverton Redwood.[2]

TABLE V.—EVAPORATION OF PETROL BY DRY AIR

Temrature of petrol.	Vol. Evaporated by 100 Vols. of Dry Air.		Cubic Inches Absorbed per Cubic Foot of Air	
	Specific Gravity 0.679.	Specific Gravity 0.700.	Specific Gravity 0.679.	Specific Gravity 0.700.
40° F.	0.11	0.095	1.9 cu. in.	1.64 cu. in.
60° F.	0.175	0.170	3.10 „ „	2.94 „ „
80° F.	0.340	0.360	5.87 „ „	6.22 „ „
100° F.	0.650	0.480	11.20 „ „	8.30 „ „

The proportion of spirit vapour which air is capable of taking up varies with the volatility of the liquid, **also directly as** the **temperature,** and **inversely** as the **humidity of the air.**

When the temperature of petrol **vapour** is maintained at **60° F. a pressure** of about 2 inches of water can be sustained by the vapour.

43. Minimum Temperature of Fuel Vapour.—The principal reason why a cold engine cannot be started with a heavy spirit is that the vapour from such a spirit cannot exist, as such, at ordinary temperatures. So for every particular spirit there is a critical or minimum temperature below

---

[1] It is essential to know the relation which exists between the vapour pressure and temperature of the fuels in order to thoroughly understand how to secure complete vaporisation of the spirit. Unfortunately, the many works that deal with this subject usually treat on pure substances, whilst all commercial liquid fuels are, strictly speaking, mixtures.

[2] "Petroleum and its Products," vol. ii. p. 686.

which it must not fall if liquefaction is to be avoided, and
this temperature becomes less as the proportion of air in the
mixture is increased. This and some other points of great
interest are made clear by an examination of the following
tables, worked out by Mr. G. H. Baillie,[1] for the range of
mixture ratios of from 20 per cent, less air than the right
amount (that which is chemically required) to 40 per cent,
more air, from which it will be seen that octane, decane, and
alcohol vapour cannot exist under ordinary atmospheric
conditions, except in mixtures that are very weak.

TABLE VI.—MINIMUM TEMPERATURE AT WHICH FUEL CAN EXIST AS VAPOUR

Name of Spirit.	Formula.	Density at 15° C.	Boiling Point.	20 per Cent less Air.	Right Amount of Air.	20 per Cent. more Air.	40 per Cent. more Air.
Hexane	C_6H_{14}	.674	68.5° C.	-14.2° C.	-17.7° C.	-20.6° C.	-24.2° C.
Heptane	C_7H_{16}	.688	98°	7.3°	3.6°	0.7°	2.0°
Octane	C_8H_{18}	.719	120°	29.9°	19.0°	16.0°	13.0°
Decane	$C_{10}H_{22}$	.738	160°	46.1°	42.0°	39.0°	36.5°
Benzene	C_6H_6	.884	80.4°	-0.7°	-4.3°	-6.9°	-8.3°
Ethyl Alcohole	C_2H_6	.794	78.3°	26.5°	23.3°	20.7°	17.8°

44. Fall in Temperature due to Evaporation.—
Before a liquid can be vaporised a quantity of heat (known
as the **latent heat of vaporisation**) must be taken up by
the spirit, and if this heat is imparted to it by the air a fall
in temperature occurs Mr. Baillie has calculated these falls
for the same fuels, and they are given in the following table.
When the **induction pipe** connecting the carburettor to
the inlet valve is **long,** the **temperature** of the mixture
may be still further **reduced,** and this tends to produce
condensation of the petrol vapour into a mist or cloud of
finely divided liquid drops suspended in the air, this action
being encouraged to make a start by the presence of minute
particles of moisture or dust.

---

[1] "Petrol and Petrol Tests,"a paper read before the Royal Automobile Club, May 14,
1908. See also Ernest Sorel's "Carburetting and Combustion in Alcohol Engines,"
pp. 128–158.

RATE OF VAPORISATION

TABLE VII.—DROP IN TEMPERATURE DUE TO EVAPORATION

Name of Spirit.	20 per Cent. lean Air.	Right Amount of Air	20 per Cent. more Air.	40 per Cent. more Air.
Hexane	23.3° C.	19.0° C.	16.3° C.	14.2° C.
Heptane	22.4°	17.9°	15.0°	12.8°
Octane	21.5°	17.2°	14.3°	12.3°
Decane	18.5°	14.8°	12.4°	10.6°
Benzene	47.3°	32.2°	23.2°	20.9°
Ethyl Alcohole	95.5°	76.3°	63.7°	54.6°

An examination of this table (No. VII) brings out the fact that **benzene** produces nearly twice the amount of drop that **heptane** does, and it will be seen that **alcohol** lowers the temperature twice as much as **benzene** does.

45. **Minimum Temperature of Air before Evaporation of Fuel.**—All practical motorists sooner or later have occasion to notice how the temperature of the atmosphere affects the starting of the engine, for in **cold weather** the heavy or **stale petrol will not vaporise,** and the engine must be primed with fresh petrol. The following table, which is made up by adding the figures of the two previous ones, gives the minimum temperature which the air must have before the spirit can be evaporated. It will be seen that with the right amount of air only hexane can be vaporised in a cold cylinder, but with 20 per cent, more air than the right amount, heptane and benzene can also be evaporated cold. The figures relating to alcohol are also of interest, as they show how much the temperature must be increased if there is a shortage of air-supply below the right amount required for combustion, and how mixtures with extra air require less heat. Further, it also shows how entirely out of the question is complete vaporisation without the use of external heat.

Name of Spirit.	20 per Cent. less Air.	Right Amount of Air	20 per Cent. more Air.	40 per Cent. more Air.
Hexane	9.1° C.	1.3° C.	-4.3° C.	-10.0° C.
Heptane	29.7°	21.5°	15.7°	10.8°
Octane	44.4°	36.2°	30.3°	25.3°
Decane	64.6°	56.8°	51.4°	47.1°
Benzene	46.6°	27.9°	16.6°	12.6°
Ethyl Alcohole	122.0°	99.6°	84.4°	72.4°

46. Rate of Evaporation.—No matter how volatile the liquid fuel may be, evaporation is not absolutely instantaneous; but for internal combustion engines the time of contact during which vaporisation must take place is very short; as, even with a heavy slow-running engine, making 180 revolutions per minute, the **time** (of one stroke) available for **carburetting** cannot exceed $\frac{1}{6}$ of a second, and with a light high-speed engine, running at 1800 revolutions per minute, $\frac{1}{60}$ of a second. On the other hand, the time required for the vaporisation of a spirit and the complete saturation of the air of the mixture increases with the density of the former, and can be calculated[1] when all the conditions are known. But, as we have seen, the **evaporation** can be **hastened** by **raising the temperature** (by using the heat of the exhaust), or by introducing an **excess of air,**[2] or by a combination of both means; and, if space would permit, we could show that the temperatures given in the above table would have to be sensibly increased for engines running at the higher speed to ensure complete carburation.

47. **The Use of Oxygen in Petrol Engines.**—We have seen that when a liquid fuel is used in an internal combustion engine, the oxidation of the carbon of the fuel is performed

---

[1] By the simple law of August : *see* Ernest Sorel's "Carburetting and Combustion in Alcohol Engines," p. 146.

[2] This is the primary reason for that necessary evil, excess of air, for such engines using liquid fuel. The evil effects of extra air are represented by (a) lowering the temperature of combustion; (b) lowering the maximum pressure in ignition; (c) greater quantity of heat carried away by the exhaust gases.

by the oxygen of the air, and that nearly **four-fifths the volume** of the air is **nitrogen,** an inert gas which is of no direct use in assisting combustion or taking an active part in the chemical processes; in fact, it merely **acts as a diluent,** and is swept into and out of the cylinder, forming a considerable part of the exhaust gases. Obviously, this mechanical process represents a loss of energy which does not occur when oxygen alone is used to oxidise the hydrocarbons of the fuel. The use of oxygen has the further important advantage due to each cylinder charge being a heavier one of pure combustibles. So it follows from these considerations alone,[1] that an ideal way of using petrol for power purposes is to supply it with oxygen instead of air, and this has been occasionally done in racing competitions (at critical points in the race), where the important factor of cost is often not much considered. But, unfortunately, we can never hope to have oxygen cheap enough to use in this way for commercial purposes. And there is the further disadvantage that it has to be stored at great pressure in very strong and heavy iron bottles. However, there are some cases where the cost, however great, would not much stand in the way of an ideal fuel. For instance, an **oxy-hydrogen mixture,** produced from liquid oxygen and liquid hydrogen, with a convenient apparatus permitting their re-vaporisation and mixture in their combining proportions, also a suitable means of storing them, would appear to be a promising if not a **perfect fuel for high-speed long-distance torpedoes.**

48. **Combustion Tested by Analysis of Exhaust Gases.**—If space permitted, it would be instructive to further consider under what conditions of temperature, pressure, and proportions a combustible mixture gives the highest efficiency, but, as a matter of practice in running, **the most economical mixture** to be used in the cylinder of a motor is usually determined by trial and error at average speed, or, in other words, by **hand control,** the carburettor being adjusted to give the best results, without the exact proportion

---

[1] Not taking into account the cooling effect on the cylinder walls due to the production of steam or water by the oxidation of the hydrogen, &c.

of air and petrol vapour passing through it being known: for a **perfect automatic carburettor** does not exist, and it is **only by analysis of the products** of combustion from the **exhaust that we can learn whether our ratio of fuel to air is correct,** the result of **incomplete combustion** being the production of the invisible, insidious, and poisonous carbon **monoxide (CO)** or of visible **smoke.** With perfect combustion, the petrol will be completely burnt to carbonic dioxide (CO_2) and water. Any **oxygen** in the **exhaust** indicates that **too much air** has been used; but, of course, when **running light** an excess of air is generally supplied to minimise the violence of the explosion.

Bearing in mind the points we have explained in connection with the combustion of petrol, and that the ratio of oxygen (O) to nitrogen (N) in air is nearly **in the ratio of 1 to 4 by volume** (the more exact ratio being 0.266 to 1), we may state the relationship between the constituents of the explosive mixture of petrol (heptane, C_7H_{16}) and air, and its products of perfect combustion, by the following equation representing the reaction, the O required for the combustion of the C and H being shown separately.

$$C_7H_{16} + 7O_2 + 4O_2 + 44N_2 = 7CO_2 + 8H_2O + 44N_2$$

1 vol. 7 vols. 4 vols. 44 vols. = 7 vols. + X + 44 vols.

The lower line shows the relative volumes of the gases. The volume X of the H_2O is practically nil, as it appears as water from the condensed steam, the analysis being made at ordinary temperatures.

We see from the equation that the residual gases of the burnt fuel contains 7 volumes of CO_2, the total volume being $7CO_2 + 44N_2 = 51$ volumes, or there is **13.727** per cent, of CO_2 present. The left-hand side of the equation shows that 1 volume of the petrol vapour requires $7 + 4 + 44 = 55$ volumes of air to burn it.

If in the **analysis** of the exhaust or **residual gases CO** be found, it shows that the **air-supply** has been

insufficient;[1] on the other hand, the presence of extra O_2 indicates that too much air was present in the mixture.

In this connection Mr. Dugald Clerk remarked in his admirable paper[2] on the "Principles of Carburetting" : "From these tests it appears probable that many cars must be running upon the road as ordinarily adjusted, discharging as much as 7 per cent, of carbonic oxide into the atmosphere, ... I find that at full load, with a particular engine, very similar variations occur, the carbonic oxide sometimes sinks as low as 0.8 per cent., and sometimes rises as high as 3 per cent., whereas, with light load, the carbonic oxide appears to sometimes attain from 6 to 8 per cent." He further remarked: "The key to the position, then, so far as best results, purity of exhaust, and maximum thermal efficiency are concerned, is found in adjusting the carburettor so that the engine gives its most economical petrol consumption for a given power. This power is somewhat under the maximum power possible, but not greatly under it. The conditions of innocuous exhaust and maximum efficiency are to be found together." In concluding his paper Mr. Dugald Clerk remarked: "So far, then, as my experiments have carried me at present, the following conditions appear to produce imperfect combustion :—

(1) Too much mixture with insufficiency of oxygen.
(2) Too weak mixture with excess of oxygen, but too slow a rate of ignition and combustion.
(3) Irregular mixture—mixture supplied too rich in composition at one part of the stroke, and too weak in another; that is bad mixture.

---

[1] This means that something less than a third of the heat due to burning C to CO_2 is only generated, as 1 lb. of C burnt to CO_2 gives out about 14,500 B.T.U., is the calorific value.

Various investigations which have been made in France concerning the behaviour of hydrocarbon in internal combustion engines have given unexpected results. Thus it appears that CO is absolutely uninflammable in the absence of water vapour. It will not take up another atom of O. The old belief that C will turn at once to CO_2 in the presence of plenty of O is not well founded. Under certain conditions it is just as likely that the lower oxide will be formed as the higher. See *The Engineer,* Feb. 19, 1909.

[2] "The Principles of Carburetting as determined by Exhaust-gas Analysis," a paper read before the Institution of Automobile Engineers, Dec. 11, 1907. Published at 1s.

(4) Engine and carburettor cold. This tends to cause imperfect combustion, due partly to low temperature, due partly to bad carburetting.

(5) Improper timing of ignition, and missed ignitions.

(6) Igniting in the body of the cylinder, instead of in a port. This will produce imperfect combustion at light loads."

The apparatus required is very simple, the best for accurate and rapid work being that of Macfarlane and Caldwell (sold by Baird & Tatlock), and the tests are easily made by any young chemist, indeed, by any careful and intelligent young engineer. With a little assistance to begin with, he should be able to make a detailed and sufficiently correct analysis in about half-an-hour by a shortened process.[1] Although it is most convenient to make the tests in the shop, garage, or laboratory, samples of the exhaust gases can be bottled on the road and afterwards tested.

49. Ideal Conditions for High Efficiency.—The conditions which the designer should endeavour to satisfy for high thermal efficiency, or at least to secure the best compromise on, have been defined by the distinguished authority, Mr. Dugald Clerk, to whose valuable work we have before referred, and may be briefly stated as follows: (1) **High compression,** the highest possible without pre-ignition. (2) **Minimum cooling surface** to which the flame is exposed. (3) Shortest **time of exposure**. (4) Lowest **flame temperature** consistent with rapid ignition.

50. Calorific Value of Petrol.—The true calorific value of a fuel, or its effective heating power, can only be determined by direct calorimetric test, but in a fuel like petrol, which we may assume consists of H and C only, its value can never exceed[2] $53,338 H + 14,540 C$ heat units; so for a lb. of the 0.700 petrol referred to in Art. 34 the **total heat**

---

[1] In an appendix to Mr. Dugald Clerk's paper referred to above, Mr. H. Ballantyne described a shortened process of analysis in which the proportions of carbon monoxide (CO) is taken as an index of the proportions of hydrogen (H) and methane (CH_4)—viz. %H=%CO x 0.36, %CH_4= %CO x 0.12. (See Proc. I.A.E., 1908, p. 101.)

[2] 1 lb. of hydrogen burns to 9 lbs. of steam, and develops 62,032 units of heat, from which must be deducted the latent heat of the steam at 212° F., which amounts to

of combustion would have a maximum theoretical value[1] of $(53,338 \times .16) + (14,540 \times .84) = 20,748$ B.T.U. (British Thermal Units), or $20,748 \times 778 = 16,141,944$ ft.-lbs.[2]

50A. **Thermal Efficiency of Heat Engines.**—Carnot proved that, no matter how we devise the engine, or what the working fluid or stuff may be, whether it be by the steam *of the steam engine,* illuminating producer or furnace gas of the *gas engine*, air of the hot-air engine, or the explosive mixture we use in the petrol engine, the greatest possible heat efficiency of the engine is equal to the quotient $\frac{T-t}{T}$, where T is the maximum **absolute** temperature, and t the **absolute temperature** at which the stuff is rejected at the **exhaust.**

Now we may assume that the maximum temperature reached by the mixture in the cylinder of our petrol engine,[3] when ignition occurs at greatest compression, is about 2000°

---

9 x 966=8694, and leaves 62,032-8694 = 53,338 units of heat available. Strangely enough, this correction for latent heat is usually overlooked by writers.

[1] Calorimeter measurements of the calorific value of petrol are constantly being made in various laboratories. The latest were published in a paper read by Mr.Bertram Blount, F.I.C., before the Institute of Automobile Engineers on March 10th, 1909, and in averaging the ten values given from different brands I find that it amounts to 20,228.6 B.T.U. per lb. The lowest value was 20,092, given by Anglo, "760," whose actual specific gravity was 0.739, and the highest 20,344 by "Carless Capel Standard," the specific gravity being 0.700.

Mr. Blount used a bomb calorimeter, with an ample excess of oxygen at a pressure of 25 atmospheres, adopting a device due to Berthelot by enclosing in a relatively deep cup provided with a celluloid envelope rising above the edge of the cup and contracted at the top so as to form a sort of sack with a relatively narrow mouth. By this means the vapour was confined sufficiently to cause it to burn at a moderate rate, and imperfect combustion and violent explosions were avoided. Thus we see that the highest value of the heat actually got out of a lb. of petrol by these experiments was 20,344 B.T.U. against the 20,748 B.T.U. as calculated above, or 98.05 per cent, the theoretical amount. But a mean of ten tests by Messrs. J. Thomas and W. Watson gives 18,603, which closely agrees with Prof. B. Hopkinson's tests, which gave 18,900 B.T.U. nearly.

[2] The number 778 is the mechanical equivalent of heat, the number of foot lbs. of work that are mechanically equivalent to one British thermal unit. Joule found this to be equal to 772, but later experiments have established the higher value. A British thermal unit is the amount of heat required to raise the temperature of one lb. of water at its greatest density (39-1° F.) 1° Fahr.

[3] This is not the temperature of the walls of the cylinder, which may reach 250° F. in water-cooled cylinders and 1000° F. in air-cooled ones, as explained in Article 85.

C. = 3632° F., or an **absolute**[1] temperature of 3632 + 461 = 4093° F. And the exhaust gases could not possibly have a lower temperature than that of the atmosphere, let us say, 60° F., or 60 + 461 = 521° F. absolute; so that with these temperatures our ideal or perfect engine would have a maximum heat efficiency[2] of $\frac{4093-521}{4093}$ = .87, or 87 per cent. Of course, this efficiency is impossible of attainment; indeed, the greatest possible depends upon the compression, as we have seen in

---

[1] Temperature, as measured by the Fahrenheit thermometer, is 461° above the absolute zero.

[2] If we could construct a perfect explosion engine working on a four- stroke cycle under ideal conditions, that is, one in which all the heat was developed instantaneously at constant volume, and in which there was no heat exchange between the working Stuff during either the compression or expansion strokes and the cylinder walls, it was first pointed out by Dugald Clerk that the efficiency of such a motor for all neat additions above the final temperature of compression would depend upon the amount of that compression and that alone. In other words, the ideal engine, with no water-jacket loss, could only convert into work done on the piston the fraction of heat evolved by combustion represented by E, the ideal thermal efficiency, and

$$E = 1 - \left(\frac{1}{R}\right)^{0.4}$$

where $\frac{1}{R}$=the ratio of expansion = $\frac{\text{compressed volume}}{\text{total volume of cylinder}}$, or the ratio of the combustion or compression space to the total enclosed volume above ratio of the combustion or compression space to the total enclosed volume above the piston when it is at its extreme out position.

Then for such values of R as obtain in petrol and alcohol motors, the following table gives the corresponding values of E in round numbers:—

R =	2	3	4	5	6	7	8	9	10	20	100
(Air Standard) E =	24.6	36	43	47	52	55	57	59	61	70	85.

Of course, these values are only useful in comparing the performances of engines running with different compressions, and referring them to the ideal values of E. The above values of R and E are given for compressions far beyond what is found practicable in any engine; the limits of R being 6 for petrol and 12 for alcohol.

As a standard of reference it is convenient to assume that the working fluid which operates the engine is air, which obeys perfectly the laws of gases, the specific heat being assumed constant at all working temperatures, and the value of γ, the ratio of the specific heat at constant pressure and constant volume, is taken as 1.4. But taking into account the change of specific heat of the gases at high temperatures the maximum efficiency which can be attained in a petrol engine in which there are no thermal losses is about 20 per cent, less than the air standard. Then with R = 4, giving E = .43 we have the ideal efficiency = .43 less 20 per cent. = .344. And the engine may have an actual efficiency of .26, which is equivalent to a relative efficiency of over .75. Thus if all thermal losses due to water-jacket, &c., could be avoided, the thermal efficiency could only be increased in the ratio of .75 to 1. With petrol engines R usually ranges from 4.5 to 2.5.

the footnote on **page 82**. Probably few motors running have a heat efficiency higher than 25 per cent.;[1] 20 per cent, being nearer the mark under ordinary running conditions. But the motorist is more interested in the power this useful portion of the total heat of the fuel is capable of developing if used in the motor in a given time, so this brings us to the consideration of—

51. **Horse-Power.**[2]—In speaking of power we must be careful to distinguish it from the term **force,** as the two words are not synonymous. The former term was very loosely used by the older writers on mechanics when referring to force; but **power,** it should be understood, **is the rate of doing work**—that is to say, if we are to measure work we must know the amount of work done in a given time, then the quotient $\frac{\text{work}}{\text{time}}$ equals the power. The unit of power was fixed by James Watt, who found by experiment that the maximum amount of work a powerful dray-horse could do when pulling regularly at a slow speed for eight hours a day was at the rate of 33,000 foot-lbs. per minute.[3] Hence, in Great Britain one horse-power = 33,000 foot-lbs. per minute.[4] So, to determine the *horse-power* (usually abbreviated to H.P.) of any motor, we have simply to *calculate in foot-lbs. the work done by it in one minute and divide by* 33,000.

But we must decide first whether we wish to measure the

---

[1] Of the heat evolved during an explosion stroke, under the most perfect conditions, only a portion is converted into useful work (say, about 28 per cent); a further quantity is taken up by the jacket water and radiation (say, about 25 per cent) and lost. And a cylinder full of exhaust gases at 1000° to 1800° F. is discharged into the atmosphere each cycle, and another, about 45 per cent, of the heat, absolutely lost. And there are smaller sources of waste, such as radiation, friction, and heat transformed into kinetic energy of the exhaust gases.

[2] The new taxes on motor cars, to be graded in proportion to their horse-power, are sure to revive the vexed question of the rating of cars. Probably the R.A.C. rating for the estimation of the taxable horse-power will suffice for some time, but it is safe to predict that great improvements in efficiency will be made all round, with the object of producing powerful cars whose rating will be low. Refer to Article 53B.

[3] It is well known that the ordinary draught horse is not capable of doing more than about 22,000 ft.-lbs. per minute, or about two-thirds of the standard amount.

[4] The French force-de-cheval, or metric horse-power=75 kilogram-metres per second = 542.48 ft.-lbs. per second, or 0.986 the British horse-power.

power of the motor to do work outside itself, the **effective power** available to drive the car through the gear, or do work in overcoming the friction of a clutch or brake applied to its fly-wheel, which is called **brake horse-power (B.H.P.);**[1] or, on the other hand, whether we are to **measure the indicated horse-power (I.H.P.)**, the power developed in the cylinder of the motor by the varying pressure of the expanding gases acting on the piston, **called indicated,** because an instrument known as an **indicator** is used to declare or indicate the variations in the pressure on the piston, from which mean pressure can be easily found, and this, multiplied by the distance in feet per minute the piston travels in performing its **power strokes,** and divided by 33,000, gives the **indicated horse-power.** The following example will serve to make this more clear.

52. Indicated Horse-Power of a Petrol Engine.—It

---

[1] The brake horse-power is often measured by using a friction brake or dynamometer. It is the power *some makers* refer to when advertising their cars. There is, as motorists well know, and as shown in Article 53A, a marked want of uniformity in accurately defining the power of cars.

The friction brake often consists of a weighted rope, lapped over the fly-wheel, one of its ends having attached to it a spring balance, fastened to the bench, and the other a weight which, with the assistance of the pull from balance, is supported by the friction between the rope and wheel, which tends to lift the weight Then if W = the weight in lbs., P=the pull on the balance in lbs., and R=the distance of the centre of the rope from the crank-shaft axis in ft, then (W - P)R=the mean turning moment of the engine, and the

$$\text{B.H.P.} = \frac{(W-P)R \times 2\pi N}{33,000 \times 2},$$

where N is the number of revolutions.

NOTE.—The braking surface is oiled, and the heat generated carried away by running water.

The electrical method of engine-testing, where practicable, is much more satisfactory. The complete engine with the radiator is mounted on a bed-plate, and it is coupled up to a dynamo, which it drives; the power generated in the dynamo is absorbed by a rheostat or water resistance, the amount of the resistance being regulated by the raising or lowering of a plate in a barrel of water. The speed of the engine and the amount of the load can be varied between wide limits, while at the same time the power being developed can be seen by reading the ammeter and voltmeter; or the current generated by the dynamo may be conducted through a saline solution, the resistance of the circuit being altered by varying the immersion of the iron plates, which serve as the electrodes in the solution. And the current may be measured by means of a special ammeter, which is **calibrated to read horse-power direct**, so that no calculations are needed.

is found that when an efficient petrol engine is working under favourable conditions, the **mean indicated pressure** during the explosive or power stroke is 80 lbs. per sq. inch, (the initial pressure being about 300). Then, having regard to the explanation given in the previous Article, we may

Let P = mean pressure during explosive stroke = say, 80 lbs. per square inch.

„ L = length of stroke of pistons in feet = say, $\frac{5}{12}$.

„ A = area of pistons in square inches = d^2 x $\frac{\pi}{4}$ = say, 4^2 x $\frac{22}{28}$,

„ N = No. of cylinders = say, 4.

„ S = speed in revolutions [3] per minute = say, 1000.

Then I.H.P.= $\dfrac{\text{PLANS}}{33,000\text{x}2}$

„ $= \dfrac{80 \text{ x } \frac{5}{12} \left(4^2 \text{ x } \frac{22}{28}\right) 4 \text{ x } 1000}{33,000 \text{ x } 2}$,

that is, I.H.P. = 25.396; say, 25.

NOTE.—As there is only one power stroke per 2 revolutions, the 2 appears in the denominator of the above.

53. **Horse-Power Rating Formula.**—To enable the public to arrive at an **approximate power** of any given engine in comparison with others, the Royal Automobile Club have adopted the following **Rating Formula** (for max. B.H.P. per cylinder, see p. 312):—

$$\text{H.P.}=\frac{D^2 \text{ x N}}{2.5},$$

where D = the diameter of the cylinders in inches, and N = the number of cylinders.

Thus for a 4-cylinder engine, whose cylinders are 4 inches diameter—

$$\text{H.P.}=\frac{(4\text{x}4) \text{ x } 4}{2.5}=25.6$$

This formula, which is for rating purposes only, and is not put forward as an accurate or scientific calculation of actual horse-power, the council of the Society of Motor Manufacturers and Traders have recommended their members to adopt for their catalogues. It will be noticed that it gives practically the same power as the preceding one for **I.H.P**. But having regard to the extraordinary achievements in the 4-inch cylinder competition which recently so much astonished the motor world, due to designers resorting to every known expedient to increase the engine power; such as reducing the weight of the reciprocating parts to make higher piston speeds possible, increasing the size of the valves to freely admit fuel enough for longer strokes, increasing the compression up to the practical limit, and securing the most perfect carburation; it is safe to predict that some modification of the above rating will ere long be made. The problem of evolving a suitable formula has for years been a vexed one, as the want of uniformity in rating has led, and is at present leading, to endless confusion. In the past this has been not a little due to cars in France and Germany being taxed by horse-power, which naturally caused manufacturers in those countries to rate their cars as low as they possibly could, with the result that a 10 horse-power machine is really 18, and an 18 really 30, or even more. Then, of course, there have been temptations to minimise the real power of cars when it has been a question of handicapping for racing or hill-climbing. But evidences are not wanting in this and other countries of a general and real desire to abandon this strange mixture of meaningless terms, and to secure the use of some official rating for commercial purposes that every layman could understand. Strangely enough, no manufacturer (so far as the author is aware) gives any particulars as to the **efficiency of the transmission gear from engine to road-wheels**, a very important thing to know about any given car, for a highly efficient engine may be mated to a mechanism, transmitting its power to the road- wheels, which has a very poor efficiency. Of course, what the purchaser ought to know is the results of some official test, not necessarily of the actual brake horse-power of the engine when tested on a bench, but of the actual horse-power delivered at the treads of the road-wheels by the whole machine fully loaded, at different speeds of the engine and on the different gears, with the approximate mileage for each per gallon of fuel. These are tests which can quite easily be made in any properly equipped laboratory, and, if officially done, a certificate could be issued that would enable a purchaser to make some really useful comparisons in considering different cars. Failing such a system as this a formula of the type adopted by the Verein Deutscher Motor-fahrzeug Industrieller (or German Motor Manufacturers' Union), which gives the approximate horse-power developed at the road-wheels, appears to be preferable to the many that have been suggested to measure the probable power of the engine alone. The German formula is given in Art. 53B, in which the symbols have been slightly modified by the author.

53A. **Relation of Catalogue Horse-Power to Cylinder Capacity.**—The following table, compiled by Mr. S.F. Edge, forcibly brings out the unsatisfactory system (or want of system) in rating the power of cars, which is so perplexing to the purchaser.

TABLE IX.—RELATION OF CATALOGUE HORSE-POWER TO
CYLINDER CAPACITY

Catalogue h.p	Make.	Cylinder Dimensions in Ins.		Cubic. Inc.	Cubic Inc. per Catalogue h.p.
40	Napier	4	x 4	301	7.25
60	Napier	$5\frac{1}{4}$	x 4	471	7.85
40-60	Pilain	$5\frac{1}{2}$	x $5\frac{1}{2}$	522	8.7
35-50	Pipe	$5\frac{1}{16}$	x $5\frac{1}{4}$	497	9.94
30-40	Peugeot	$5\frac{1}{2}$	x $4\frac{7}{8}$	405	10.1
45	Beaufort	$5\frac{7}{8}$	x $5\frac{7}{8}$	457	10.15
30-40	Daimler	$4\frac{1}{4}$	x $5\frac{7}{8}$	441	11.0
35-45	Daimler	$5\frac{1}{2}$	x $5\frac{1}{8}$	513	11.4
40	Darracq	$5\frac{7}{8}$	x $5\frac{7}{8}$	457	11.4
35	Arial	$5\frac{1}{4}$	x 5	596	12.0
60	De Dietrich	$5\frac{1}{4}$	x 6	732	12.2
32	Siddeley	$5\frac{5}{16}$	x $5\frac{1}{2}$	432	13.5
35	Brooke	$5\frac{5}{16}$	x $6\frac{1}{2}$	570	16.3
24	Panhard	0	x 5	416	17.3
24	Fiat	4	x 5	444	18.5

53B. **German Rule, Approx. H.P. at Road-wheels** = $\dfrac{3 \times N \times d^2 \times S}{1000}$,

where N = number of cylinders, d=diameter of pistons in centimetres, S = stroke of pistons in centimetres.[1]

---

[1] Obviously this is, like our own rating formula, a "crude, rough and ready" method of rating; one that answers fairly well with the ordinary car, but fails to give even the approximate power of such a car as the Sizaire racer, which has a brake

Assuming that a car is fitted with the engine whose indicated power we found in Art. 52, and applying the above formula for finding the probable horsepower at the road-wheels, we have, first converting British dimensions into metric, $d = 4" = 4 \times 3.54 = 10.16$ cm. and $S = 5" = 5 \times 2.54 = 12.7$ cm. The Probable H.P. at road-wheels =

$$\frac{3 \times 4 \times (10.16 \times 10.16) \times 12.7}{1000} = 14.532,$$

or $\frac{14.532 \times 100}{25.396}$ = 57.222 per cent. of the Indicated H.P.

The following three Articles will probably make these relationships more clear.

54. **The Mechanical Efficiency of the Engine** takes account of all the frictional resistances, and compares the work given out by the crank-shaft with that done in the cylinder. Thus, **mechanical efficiency** = $\frac{\text{brake horse-power}}{\text{indicated horse power}}$. The value of the quotient varies; it decreases somewhat as the size of the engine becomes very small, and also decreases in any given engine as the power at which it is being worked is reduced much below that which it was designed to develop; this is due to the fact that its frictional resistances are somewhat less at full power than at any lower power, although, of course, they increase with the power, but not quite in the same proportion. Thus a 20 horse-power motor (if well designed for that power) would probably give at least 17 horse-power at the brakes, and would therefore have a mechanical efficiency of $\frac{17}{20}$ = .85, or 85 per cent.,[1] but the same engine throttled down to 5 horse-power would probably not give out more than 2 **H.P.** at the brake, and would have a mechanical efficiency of $\frac{2}{5}$ = 0.4, or 40 per cent.

This shows what has to be paid for the luxury of driving a car that is powerful enough to negotiate hills at a high speed, and is running at other times much below its full power.

---

horse-power of 23 at the road-wheels although it is only rated at 6 h.p. This seems to suggest that the ultimate, and no doubt fairest, way of rating power will be at the road-wheels.

[1] A good average result. When working under favourable conditions, this efficiency varies from 90 to 70 per cent., that is to say, from 10 to 30 per cent. Of the full power developed in the cylinder (the indicated horse-power) is lost.

55. **Fuel Efficiency of the Engine.**—We have remarked (Art. 50) that few motors running have a **heat efficiency** higher than 25 per cent., and that probably 20 per cent. is nearer the mark most cars reach when running under ordinary conditions. And, if we assume their **mechanical efficiency** to be **75 per cent.,** and take the product of these quantities, namely, $\frac{20}{100}$ x $\frac{75}{100} = \frac{15}{100}$, we get **15 per cent,** of all the energy of the fuel given out in the form of work by the **crank-shaft**.

Now with this data before us, we will see what power should be developed at the **crank-shaft** if we are using a **gallon** of 0.680 **petrol** per hour when running. A gallon of this spirit will weigh 6.8 lbs.,[1] and we have seen (Art. 50) that the heat units in one lb. of petrol may[2] = 20,748, therefore the number in one gallon = 6.8 x 20,748 = 141,086.4 **B.T.U.** (equal to 141,086 x 778 ft.-lbs.), and therefore the **brake horse-power** = $\frac{15(141,086 \times 778}{100(60 \times 33,000)}$ = 8.315[3]; so, on these assumptions, the horse-power an engine that is burning a gallon of petrol an hour can be expected to give out is an average of $8\frac{1}{3}$, nearly equivalent to $\frac{8.315 \times 100}{75}$ = 11.08; say, **11 indicated horse-power.**

As some cars run 30 miles[4] (at about 20 miles per hour) on a gallon of petrol, it follows that their brake horse-power and indicated horse-power can very little exceed an average of $\frac{2}{3}$ x 8.315 = 5.543, and $\frac{2}{3}$ x 11.08 = 7.386 respectively.

Obviously, the heavier spirit now used gives more power per gallon, as the calorific value per gallon may for practical purposes be taken as proportional to the specific gravity.

[1] The weight of a gallon of liquid is found by multiplying its specific gravity by the weight of a gallon of water (or 10 lbs.), so 0.680 x 10=6.8 lbs., which is the weight of a gallon of 0.680 petrol at 59° F.

[2] In Art. 50 we referred to petrol of specific gravity 0.700, but so long as the ratio of H to C remains constant, the theoretical thermal value *per lb.* is the same for all densities. We have also seen that there is very little variation in calorific values for different densities, the lightest spirits having the highest values by weight.

[3] This is the power given out at the crank-shaft. There are further losses in transmitting it to the road-wheels, as we shall see.

[4] In the small car trials of Sept. 1904, the 7 H.P. Clyde car averaged 47.2 miles per gallon, its best performance giving 3.51 H.P. at the driving-wheels.

Thus, with 0.700 petrol the horse-powers would be $\frac{70}{68}$ the above values.

Of course, engines fitted with **ball bearings** have a **higher mechanical efficiency,** and give out a proportionately higher **B.H.P.**

56. **Fuel Efficiency of the Car.**—We have seen in Art. 23 that all the energy of the fuel we can expect to get in the form of work at the crank-shaft is 15 Per cent, but there are further **serious losses, due to friction,** before power is available at the driving-wheels. Thus we must expect a loss of about 15 per cent, from crank-shaft to propeller-shaft through the **friction in the gear-box,** and a further loss of, say, 20 per cent, from propeller to cross-shaft after the bevel wheels have worn a bit, and a still further loss of 15 per cent, from the cross-shaft to the road-wheels through the more or less **dirty chains** in chain-driven cars; this, of course, means that the **total efficiency** may be $\frac{85 \times 80 \times 85 \times 15}{100 \times 100 \times 100 \times 100} = 0.0867$, or 8.67 per cent., or approximately

only a little more than **one-twelfth** of the potential **energy of the fuel** is available as **useful work** at the tyres of the **driving-wheels**[1] of such a car. Of course, in high-grade cars, kept in the pink of running condition, these frictional losses will be appreciably less and the efficiencies proportionally greater; in fact, the former may not amount to more than about 20 per cent, from the engine to the road-wheels, whilst the above extreme case gives us $\frac{85 \times 80 \times 85}{100 \times 100 \times 100} = \frac{58}{100}$ nearly, or a loss of a little over 40 per cent. So that the range may be taken as between 20 and 40 per cent.

56A. **Horse-power at road-wheels to drive a car** at about 20 miles per hour. This can be easily approximately determined, either for (a) on the level; (b) up a hill.

(a) **On an ordinary level road** a car takes about 3.75 lbs. per cwt. to propel it against a pretty stiff wind at 20 miles

---

[1] In the best practice, with a loss of only 20 per cent between engine and car, it can be seen that the total efficiency will be 12 per cent.; or a little over an eighth of the heat of the fuel will be utilised for horse-power at the road-wheels.

per hour. Then we have Approx. H.P. of car at the road-wheels on the level

$$= \frac{(\text{Wt. in cwts. x 3.75}) \times \left(\frac{5280 \text{x speed in miles per hour}}{60} \right)}{33,000}$$

Cancelling, we have Approx. **H.P.** of car on level

$$= \frac{\text{Wt. in cwt. x speed in miles per hour}}{100}$$

Example.—A 30 cwt. car is run at 20 miles—

$$\text{H.P. at the road-wheels} = \frac{30 \times 20}{100} = 6.$$

(b) **Up a hill.**—When a car of weight W is driven up a gradient of one in G (say, 1 in 10) it has to raise its own weight 1 ft. for every 10 ft. it moves up the plane, or the additional tractive force the car must exert due to the gradient will be $\frac{W}{G}$ (in this case $\frac{W}{10}$), so the additional H.P.

$$= \frac{\text{Wt. in lbs. W} \times \frac{5280}{60} \times \text{speed in miles S}}{\text{G} \times 33,000} = \frac{\text{W lbs. x S miles}}{\text{G} \times 375}.$$

Example.—Additional H.P. for the **30** cwt. car at **20** miles per hour $= \frac{(30 \times 112) \times 20}{10 \times 375} = 17.92$; say, 18. So that the power at the road-wheels required to drive this car up a gradient of 1 in 10 at 20 miles an hour will be approximately 6 + 18 = 24 horse-power.

57. **The Effect of Altitude on Horse-Power.**—The question as to the effect of altitude on horse-power has often been raised, more particularly since cars have been freely used in such mountainous places as the heights of India, the western part of the United States, the great plateau of Mexico, and the mountain roads of Italy and Switzerland, most of which are several thousand feet above the sea-level; but apparently it has not received anything like the attention it deserves, or must sooner or later receive from the scientific investigator, to provide the designer with **suitable data** for the production of highly efficient **engines for aeroplanes and dirigible balloons**. It is known in a general way that as we ascend the air becomes more rarefied, due to the height or head of the atmosphere decreasing, and that this corresponds to a lower

barometric or atmospheric pressure. This decrease in the density of the air as we ascend means that a larger volume of it must be provided per lb. of fuel, and that fall in the pressure reached by compression occurs, which causes a reduction of thermal efficiency and a falling off in the output of power: how great this may be is indicated by some very interesting experiments that were carried out by a French investigator and described in an article in *La Technique Automobile*, Paris, a translation, by Mr. Charles B. Hayward, of which appeared in the *Automobile* of August 22, 1907. The apparatus, which was very simple but admittedly crude, consisted of a four-cylinder engine with 100 mm. bore, and 120 mm. stroke, which gave 33 brake horse-power at 1350 revolutions per minute, with the normal atmospheric pressure of 760 mm. The engine was connected direct to an electric brake, and the air-supply to the carburettor was taken through a large tank provided with a cock at the opposite end to permit the operator to vary the pressure in its interior at will, the latter being indicated on a mercurial manometer mounted on the end of a spiral tube communicating with the tank. The automatic carburettor was adjusted so as to permit the engine to develop its full-rated power of 33 horse at the normal speed of 1350, and was not touched throughout the experiments.

In starting the experiments the air-cock was opened, and, after regulating the rheostat, the pressure and power were read off directly and converted into terms of altitude and effective output, with the following results:—

TABLE X.—RESULTS OF ALTITUDE AND HORSE-POWER EXPERIMENTS

Altitude in Metres.	Preasure in mm.	Ratio[1]	Break Horse-Power.
0	760	1.00	33
1000	670	0.84	28
2000	590	0.72	24
3000	522	0.60	20
4000	462	0.50	16.5

It will be noticed that at 1000 metres altitude the above table shows the fall in horse-power to be only slight, whilst at 4000 it is nearly 50 per cent.

IGNITION

58. There is no part of the petrol motor of greater importance than the ignition apparatus, the slightest disarrangement of which invariably causes trouble, as every driver soon discovers, for he finds that most stoppage are due to something abnormal occurring to this all-important part of the motor's mechanism. Of course, the **function of the ignition apparatus** is to ignite the charge of explosive mixture in the cylinder on or about the completion of the compression stroke, when the charge is at its maximum pressure due to compression, and a working stroke is about to commence. This ignition was formerly very generally effected by what was called tube ignition, and although this system is obsolete for motor car purposes,[2] it should still have at least a historical interest, and therefore we will briefly describe it.

59. **Tube Ignition.**—A small platinum tube, closed at one end, was fitted to the cylinder in the combustion chamber, the closed end projecting outside, and heated to

---

[1] In the article referred to the writer states that "several authors have estimated that the power of a motor should be proportional to the mass of the mixture aspired in a certain unit of time," so assuming a constant speed he demonstrated that the altitude increasing in an arithmetical progression, the power will decrease in a geometrical progression, so that at 1000 metres the result would be $\frac{P}{P^\circ} = 0.88$. Unfortunately this theory is inexact, because he does not take into account the diminution of compression in the engine cylinders, due to the decrease of the density of the air as the altitude increases.

[2] It is still very largely used in stationary gas engines.

incandescence by a blow-lamp of the Bunsen burner type[1]
fed from the petrol tank, the mixture being forced into the
tube and ignited each time compression occurred. It might
be supposed that with this arrangement the charge would be
apt to ignite before the completion of the compression stroke
(indeed, this pre-ignition did sometimes occur, accompanied
by a peculiar sound, which if once heard is easily recognised),
retarding the piston as it neared the end of its stroke, and
putting a severe strain upon the crank and all the bearings;
but by moving the lamp to another part of the tube, farther
away from the cylinder, the time of firing could be retarded,[2]
and this retardation made to vary the power and speed of
the engine. Thus the singular synchronism of pressure and
ignition, due to the mixture becoming rapidly more explosive
as its pressure increased, was capable of being adjusted.
Of course, when the valves were leaky, the compression
suffered, and the mixture was not forced to the part of the
tube directly over the flame (which was more or less filled
with the burnt gases from the previous stroke), the **timing**
or moment of ignition being affected with constant reduction
in power. Again, with this arrangement, when the lamp was
adjusted for a certain speed, it was not right for a higher or
lower one; but the arrangement has been made to give very
good results on comparatively slow-running engines, with a
limited range of speed. Thus the principal reasons why tube
ignition died out were, the time of firing the charge was not
sufficiently variable at the hands of the driver, and the use of
a naked light on the car was a very real danger. To the use of
an **electric spark** to ignite the explosive mixture in petrol
engines at a moment which can be controlled by the driver,
giving him **command over a wide range of speed,** not
a little of the wonderful development of the motor is due, and
we must now give some attention to—

60. **Electric Ignition,** which is a great advance over
the method just described, as, with it, greater compression
is possible, and there is absolute immunity against fire.

---

[1] There was some difficulty in keeping the lamp alight when the wind caught the
car in certain directions, and the flame was apt to get deflected from the ignition
tube, allowing it to cool down enough to cause late firing, with weaker explosion,
and consequent loss of power.

[2] Another arrangement used to advance and retard the ignition was a nipple
whose orifice could be regulated.

ELECTRIC IGNITION

Needless to say, the object of the electric ignition apparatus is to automatically produce a very hot electric spark (as blue as possible) in the midst of the explosive mixture, at or about the moment the working stroke commences. In a broad sense there are two systems at present in use—(a) the well-known **high-tension ignition**, involving the use of **induction coils,** with either **accumulators or batteries**, and (b) **electro-magnetic ignition**, in which a permanent magnet is the agent, and the rotation or oscillation of an armature or field-piece is used to generate the necessary current.

In the former (a) the **electric current** is produced by what we may call **chemical means,** whilst in the latter system (b) small dynamos or magnetos, driven by the motor itself, **mechanically** generate the current used for firing the mixture; but as they only work when the motor is running, the electric current required to start the engine has to be generated either by giving a certain speed to the engine, by working the starting-handle, or the current for starting is supplied by an accumulator, which, when necessary, is recharged by the dynamo. On the other hand, these machines have many advantages, not the least important of which is freedom from stoppages due to short circuits and leakage; they also **can be made to give a hotter spark** than primary batteries and accumulators, and are therefore more capable of causing complete ignition of a big charge; but, as at present made, their delicate construction makes them liable to give a deal of trouble. However, there are several types striving for supremacy,[1] and it is not yet possible to predict the ultimate issue.

Although the usual form of ignition is of the electro-magnetic type, the high-tension ignition system, with accumulators and induction coils, previously referred to, is still to be met with, but as a supplementary system working on to separate plugs, therefore it may be briefly examined, but the exigencies of space forbid the author dealing with the other systems in use; he must refer the reader to works that

---

[1] There is sure to be some further marked improvements and interesting developments in this direction.

treat specially on ignition systems.[1] Referring to **Fig. 1,** it will be seen that **this electrical system consists** of (1) the **accumulator** or **battery,** (2) the **coil,** (3) the **commutator** or **contact maker and breaker,** (4) the **sparking plug,** (5) the **switch.** And we may now proceed to describe these parts before attempting to explain how they must be linked up to form a complete system; so we may commence with—

61. **The Battery or Accumulator.**—This is called a **primary battery** if it is so arranged that electricity is created by the chemical action of acid solution upon zinc and carbon plates, but if it consists of a series of lead grids or plates, some filled with a paste of peroxide of lead, forming the positive element, and others filled with pure lead in a finely divided or spongy condition, forming the negative element, placed in a liquid-proof receptacle filled with water acidulated with sulphuric acid, it is an **accumulator** (or secondary or storage battery), which can accumulate or store[2] within itself a charge of electricity from a dynamo, or a primary battery of suitable construction. When discharged, both the positive, or lead-peroxide plates, and the negative, or spongy lead plates, are largely converted into lead sulphate. When being charged, the lead sulphate undergoes a chemical change, due to the electrolytic action of the charging current, which converts the positive plates once more into peroxide of lead, and the negative plates into spongy metallic lead. These two elements in the sulphuric acid solution give an electro-motive force of about 2.2 volts. Thus the accumulator creates electrical energy in the same sense as a primary battery does, *i.e.,* by chemical

---

[1] "Electric Ignition for Motor Vehicles," an admirable little work, by the author's colleague, Mr. W. Hibbert, contains much instructive matter

[2] Strictly speaking, it does not actually store electricity. The lead plates and lead-peroxide, by means of a continuous current or charge from some outside source, are so changed that they become capable, owing to their chemical condition, of themselves creating a flow of electricity when the circuit is closed. The usual cells are of two distinct types—namely, the **Plante,** in which the active material is chemically or electrically formed out of the surface of the leaden conductor, and the Faure, in which the active material is formed into a paste, and is caused to adhere to a lead grid or conductor. The former type is superior for durability, but the latter has the great advantage of being much less expensive in manufacture. Most of the accumulators now made are one or the other of these types, only differing in constructional details. They all have a **very low internal resistance** compared with any form of primary battery. Some automobile makers now use accumulators fitted with Plante positive plates and Faure negatives for traction.

action, but is renewable, when exhausted, by passing through it a current of electricity from another source, in the opposite direction to that taken from it in discharging.[1]

Accumulators are more generally used than primary batteries, for although they have not the same capacity (will not be efficient for so many miles) bulk for bulk, when properly used they have not to be replaced by new ones after they have become exhausted, as must be done with the latter.[2] As in both cases the method of using them and their function is the same, either can be used in this system of ignition, but for the reasons given we will assume that accumulators are preferred. Now, each accumulator is fitted with two **terminals**, called **positive**[3] and **negative poles**, arranged so that wires can be connected to them by means of set screws. If these terminals be connected by a wire (completing the circuit), electricity will flow from the positive to the negative terminal continuously, and in so doing will gradually **discharge the accumulator**. Electricity flows with very little resistance through all metallic substances, and with more resistance through water or across any moist or wet surface. If a wire carrying a current comes into contact with any metallic substance in more than one place, the current will divide between the two; in this case the wire is said to be **short-circuited** at that part. Therefore, in conveying current from one part of the motor to another,[4] the wires must

---

[1] The **life of the accumulator** greatly depends upon the **care taken in charging and discharging,** and upon the **purity of the materials used,** and it is false economy to buy anything but the best cells.

[2] **Primary batteries** are usually **dry ones,** modifications of the simple voltaic elements, zinc and carbon, of constant or non-polarisable type, **filled** with some material to prevent the liquid electrolyte from spilling. A **battery** usually consists of **four cells,** and although the initial **cost of** these is far **less than that of accumulators,** and they are capable of standing **rougher** and more irregular **treatment,** they are **not** so **economical,** as their energy depends upon the consumption of the zinc **plates, and** when these have been **used up,** the cells are practically **worthless, and must** be **replaced.** So, **for continual use,** this **makes them ultimately twice as costly as accumulators.**

[3] **The positive** terminal on an accumulator or battery is coloured red.

[4] To reduce the resistance to a minimum, and avoid the chance of leakage, these connections should be as direct and short as possible, and great care should be taken in making them.

be (**insulated**) covered with insulating materials, those of an india-rubber nature being found most efficient. The higher the tension or pressure used to urge the current through the circuit, the thicker must the non-conducting cover be, for if the insulation be not sufficiently good, electricity may **leak** through the engine frame to the negative pole (*become short-circuited*, or **shorted**, as it is sometimes called). Now the electrical current, as it is discharged from the accumulator, is not lacking in **quantity (amperage),1** but it is of too low voltage[2] or pressure, and to get a current to pass, in the form of sparks, across the small insulating gap at the end of the sparking plug, the pressure must be **raised from** that of the accumulator cells, viz., about 4.4 volts, to some **thousands of volts**; so, to transform it into the **high-tension** current necessary for this purpose, it is passed through—

62. **The Induction Coil.**—When the current flows from the accumulator, it is conducted through several turns of insulated wire (about 20 gauge), wound round a **central core** of soft iron wire. This is known as the **"primary"** or **"low-tension" winding.** From there it passes to a **contact-breaker,** which automatically opens and closes the circuit, and then flows back to the accumulator, so completing the circuit. Round this primary coil (but well insulated from it) is wound a second coil of *very many* turns of fine wire (about 32 gauge), the ends of which are connected to the terminals of the sparking plug. This coil is known as the **"secondary"** or **"high-tension"** winding. When the primary current flows, it magnetises the iron core, and the magnetic field established interlinks with the very many turns of the secondary coil; it also immediately attracts the iron armature of the contact-breaker, and so breaks the circuit. The **magnetic field** then disappears, and the spring of the contact-breaker pulls the armature back to its original position. This again completes

---

[1] The ampère is the unit of current, or the unit rate of flow of electricity; and the ampère-hour equals the ampère flowing for one hour.

[2] The volt is the unit of pressure, electro-motive force (E.M.F.), or potential difference (P.D.). The unit of resistance which the conductor offers to the flow of current through it is the Ohm, and E. M. F. = Ampères x Ohms.

The watt equals the ampère multiplied by the volt, and the watt-hour equals the energy expended in one hour by one watt, which equals 3600 joules, or 3600 x .7373=2654.28 foot-lbs.

the circuit, and the magnetic field once more interlinks with the secondary coil, and the whole operation is repeated in this way several times a second.

The **magnetic field,** in surging through the secondary coil of many turns, induces in it an electrical pressure high enough to break down the insulating gap at the sparking plug points, resulting in a **discharge** across it in the form of **sparks,** which ignites the explosive mixture in the cylinder. The **power** and **efficiency** of the coil is greatly increased by being fitted with a **condenser,** made up of a series of alternate layers of fine tinfoil and paraffin-waxed paper, the connections being *so* made that when the current through the primary winding is interrupted by the vibration of the trembler, the condenser acts as a **"shunt circuit,"** and stores up the energy which would otherwise dissipate itself in a very destructive spark at the platinum contacts of the circuit-breaker,[1] and this stored-up energy helps the current to rise quickly in the primary coils at the next making of the circuit. **The efficiency** of the **spark** depends on the large **number of turns** in the secondary winding as compared with the primary turns, also on the **rapidity** with which the primary **circuit is broken,** and on the strong magnetic field of the soft iron core when temporarily turned into a powerful magnet. Another important detail of the system is—

63. **The Contact-Breaker or Commutator.**[2] —This is generally of the **wiping contact type**[3] as shown in Fig. 1, and consists of an insulated disc (usually made of fibre) fixed to the half-speed shaft. At a fixed point on this disc is

---

[1] If an inefficient condenser be fitted, a strong spark is obtained when the circuit between the platinum-pointed screw and trembler is broken, which quickly causes unsatisfactory working by burning away the contacts, necessitating readjustments, and wasting current.

[2] The two terms contact-breaker and commutator are not synonymous, therefore they must be correctly used. A contact-breaker is fitted to a single-cylinder engine, and a commutator to a multi-cylinder one, though in both cases types and designs may be precisely similar. In the latter case its function is to commute the current from one path to another, or, more explicitly, from one cylinder to another. In the well-known apparatus introduced by Mr. F. C. Blake of Kew, two or more cylinders are fired by means of a single coil with a high-speed trembler.

[3] The other type, which was formerly bo much used, is the spring blade or trembler contact-breaker.

a **sector N** of brass, connected directly to the shaft, which again is in metallic contact with the frame of the motor.

A metal **brush or collector O,** insulated from the frame of the engine, and in metallic contact with one terminal of the primary coil, ordinarily rests on the insulated disc, and wipes it as the latter rotates, acting as a **contact-breaker,** and we shall explain directly what part this **detail** plays in the complete system.

64. **The Sparking Plug.**—The principal features of the sparking plug or igniter are shown in Fig. 11, which represents the De Dion Bouton new pattern plug. Into a brass or gun-metal shell **S** (which is screwed into the cylinder wall, and is in metallic contact with it) a hollow non-conducting plug **D**, made of porcelain (or compressed mica), is held in position by the gland nut **N**, and through plug **D** a wire is fixed, the pointed end **P** being of platinum, and the other end **E** being in metallic contact with the brass cap **C**, on to which the insulated copper wire from the induction coil, carrying the high-tension current, is screwed by the brass fly-nut **F**, placing the platinum point **P** in metallic contact with the wire from the coil. The other platinum point **Q** is fixed in the brass shell **S**, so that **PQ** forms the **spark gap,** and we shall explain directly what occurs when the plug is in use.

65. **External Plug Gap.**—By introducing a second gap of about $\frac{1}{16}$" into the high-tension circuit, a spark can be maintained inside the cylinder under conditions which would otherwise prevent any effective ignition taking place, and contrivances have been introduced for attaching to the **sparking plug,** so that external sparks can be obtained. This not only **intensifies the spark,** but assists in preventing trouble due to sooting of the plug, and enables the driver to **see** at a glance whether **current** is **passing** through each of the **plugs;** and another advantage is, he has not to resort to the common but clumsy method of discovering an erring plug by opening the coil box and holding down the trembler, so that one cylinder is left in at a time. If required, the spark gaps can be attached to the induction coil instead of to the plugs, or to a board on the dash, where the sparks can be seen by the driver, and the failure of the sparking arrangements in a cylinder detected at once.

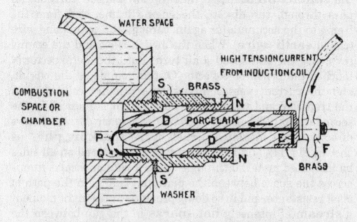

FIG. 11. DE DION BOUTON PATTERN SPARKING PLUG

However, it should be mentioned that plugs fitted with external gaps are not often used now.

66. **The Switch** is a simple contrivance by means of which the primary circuit can easily be made or broken by a small movement of a metal connecting- piece. The switch is used for **momentary breaks in running the engine;** by its use the **current** from the accumulator is **switched on or off** the induction coil. Of course, the switch is used to break or make the circuit when the engine is stopped or started. There are several types of switch, the latest and most convenient for motor cycles being that operated by the preliminary movement of applying the brake.

67. **An Interrupter** is merely a means of conveniently **breaking the circuit** when the **motor is not** to be used for a considerable period. Motor bicycles are generally fitted with a plug interrupter, which can be carried in the cyclist's pocket when the machine is not being used, or is standing during a halt.

68. **The Complete Ignition System.**—We may now summarise the various parts which, connected together, form the complete system. Commencing with the **accumulator,** Fig. 1, we have one of its poles connected with one end of the primary coil of the **induction coil,** the other

end being connected (through the switch) to the brush of the **contact-breaker,** so that the low-tension current can pass through the disc to the engine frame, and from the frame to the accumulator again, through the connecting wire (called **earth**[1] **wire**). When the switch is on and the engine revolving, the half-speed shaft turns until the metal sector **N** touches the brush or collector **O**; this completes the circuit, and the current passes through the primary coil, agitates the trembler, and the high-tension current is induced in the secondary coil. This high-tension or secondary current passes directly to the insulated portion of the **sparking plug** (as shown, Fig. 11), and being, as it were, imprisoned on all sides by insulated material through which it cannot escape, jumps across the space between the platinum points, in the path of least resistance, and in so doing produces at the right moment a **stream** of intensely **hot sparks** in the gap between the sparking plug points, **igniting** the **explosive mixture** surrounding it, the high-tension circuit being completed through the engine frame and earth wire to induction coil.

69. **Accumulators, Charging, &c.**—The accumulator used for our purpose[2] usually consists of two cells, each with a voltage of 2.2, and being **connected in series,**[3] as they always are for this ignition apparatus, the result is a **working voltage** of 2 x 2.2 = 4.4; but when the cells are fully charged, it may almost reach 5 volts. There are several methods of charging accumulators, but we need only mention the following three:—

70. **(1st.) Charging from Primary Batteries.**— This is a method that is within the reach of every motorist who is not afraid of a little trouble. The first cost of a **good four-cell primary battery** does not amount to much, and the same remark applies to the cost of charging, if all the materials are used up before they are replaced. If the motorist has only a very limited knowledge of electricity, he would be wise to get an electrician to arrange everything for him at first, and this advice also applies to the other two methods to be explained;

---

[1] We have explained that this word is a misnomer, as there is no direct connection with the earth.

[2] Accumulators are used for lighting as well as for ignition and traction.

[3] In series, the positive or peroxide pole of one cell (usually painted red) is connected to the negative or spongy lead plate of the next cell.

indeed, many ear- owners prefer to send their accumulators to the makers, or to an agent who undertakes the work, to be recharged, rather than be bothered or run any risk of making mistakes; but they should make an effort to understand these things, to protect themselves, and to be able to put things right in case of emergency. The second method is by—

71. (2nd.) **Charging from electric mains,** using **lamps** solely as a **resistance:** this is by far the most popular, but, unless several cells can be charged at the same time, it is the **most extravagant.**

72. (3rd.) The **third method,** which is by far the **best when practicable,** is to also **charge from electric mains,** but using, **as a resistance, lamps which would in any case be used for lighting purposes.** It entails a small outlay for slightly altering the wiring of the room to be used, but should the car-owner have the electric light in his coach-house, it can be easily arranged for the purpose, and the accumulators can then be charged when the lights are used for ordinary purposes, the only noticeable effect of this being a slight decrease in the intensity of the light; the current then practically costs nothing. An additional advantage due to this way of charging is that accumulators can be kept nearly always fully charged. Indeed, they should be charged whenever possible, to keep them in order. Of course, it must be **direct current electricity,** as an alternating current would charge and discharge with each alternation. Now, **to keep the cells in order,** it is best not to withdraw more than about 25 per cent, of the total charge from them before **recharging;** but much more, say up to 70 or 75 per cent., can be discharged if the cells are recharged immediately. They should always be fully charged before being put out of action for any considerable time, as there is a constant **tendency** for an **automatic discharge** to occur.

73. **Discharge Rate.**—The normal **discharge rate** through a coil of good construction is about **half an ampère,** so that if the accumulator cells have a **capacity,** as many of them have, of 40 ampère-hours,[1] and the reading of the

---

[1] The quantity of electricity flowing into or out of an accumulator is computed in ampère-hours, and the rate at which it passes a given point in the circuit is indicated in ampères.

ammeter[1] is half an ampère, and about 50 per cent, of the total charge be withdrawn, it can be used for about 40 hours; but suppose the commutator only makes contact for one-fourth of a revolution, the accumulator is only giving **current** for one-fourth of the time, then it can be run for 4 x 40, or 160 **working hours.**

All accumulators are **constructed to charge** and **discharge** at a **certain rate,** and any attempt to **force the rate** of either charging or discharging inevitably results in the peroxide paste being forced out of the **grids,** and the latter being bent and **buckled** by the stress. This often occurs due to **shorting,** when the terminals are connected by a good conductor to ascertain what charge, if any, remains in the accumulator. Of course, this should never be done without a **resistance,** such as the coil, in circuit, nor should the **ampère-meter** be connected direct across the **terminals,** as in either case it would allow the accumulator to **discharge** at many times its correct rate. On the other hand, a **volt-meter**[2] may be connected in this way to take the reading, as it has a **high resistance,** and takes but an infinitesimal current.

This brings us to the question of measuring the charge in the accumulator.

74. **The Voltage of the Current.**—Let us assume that we have before us an accumulator consisting of the usual **two cells fully charged**, each to a voltage of 2.2, giving a voltage of 4.4 when connected in series and tested with the voltmeter. "We may also assume that on being tested with an ammeter[3]

---

[1] The ammeter, or ampère-meter, is an instrument for indicating the rate of charge or discharge in ampères.

[2] An instrument for indicating the electro-motive force, or the electrical pressure in a circuit, or at the terminals of a battery or dynamo.

[3] In testing dry batteries for capacity an ammeter should be used, not a *voltmeter,* because the voltage indicated when the battery is nearly run out is almost the same as when new; the resistance of tho battery and voltmeter together to the passage of a current being relatively high, whether the battery be nearly exhausted or almost new. On the other hand, an *ammeter* offers small resistance, and, if used just long enough to obtain a reading, will indicate by the quantity of current, passing through it the condition of the battery; for as the battery becomes exhausted its resistance increases, and its capacity for giving out current becomes reduced.

(connected up to the coil whilst working and included in series connection[1]) its discharge rate is found to be half an ampère, and that the charge is 30 ampère-hours,[2] we should find that as the **current is discharged** there is a gradual **fall in the voltage,** until, when about half has been withdrawn, the voltage would be only about 4, and if the withdrawal of current be continued, the **fall** in voltage becomes far more rapid till it drops to 3.6, at which reading the accumulator is considered to be **exhausted** or discharged.

75. **Spare Accumulators.**—It is usual to carry a spare set of accumulators, and these are often connected up by a **two-way switch,** so that they can be put in circuit and the others disconnected at any moment. This arrangement takes up no more room than the four-cell primary battery it often replaces, and is a great safeguard against involuntary stoppages.

76. **Testing on a Closed Circuit.**— The expedient of using a small **incandescent lamp** of the same voltage as the accumulator is a good one. This is **connected across** the **terminals** for a moment or two, and if it lights up brightly and the light is sustained, then there is a charge in the accumulator, but if it becomes **dim,** then the **accumulator** is **exhausted**. This test should always be **made at the conclusion of a run,** as the accumulator is capable of **recovering** sufficiently **while standing** to give a fairly bright light for a few moments, even when almost **exhausted.** As this is a **test of current and voltage,** it is very reliable, for a reading with a voltmeter (*testing an open circuit)* will sometimes be almost normal, and a fall of voltage occur as soon as current is withdrawn.

GOVERNING AND CONTROLLING

77. One of the most difficult problems the designer of a petrol engine has to deal with, is the governing of its power

---

[1] The internal resistance of the accumulator being very low, unless a resistance, such as the coil, be placed in the circuit, both the ammeter and accumulator would be damaged, the latter being quickly run down, and the winding of the former seriously over-heated.

[2] The amount of electric energy given out by an accumulator is always less than the amount put in; and the former, compared with the latter, represents the efficiency, which varies from 70 to 80 per cent., according to the age of the accumulator and the rate of charging, being highest when new and slowly charged.

and speed. He is called upon to arrange its mechanism in such a way that the engine *automatically* prevents the production of more power in itself than is actually needed for the propulsion of the car at any particular speed. To give practical effect to this condition, designers have exercised their ingenuity in a variety of ways, but they have a more difficult task to deal with in the petrol engine than in either the steam engine or ordinary gas engine, as we shall see directly.

The function of governing differs from that of controlling; for the engine is *governed automatically,* but *controlled by hand.*

Up to a year or two ago it was the general practice to fit a governor to an engine to so regulate it (by cutting out the exhaust) that it ran at a fairly constant speed; the speed of the car being altered, when the engine showed signs of pulling up, by a change of gear; using the clutch and brake, when in traffic, for momentarily slowing down. But the introduction of the practice of using a variable charge, by **throttling the mixture** (made by Duryea), and the use of more **flexible carburettors** (Kreb's being one of the first) supplemented by varying the ignition, has led to almost **perfect control** over the speed of the engine being obtained; so that there is **now very little use for a governor,** and this accounts for its practical disappearance as a feature of the motor. Indeed, the only excuse for using one now is to prevent the **engine racing,** when it becomes necessary in an emergency to declutch suddenly when the spark and throttle are fully advanced.

It is easy to make arrangements to enable the driver **to control the engine;** and we may proceed to explain how the amount of useful work done by a petrol engine during a cycle can be varied. There are several ways of doing this, the following being the best known:—

(1) Advancing and retarding the ignition, the charge being constant.

(2) Varying the amount of charge by throttling, *the proportion of the mixture being constant.*

(3) Advancing and retarding ignition with fluctuating charge.

(4) By throttling the exhaust.

In order to grasp the general principles that underlie the working of the 1st and 3rd methods, the reader must become familiar with the effect of—

78. **Advancing and Retarding Ignition.**—The power of the engine can be varied between fairly wide limits by varying the time of ignition. If the explosion is to occur at the beginning of a power stroke for running the engine at its full power, the brush of the contact-breaker or commutator (Figs. 1 and 16) should commence to come into contact with the metallic sector on the insulated disc slightly before the piston has completed its compression stroke; as there is always an interval of time between sparking and exploding, the time required to explode the mixture depending upon the proportion of air to spirit vapour forming it, upon the amount of compression, and also upon the proportion of the exhaust gases mingling with the explosive mixture; the interval[1] being shortest when the mixture is perfect and at maximum compression, and increasing as the mixture becomes throttled, causing a smaller quantity to enter the cylinder; which, mixing with the normal quantity of exhaust gases in the clearance or combustion space, results in an impoverished mixture at a lower compression,[2] and in a later explosion. This being the case, the expedient of causing sparking to occur a little earlier, that is, by advancing

---

[1] The explosion arises from the rapid spreading of the flame throughout the whole mass of the mixture; but this is not instantaneous, as, when the spark occurs it explodes the mixture around the points, the flame rapidly spreading through the rest of the mixture; the time of the explosion being the interval which elapses between the beginning of increase and maximum pressure. Thus there is a brief interval between the spark and the full force of the explosion, so the spark must occur sometime before the compression stroke is completed, that is, it must be advanced; the exact amount being decided by trial, and the beat of the engine.

[2] The more the mixture is throttled, the smaller is the volume which is compressed in the cylinder and the lower the pressure due to compression. Thus, if when the cylinder is fully charged at atmospheric pressure, the charge bo compressed to one-fourth the initial volume, then at greatest compression, neglecting refinements, the resulting pressure would be 4 times atmospheric pressure, or, say, 4 x 15 = 60; but if, on the other hand, due to throttling, the cylinder is charged with only half a full volume when the compression begins (this means doing negative work during suction stroke), then obviously the compression cannot exceed 2 x 15 = 30 lbs. per square inch. And with the lower compression there is a marked fall in initial explosive pressure and in thermal efficiency.

the spark, is one that would suggest itself; indeed, it is the one that is generally employed, although in most cases in a somewhat casual way. The object should be to so time the ignition that the greatest pressure due to it occurs at the commencement of the working stroke at all speeds. Therefore the usual practice is to advance the spark as the speed of the engine increases, and, conversely, to retard it as the speed is reduced. If the sparking is so timed that explosion occurs after the piston has started on its power stroke, the ignition is said to be retarded, and the effect of this is to reduce the amount of work done in the cylinder during this stroke.[1] Engineers are able to examine the variation of pressure in the cylinder, during the complete cycle, by using an instrument called an indicator. When using the ordinary form of this instrument, a pencil point traces out a curved figure on a sheet of paper or card,[2] as it is called, and from it the pressure on the piston at all points in its stroke can be measured, a mean of these pressures giving the mean pressure[3] throughout the stroke. The area of the figure formed by the expansion and compression lines (3 and 2, Fig. 12[4]) is a measure of the work done during the stroke, whilst the area of the figure bounded by the exhaust and suction lines 4 and 1 (same Fig.) represents the negative work done by the engine when acting as a pump during the suction stroke. The indicator diagram not only shows the behaviour of the working fluid in the cylinder, but it **reveals any defect** in the valve setting, timing of ignition, and general action.

79. **Late Ignition.**—The diagram (Fig. 13) shows what occurs when the **spark is retarded to** reduce the power

[1] Giving an additional way of regulating the speed. Of course great care must be taken to avoid pre-ignition, with its attendant damaging effects. Refer to p. 120.

[2] The ordinary instrument does not give satisfactory results at very high speeds, but the beautiful **Hospitalier-Carpentier Manograph,** an optical instrument of the type invented by Professor Perry, indicates efficiently at **2000** to **3000** revolutions, when skilfully arranged with **short** and **direct** connections to the engine.

[3] This is the pressure which is used in measuring the indicated horse-power of the engine.

[4] The Figs, are slightly contorted, so that all the lines may be clearly seen.

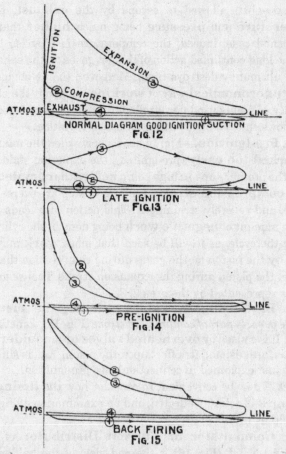

EXPANSION

IGNITION

COMPRESSION

ATMOS 15 EXHAUST LINE

SUCTION

NORMAL DIAGRAM GOOD IGNITION
Fig. 12

ATMOS LINE

LATE IGNITION
Fig. 13

ATMOS LINE

PRE-IGNITION
Fig. 14

ATMOS LINE

BACK FIRING
Fig. 15.

of the engine. It will be seen that the piston has travelled to nearly half stroke before the **highest pressure** (which is much **less** than in the **normal** case) of the burning gases is reached, the **smaller area** of the part 2, 3 showing the **reduced** amount of **work** done, although the same amount of mixture may have been drawn into the cylinder as for Fig. 12; but the rate of **propagation of the flame** throughout the charge **is slow** compared with the piston velocity, due to the **lower compression**,[1] and the gases are only **partially**

---

[1] With late ignition the compressed mixture continues to expand and fall in pressure as the piston moves down till ignition occurs.

burned when allowed to escape by the **exhaust**, their **temperature** and **pressure** being much **higher** than in the normal case; indeed, the temperature is often so high that the long-continued action of the hot gases on the exhaust valves ultimately destroys them. Moreover, this is obviously a very **uneconomical** way of **working,** as about the same quantity of fuel is used per stroke for different powers, so all this shows the evil of governing by spark variation.

80. **Pre-Ignition.**—Fig. 14 shows how, when the mixture is **sparked too early** (pre-ignited), the explosion suddenly sends the pressure up to a high point, **before** the **completion** of the **compression stroke,** tending to stop or reverse the engine, and severely straining it. This action also leads to a certain amount of **negative work** being done in the cylinder during the cycle, as it will be seen that more **work** may be **done by** the piston on the gases during compression than is done *on* the piston during the expansion stroke. This *negative work* is represented by the area 2, 3.

81. **Back-firing,** or **explosion during the suction stroke** or *early part of compression stroke* (Fig- 15), sometimes occurs. It is caused by **overheated valves or smouldering exhaust gases,** and its effect upon the piston, &c., is similar to that just explained in connection with pre-ignition.

It will now be convenient to consider how the **timing of the spark** is actually effected, and an examination of Fig. 16 will help us in this matter. It represents a—

82. **Commutator or Current Distributor** of the Panhard type. **T** (Fig. 16) is the end view of the half-speed shaft, and **M** that of the disc, made of a non-conducting material, usually of a fibrous character; it is keyed to shaft **T**, and is fitted with a metal plate **K**, which is put in metallic contact with the shaft **T**, which is in the electric circuit, by means of a screw or pin **N**. The shell or body **G** has a boss at the back which is bored to fit the shaft, so that its arm or lever **C** can move it and its fittings freely in either of the directions shown by the arrows; into the projecting bosses **HH** insulating sleeves or brush-holders **FF** are screwed, and into these again the brass tubes **VV** are screwed.

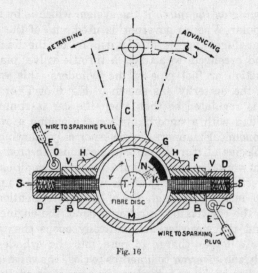

Fig. 16

These tubes contain the *brushes* **BB**, which are made of coiled wire gauze, held in contact with the edges of the disc by the helical springs **SS**, which press against the brass split caps **DD**; bolts or screws **OO** clipping the cap on the tube, the wires **EE** placing the brushes **BB** in metallic contact with the coils. Obviously, this **commutator** is arranged to **serve** two cylinders with cranks side by side, as in the Mors engine, the number of bosses **HH** and their fittings corresponding with the number of the engine's cylinders (with cranks at 180°, the bosses would, of course, be at 90° to one another). The link J is connected to the working handle by suitable rods, wire cables, and levers. A movement of **C** to the left, as can be seen, will cause ignition to occur later, or the **spark** will be **retarded,** just as a movement in the opposite direction will bring the brushes nearer the advancing metallic contact piece, and hasten ignition or **advance the spark.**

COMMUTATOR, OR CURRENT DISTRIBUTOR (Panhard Type), FOR CRANKS SIDE BY SIDE

83. **Governing and controlling by throttling the mixture,** sometimes called **charge volume throttling**

(or governing on the inlet), is the system which is by far the most popular. When a governor[1] is used, one of the crank-shaft centrifugal type is fitted,[2] usually on the half-speed shaft, and arranged, to actuate a throttle valve[3] placed in the induction or fuel pipe of the cylinders—this valve is either of the butterfly[4] (as shown in Fig. 6 at T) or piston type. It is regulated so that when the car is running on level ground with a smooth surface, the engine is working in an economical manner; the governor only allowing suffi-cient explosive mixture to enter the cylinder to produce the amount of work that the resistance due to the condition of the road, direction, and velocity of the wind call for. Should this resistance increase, through any of the causes mentioned, or owing to the car coming to rising ground, the engine slows down, and the governor automatically opens the throttle to enable a larger charge to pass into the cylinder, and, conversely, the governor commences to close the valve as soon as the engine begins to race above its normal speed. But now, in standard practice, engines of pleasure cars are fitted so that the throttle is controlled by a pedal- accelerator, also in most cases by hand (the latter for setting the engine to run at a slow speed), usually through a lever on a toothed quadrant above the steering-wheel.

84. **The Accelerator.**—To enable the engine to exert its maximum power for hill-climbing, and to control its speed in gear-changing, &c., an arrangement called an *accelerator* is fitted; it is a combination of levers, wire cable, and spring, connected to a third pedal projecting through the foot-board, so that by a depression of the pedal the throttle valve is further opened. When a governor was used, the system of levers, &c.,

---

[1] As we have explained, governors are now rarely used on pleasure cars.

[2] Working drawings of a governor are shown in the author's "Drawings of and Notes on a 4-Cylinder Petrol Engine," Longmans & Co.

[3] The quantity is regulated in the Duryea, Bollee, and many other cars by giving the inlet valve a variable lift.

[4] The tendency of many engines fitted with this valve is to run in jerks, first gain-ing speed then slowing down too much, under the action of the governor, or, in other words, the governor hunts; but this un-uniform action may be largely checked, and the running much improved, by drilling a hole about J inch in di-ameter through the disc of the valve, to form a by-pass. Probably in some cases the uniformity of running would be much improved by the governor being fitted with a dash-pot arrangement, but at the best, with light loads, throttle governing is more **or** less unstable.

from the pedal prevented the weights of the governor from exerting their power to close the throttle; in other words, it cut out the governor's action, the throttle remaining open, allowing the speed of the engine to increase above its normal rate, and the engine to work at its maximum power, which is obviously what is required if a steep grade is to be mounted without changing gear; when a car thus fitted failed to make headway, the gear was changed to a lower one[1], and the accelerator thrown out of action, allowing the governor to act again and the engine to run at its normal speed.

Thus when the **use of governors** on pleasure cars was abandoned as an unnecessary complication, the accelerator was retained, as we have seen, the pedal being connected to the throttle valve direct, instead of acting through the governor. But now there is some tendency to discard the accelerator and rely entirely upon the hand-control. The wisdom of this is questionable, and many would miss an old friend, whose only fault is that the pedal has to be depressed all the time the engine is going fast, but this is a fault that can be remedied.

84A. **Governing on the Exhaust.**[2]— In this system a hit-and-miss arrangement, actuated by a centrifugal governor of the crank-shaft type, permits the **exhaust valve** to be raised in the **ordinary way** when the engine is working within its maximum **speed limit,** but when the latter is **reached** a **digger** is **withdrawn** from the exhaust valve spindle or plunger by the action of the governor, so that the **valve remains unlifted,** and the burnt **charge** is **retained** within the cylinder; or the opening of this valve is retarded, a portion of the burnt gases remaining in the cylinder to dilute the next charge admitted. This so reduces the speed of the engine, that the next exhaust stroke is a

---

[1] Drivers easily get into a way of **manipulating the clutch** to enable them to mount the crest of **rising ground without changing gear**. As the engine slows down, the clutch is momentarily withdrawn to allow the engine to gain speed, and is let in again before the car has had time to be much reduced in speed. For obvious reasons this expedient must be worked with moderation; but with the more powerful engines of modern cars it is not often necessary to use it.

[2] As we have explained, governors are no longer used on pleasure cars; but, on the other hand this system of governing has much to recommend it for some stationary purposes.

normal one, and the ordinary cycle of operations is taken up again. With this system there is, of course, a loss due to back pressure, but the cylinder being kept full the compression does not suffer, and the mixture is therefore more economically consumed, although when the engine runs light there is a loss of economy, as the in-coming cold charge mingles with the hot burnt gases, making a high temperature mixture before compression. Not a little of the economy of the Daimler, the Gillet-Forest, and other motors was claimed for this system of governing, but it has died out, and is only now seen on old cars which are still running. However, for stationary work it has advantages which are well worth considering.

CYLINDER COOLING

85. **When** it is remembered that somewhere in the **cylinder** during each working stroke there may be a **temperature** of some 3600° F., tapering off to about 1800° to 2000° F. as the burnt gases pass out of the cylinder, and that the **temperature** of the **cylinder-wall** must be **low enough** to allow of the piston being efficiently **lubricated,** the importance of providing suitable arrangements for keeping the cylinder sufficiently cool can be realised. To make the conditions under which the piston can satisfactorily work in the cylinder a little more clear, it should be explained that the maximum temperature referred to is more or less evolved at the **kernel of the mixture,** the **temperature** near the cylinder-wall probably being not much more than half that amount, and that of the wall itself about 250° F. Further, these high temperatures are much reduced during the suction stroke, when the cool mixture enters, also during the compression stroke, although not to the same extent,[1]

so that the heat imparted to the cylinder each cycle is not so much as might at first be expected; never theless, as an engine making 1000 revolutions a minute will perform a cycle in $\frac{1}{500}$th of a minute, or rather less than $\frac{1}{8}$th of a second, the rapid succession of heat increments could soon raise the temperature of the cylinder to a point when effective

---

[1] A great deal of heat is generated in compressing the mixture, the work done in compressing being converted into heat; but all of this is not lost.

lubrication would be impossible; so to keep the temperature of the cylinder down to a safe point special arrangements have to be made. So far as very **small engines** (such as are used on low-power **motor bicycles**) are concerned, it is sufficient to increase the outer surface of the cylinder by an arrangement of either radiating or circular flanges or ribs,[1] so that in passing through the air it may be **cooled** as much as possible. **The cooling efficiency** of this arrangement (or of the air-cooled tubes of a radiator) **depends upon** the **velocity** of the encountering air, the **extent** of the **surface** in contact with that air, and the **difference in temperature** between the inner surface and the air in contact with the exterior surface. It is found that when this simple method is intelligently carried out, the cylinders of engines up to about 3 horsepower can be effectively cooled, but with larger powers the problem becomes one that requires the assistance of an **additional cooling** agency to solve it; hence the evolution of the arrangement diagrammatically shown in **Fig. 1,** where it will be seen that the cylinder has a **jacket** surrounding it, through which **water** is circulated by a centrifugal pump[2] (P.C.) which forces the water to circulate through the cooling system, entering the jacket at the lowest part a, and leaving it at the top b, passing through the connecting pipe[3] into the **radiator** to the tank[4] at a level of

---

[1] Circular flanges are best, as the air can more completely sweep round them, and they materially add to the strength of the cylinder.

[2] This **pump** is found, on the whole, to be the most satisfactory for the purpose. If made a decent size, not requiring to be run at a high speed, and gear driven, as many now are, it works well, and is not affected by dirt in the water. Other types, such as the **eccentric**, the **rotary-force** or simple **gear-wheel**, have been tried and used by a few makers, but although they give an excellent circulation when perfect, they **soon wear out**, and their first **cost is greater**, to say nothing of the difficulty of keeping their wearing parts **lubricated** without introducing into the cylinder jacket and tubes an oily viscous coating that much impairs their efficiency.

[3] These pipes are often made too small, and with **bends** much **too sharp**, to allow of a free and unrestricted circulation. They should not be less than | inch diameter, and the bends should have a radius of at least some five diameters when practicable.

[4] The connections c and d to the tank should be as far away from one another as possible; so as to get a good circulation of water in the tank, they are usually placed at opposite ends, as shown. The tank is fitted with a filling hole, usually

about its centre c, and leaving it at its bottom *d* to enter the pump again. If the tank and radiator be sufficiently large, and the former fixed high enough above the engine,[1] a very fair natural circulation results without using a pump; in fact, this gravity or thermo-syphon system has the great advantage of simplicity to recommend it, and formerly was much used, and still is used with advantage on very light cars. Thus the introduction of forced circulation, with the indispensable pump, which in some form or another is almost general, has reduced the weight of the cooling system, and increased its efficiency, but has added to the number of parts which require attention and are liable to give trouble. The cooling system being a vital part of the motor, it greatly reduces the possibility of annoying stoppages when fitted so that in case of emergency the pump can be thrown out of circuit, and the engine run on low speed and power with natural or gravity circulation.

86. **Radiators**.—There are three types of radiators in use, namely, the **multitubular, honeycomb**, and **coil**. The honeycomb was first brought out on the famous Mercedes car. In this the water is made to circulate around a great number (in some cases amounting to 5000 or 6000) of small tubes fixed about $\frac{1}{16}$ of an inch apart, its **principal advantage** being the **small volume and weight of water** used, some few pints only being required. Its **drawbacks** are that the **workmanship** must be of the very **highest class**, or leakage troubles will occur. Radiators of this type are very **difficult to repair**, and the **passages** being so very small, they are liable to get **choked**. In the multitubular type, and the ribbed or gilled pipe coil, the section of the pipe is usually circular,[2] and in the latter the surface of the gills flat-although in some cases they are corrugated, the idea being that, as they expose more surface to the action of the air, they are more

---

closed with a screwed bung, and an open tube from the highest part, bent over the tank side to allow any steam that may be generated to escape.

[1] Vibration, and the slight yielding of the frame when the car is roughly used, cause the connections to become leaky; so, for this reason, armoured rubber hose is to be preferred for the connections, which should always be long enough to prevent undue straining actions.

[2] A flattened tube has a larger cooling surface than a circular one of the same sectional area, but it offers more resistance to the flow through it, particularly at the bends.

efficient; but it has been proved that this is not the case, the corrugations retarding the passage of air between them, and causing as much loss of cooling effect as was gained by the extra surface.

87. Air-fans are now generally **used to avoid carrying more water** and a **larger radiating surface** than is absolutely **necessary.** The fan is usually placed immediately behind the radiator, and is sometimes supplemented by making the **fly-wheel** act as a **fan,** forming it with fan-like blades, but of course when this is done it is necessary to close in the engine between the two fans, so as to prevent the air entering from other sources than through the radiator. A great **advantage** of the fan is that it creates a **forced draught** when the **vehicle** is **stationary,** or is going very slowly uphill or in **traffic,** whilst the engine is running fast and there is **no natural draught** to prevent **overheating.** But unless fans be skilfully designed, and run at a speed sufficiently high (which, by the way, requires a fair amount of power), they can easily *be worse than useless.*[1] The scientific determination of the most suitable fan for a given motor represents a somewhat difficult problem; doubtless with few exceptions the average fan used on cars is largely a matter of guess-work, very little calculation or science entering into its construction. Notwithstanding this, in most well-made cars it works with satisfactory results.

Fans are usually driven from a pulley fixed on the front end of the crank-shaft by a belt of either flat, round, or vee section, and occasionally by a coil **spring belt**, which has the advantage of being elastic enough to **lessen** the **shocks,** due to the quickly **varying speeds** of the engine, which are very **damaging** when the **drive** is positive through **spur-gearing**. It may be mentioned that very good results are got from fans of about 15" diameter, with six 2" blades set approximately at an angle of 45°, with a normal speed of about 1400 to 1500 revolutions per minute. But in not a few cases that the writer has come across in

---

[1] They also draw the dust from the roads and the hot air off the radiators on to the engine, which is a drawback. This is avoided in the **Renault system**, where the **fan blades** are formed on the periphery of the fly-wheel, and the radiator is placed behind the engine and next to the dash.

the past, the fans have been so small and insignificant and so badly formed that the efficiency of the motor would have been increased by scrapping the fan and paying a little more attention to the free and easy circulation of water in the cooling system, and the condition of the **surface** of the **radiator,** which should be so treated that heat leaves it with the greatest freedom. **Now,** strangely enough, **all bright and polished surfaces reluctantly part with their heat,**[1] whilst most **dull rough ones freely lose it;** therefore, the common practice of blackleading and polishing cylinders and cooling pipes, or coating them with metallic paints, impairs the efficiency of the rough surface. **The best stuff** known for coating purposes is **lampblack,** and the rougher the surface to which this is applied the more easily will it part with its heat.

88. **Air-Locking.**—Trouble sometimes occurs due to the system becoming **air-locked** in filling up with water, an **air-bubble** forming in the top of a bend and getting compressed and set instead of circulating when the pump begins to work. This of course means that the flow of water is stopped, with consequent **boiling away** of that portion of the water which is kept in contact with the cylinder, it not being free to pass through the radiator, which quickly becomes hotter at the upper part than at the bottom; so, if a sensible difference of temperature be detected in these parts after the engine has been running a few minutes, it means that there is either an air-lock or the **pump is not working;** if the former, it may sometimes be relieved by **opening** the **air-cock** which is generally fitted to the top of the radiator,[2] or, this failing to give relief, by drawing off the water and continuing to fill up the tank while the engine is running slowly.

88A. **Steam locks** may also occur if the water boils, and there are crevices in the water system in which the vapour can get pocketed.

88B. **Overheating of the cylinder,** usually referred to as **overheating,** manifests itself by **a knocking sound**

---

[1] Part of the heat is carried or *conducted* away by the air in contact with the surfaces and part by *radiation*.

[2] If such a cock is not fitted, a joint or connection in the upper water-pipe may be broken to let out the air.

or by the **engine pulling badly.** It is most often due to **imperfect water circulation,** which may be **caused** by an **air or steam lock** (as we have seen), **furring of pipes** due to hard water, **faulty** working of the **pump,** faulty lubrication of the cylinder, faulty ignition[1] or mixture too rich. When overheating occurs it causes excessive expansion of the incoming charge, so that a full one is not admitted, and the excessive heat may bum up the lubricant, causing seizing of the piston, and it may cause premature ignition, exploding the mixture before compression is completed with loss of power and possible damage to the crank-shaft, &c.

88c. **Non-Freezing Solutions.**—As is well known, water in the process of **freezing expands,** and exerts an enormous force upon any unyielding containing vessel, so, if the **material** of the vessel is **not ductile** enough, it **bursts,**[2] as **cylinders and pumps** are apt to do. The best way to **avoid** trouble due to freezing is to have **drain cocks** fitted to the **water system,** so that water from all parts, including the pump, can be run off every **night** during frosty weather. **Another method** to avoid trouble is to use a **chemical stuff** to lower the freezing point of the water. Many substances have been tried, the most efficient and safe but most expensive **is glycerine, in the proportion of about 3 parts to 7 of water.** Charges of about $1\frac{1}{2}$ pint of methylated spirits have been found effective and less expensive. Of course, fresh quantities must be occasionally added to make good that which passes off with the steam.

SILENCERS

89. No one can fail to have noticed what marked improvements have been made during the past few years in **muffling,** or *deadening,* **the sound** of the **exhaust gases**

---

[1] Which may be due, with the high-tension system, to partly broken wires, loose connections, wear of the wipes, or the fibre wheel causing imperfect contact with the sector, sooted sparking plugs or broken porcelain, imperfect contact at the trembler or exhausted accumulators.

[2] The simple expedient of making a pipe slightly oval in section is a good safeguard. Of course, lead pipes used for domestic water-supply call easily be flattened a little and made safe from rupture by freezing,

from petrol motors, and all must agree that this is a step in the right direction; indeed, one well worth making if we have not to pay too dearly for it in greatly **reduced effective power,** which is the price represented by want of skill in designing the silencer. The problem to be solved is how to deaden the noise caused by the sudden liberation of the exhaust hot gases under pressure. The engine, as used at the present time, emits the **products of combustion** at such a temperature and pressure that they **expand violently,** striking the surrounding air, and **causing** the sensation which we know as a noise or explosion. Now, the silencing method usually adopted is to muffle this noise by passing the gases into a cylinder or muffle of considerable capacity, to allow them to expand and cool[1] with little resistance till their pressure is reduced to almost that of the atmosphere; their path through the cylinder being made more or less tortuous by **baffles** and **perforated pipes,** with the object of **breaking up** the **sound-waves** and reducing their velocity, so that the gases pass out of the silencer nearly inert and noiseless.

By a variation of the above method the gases are sometimes discharged through a **large number of little holes** in a **silencer** of very **small dimensions,** the idea being to **break up** the **large explosion** into very many **small ones,** which, not synchronising, more or less cancel one another. But any attempt to reduce the dimensions of the silencer below a certain **capacity,** which **depends upon size** of the engine **cylinder** and **pressure** of the **gases as they** leave the exhaust valve, must mean an increase of **back pressure;** and this **resistance** is considerably **increased** by using **sharp bends** in the **pipe** from exhaust valve to silencer.

---

[1] The cooling causes the gases to contract, and this reduces the ultimate volume of the expanding gases at ejection.

TYPICAL SILENCER

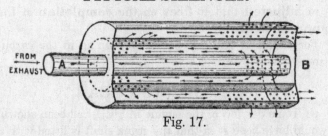

Fig. 17.

A very good idea of how a **typical silencer** works can be formed by examining **Fig. 17,** where, if the arrows be followed, it will be seen that the gases pass through in a zig-zag way, increasing in volume, and therefore decreasing in pressure, as they near the outlets to the atmosphere at the end B.

Formerly, **silencers** were largely **made** of sheet iron or steel; now **aluminium** and **cast iron,** which are less resonant, are very generally used.

89A. **Exhaust Cut-out.**—Some cars are fitted with a **by-pass valve** (called an exhaust cut-out), so that the driver can temporarily allow the gases to escape without all passing through the silencer, thereby slightly reducing the back pressure; but the noise is very objectionable when this valve is opened, and *its use on the road is now illegal;* it should only be used in the motor-house or workshop to test the proper firing of the cylinders.

90. **Back-firing or Popping** in the silencer is nearly always caused by a **misfire,** either through the mixture being too weak, or due to some **defect** in the **ignition system**. The charge is not then exploded in the cylinder, but passes out of the exhaust valve into the silencer, where it is ignited either by the heat of the exhaust pipe or passages, or by the red-hot exhaust gases which follow on the next normal power stroke. When the **speed** of a motor is **suddenly checked,** the piston does not move quick enough to suck in a sufficient **quantity of spray** to carburate the air, so the remedy is to push the mixture lever forward when suddenly reducing speed.

If the trouble is due to **faulty ignition,** the latter must be so **adjusted** that it **fires** on the **completion** of the **compression stroke.**

For causes of backing, firing, or popping in the carburettor, see Article 19.

TRANSMISSION GEAR

91. If a side-view of the engine in Fig. 1 had been shown, it would have been seen that the crank-shaft is fitted with a **fly-wheel,** whose function in a reciprocating engine is well understood, as most people are aware that not a little of the even running of a petrol engine, with its one working stroke in four, is due to this important part being of sufficient **size and weight.** Of course, it is keyed to the tail of the crank-shaft, as shown in Fig. 18 at D, and in most cases it is made with a conical hole arranged to form, with the male conical block C, a **friction clutch.** This clutch is used to connect the road wheels with the motor through a mechanism called *the transmission gear.* And two forms of this gear or drive now hold the field, one, called **chain drive,** in which *side-chains* are used to drive the back **road-wheels,** which are **loose on** the **axle,** and the other, **live-axle,** in which the power is transmitted to the back axle by tooth gearing, causing it to rotate in its outer or hollow tube and carry with it the rear **road-wheels,** which are in this case **fixed** to it.[1] **To** understand these arrangements, and to be clear about what happens when a car is reversed, or put on a different speed

---

[1] The live-axle in most cars now consists of a hollow tube or axle fixed to the rear springs in such a way that it is incapable of revolving, the ends of the tube being arranged so that they form journals for the hubs of the road-wheels to freely revolve on. The two lengths of the differential shaft run in the tube and project at the ends, where they are coupled to the ends of the road-wheel hubs, the differential gear itself being at the centre of tube, where, of course, connection is made with the differential shaft lengths. With this arrangement the whole of the weight of the rear end of the car is supported by the fixed hollow axle, and no strain, except that due to the transmission, comes on the differential shaft, which is then said to float in the hollow axle, and for that reason is often referred to as a **floating axle**. It used to be the practice (and is now in some cars) to mount the *road-wheels* direct on the ends of the **differential shaft**, causing the whole weight to come directly on it, resulting in excessive friction and difficult lubrication.

by a change of gear, the reader is referred to Figs. 18 and 19, which diagrammatically show typical examples of these gears. The former illustrates the system of

91A. Driving through Side-Chains.—It will be seen that the male part **C** of the **clutch** is kept in frictional contact with the fly-wheel part **D**, by the action of the compressed helical **spring S,** the friction between them due to the spring being great enough to enable the engine to drive the car through the clutch. A bell-crank lever, with a fork at one end and a pedal at the other, is fitted to the grooved collar **M**, as shown in Fig. 20, in such a way that when the pedal **G** is pushed, the spring is compressed and the clutch thrown out of action. Now, although this small end movement of the clutch cone **C** in relation to the shaft **N** can take place, they are so coupled that when **C** is "let in," and is rotating about its axis, the shaft **N** is made to turn with it.[1] Keyed to **N** (Fig. 18) are three wheels, E, B, and **P** (E and B are used for **running ahead,**[2] and **P for reversing),** each of the two former of which is arranged to mesh with one of the wheels on the sleeve GO. Now this sleeve is usually made with a square hole fitting the shaft **RV,** which is square to fit it.[3]

The sleeve has on it a grooved collar, which engages a sliding fork F, suitably connected at L, to the change-speed lever fixed at the right-hand side of the car, and this lever works in a quadrant with four notches, one of these

---

[1] The **end** of the **shaft** N is usually made **square** where it fits the clutch C, or the latter drives the shaft N through a feather or feathers fixed to it or forming part of it.

[2] It will be noticed that, for simplicity's sake, the **gear-box** in this example only contains two pairs of forward wheels and a reverse, corresponding to two speeds of the car for a given speed of the engine. Of course, a motor arranged in this way would be more dependent upon the elasticity of the engine (or power of varying its speed) than one fitted with three or four speeds, the advantage of the larger number of speeds being that the engine can be run at its highest speed and greatest power whilst the car is climbing a hill at a slow speed. With a four-speed gear, the **speed ratios** are usually as follows: first speed a quarter of the fourth speed, second speed half of the fourth speed, and the third speed three-quarters of the fourth speed.

[3] Or the shaft is round, and formed with a feather or feathers arranged to drive the sleeve.

corresponding to the position of the sleeve shown with the second speed[1] wheels in mesh.

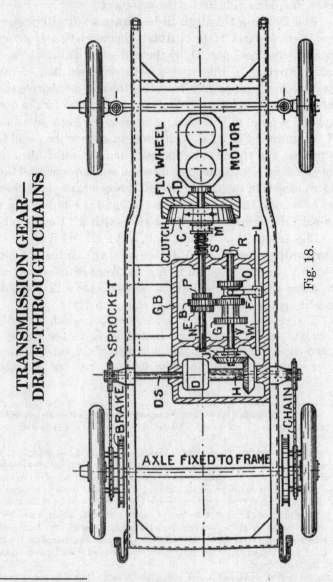

TRANSMISSION GEAR—
DRIVE-THROUGH CHAINS

Fig. 18.

AXLE FIXED TO FRAME

---

[1] In this case the top or highest speed.

Another position (due to a movement of L towards the right, and the lever into another notch) places the **first speed** wheels G and E in mesh, whilst a movement of L to the left throws all the wheels out of mesh, and the engine is free to rotate without driving the shaft **VR.** This, of course, is the position of the sleeve when the car is **standing** still and the engine is running, the change-speed lever being in the **neutral notch.** The fourth notch fixes the position of the lever for **reversing** the car. When this notch is used, the sleeve is moved to the left till the wheels O and P are opposite. O then comes into mesh with another wheel, called a change wheel, running on a third shaft above it (not shown in the Fig.) which connects the two wheels, but causes the wheel O and the shaft **VR** to rotate in same direction, thus reversing the car.[1]

It should hardly be necessary to explain that the shaft **VR** drives the differential shaft **DS,** through the bevel wheels **J** and H and the box **D** containing the differential gear;[2] the shaft **DS,** in its turn, driving the road-wheels through the side-chains as shown, and in the way that every one who owns a common bicycle understands.

---

[1] This gear is of the Panhard type, the one most generally in use, being fitted to the Napier, Darracq, Wolseley, Daimler, Mercedes, and many others, and it is some-times referred to as the **run-through gear**. The Fig. (18) shows an arrangement closely resembling that used in the De Dietrich car, but there is an increasing tendency to use a so-called direct drive for the top speed (or for the one just below), as in the Renault and the Mors cars. This is in some cases secured by fixing the bevel wheel J (Fig. 18) on the end of the gear shaft N, which of course necessitates a rearrangement of the gearing and the use of a claw-coupling, with the sleeve **JR** in two lengths, moved independently, and these may be referred to as **selective gears.** Refer to Art. 101.

It is a **noteworthy fact** that the **Panhard and Lavassor car,** when it made its first appearance in 1894, contained all the essential elements of the modern pleasure petrol car, and arranged in a similar manner.

In another type (the epicyclic or crypto), much less commonly used, but becoming increasingly popular, the change wheels are always in mesh, the changes of speed being obtained by rendering different elements active or stationary, by expanding interior clutches. A typical example of this change-speed gear is a feature of the famous and ingenious Duryea car, also of the Lanchester car, another vehicle remarkable for its original features. But with this gear it is very difficult to arrange for more than two speeds.

[2] One form of this interesting and indispensable gear is shown in section on the live-axle in Fig. 19, and its action is referred to in the next Article.

The other kind of transmission gear referred to is the—

92. Live-Axle or Cardan Drive, in which the power of the engine is transmitted to the road-wheels by *tooth-gear* throughout. This system, which is becoming increasingly popular and bids fair to become general for all but the heaviest cars, can be understood by an examination of the explanatory diagram Fig. 19. It will be noticed that, from the motor to the gear-box **GB,** the mechanism is the same as in Fig. 18; indeed, the greater part of the gear and box is identical with that previously described in connection with that figure, but in Fig. 19 the tail of the shaft **VR** is connected to the bevel pinion *c* by the propeller or Cardan shaft *ps,* two flexible or universal joints[1] *a* and *b* being fitted to the shaft to allow full play of the carriage-spring system between the road-wheel axle and the frame which supports the motor and gear-box.

Now the bevel pinion *c* is in mesh with the bevel wheel *d,* which forms part of the **differential gearbox** T, through which motion is transmitted to the axle of the driving wheels.

93. Chain-Drive *v.* **Live-Axle.**—Although during the past few years there have been an increasing number of makers who have adopted the system of live-axle and gear transmission, particularly for light cars, there are still a great many who pin their faith to chain-driving, with its rather greater simplicity and flexibility, the fact of the matter being that either system is in a way a compromise, each one having its advantages and disadvantages.

The former system, perhaps, on the whole is considered by engineers the **best mechanical arrangement,** (particularly when arranged with a floating axle Art. 91); certainly the **working parts** are better **protected,** but the **divided axle** is a **drawback** when the road-wheels are fixed directly to it, and should it and the hollow tube or **axle** accidentally get bent, it means a big job to get it right again, or even true enough to get home with, whilst a village blacksmith

---

[1] These joints are perhaps best known to the engineer as Hooke's, the inventor being Dr. Hooke, who was described by the illustrious Thomas Young as "the greatest of all philosophical mechanics," but they are best known in the automobile world as Cardan joints—Cardan being the French equivalent of Cardano, the name of an Italian engineer who invented a shaft with flexible or universal joints, in the early part of the sixteenth century.

can straighten the axle of a chain-driven car with certainty. On the other hand, chains are more or less noisy and **apt to break,** and should one give way and the other continue driving, the car may be overturned if going at a high speed; of course, most cars carry a spare chain, or at least spare links that can be fitted on the road should it be necessary.

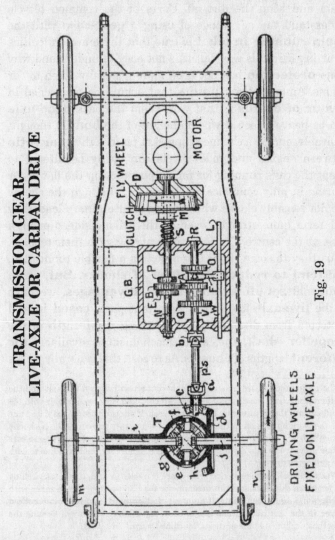

TRANSMISSION GEAR—
LIVE-AXLE OR CARDAN DRIVE

MOTOR

FLY WHEEL

CLUTCH

G.B.

Fig. 19

DRIVING WHEELS
FIXED ON LIVE AXLE

After chains have been in use some time they **stretch** (primarily due to their pins wearing) and become loose, and have to be **taken up,** either by **lengthening** the **radius rod**[1] or taking out a. link. Chains as ordinarily used are rarely run at their highest efficiency,[2] as it is quite the exception to see any attempt made to properly lubricate them and keep the dirt off. Users of the common bicycle understand the advantage of using a **gear-case** with the **chain running in oil;** it is true that there are difficulties in fitting cars this way, but it is not easy to understand why some **protection** has not been more generally given to car chains. Among **other points** that should be mentioned in **favour of chains** is that with them the back **dead-axle** can be bent to keep down the height of the **body** if thought desirable, and by a change of sprocket pinions the **gear ratio** between engine and road-wheels can easily be altered to adapt the car's running for racing purposes on the flat or for touring in hilly countries. Furthermore, although the chains are not sensibly elastic when taking their ordinary load, they are never quite straight, even on the driving side, dipping a little at the centre, the deflection varying with their tension. Thus they to some slight extent act as a flexible connection, and **tend to reduce the effect of shocks. But,** as an additional **set-off against these advantages,** we have in the **live-axle** job all the important parts **cased in** and protected from dirt, **and, by altering** the **length** of the **propeller shaft,** the, same mechanism is available **for different** lengths of **chassis.** As to cost, this generally works

---

[1] The radius rod is used as an adjustable connection between the axle and the differential shaft, the distance between which would vary considerably with the deflection of the springs were this rod not used. It also supports an axial load due to the working tension in the chain, and in many cars **prevents** the back axle from twisting round when the brakes are applied. Of course, in **live-axle** cars they prevent the axle casing from **twisting** round under the forces due to both braking and driving.

[2] When the teeth of the sprocket wheels are correctly formed, it is mostly rolling friction which occurs, and this accounts for the liberties that can be taken with chains in lubricating them. But the want of **alignment**, that is so often noticed even in the best cars, means loss of efficiency. The correct way of forming the teeth is explained in the author's "Machine Design," &c., p. 237.

out to **about five per cent, more** than for a chain-driven chassis.

It will now be convenient to give a little attention to some of the details that have been referred to in connection with the two systems of transmission, so we may commence with—

94. **The Differential Gear is a train of wheels** elegantly arranged **to average the speeds** of the two **driving wheels,** for, when the car turns a corner or runs round a bend in the road, the outer road-wheel will be travelling faster than the inner one;[1] but the propeller shaft can only revolve at one speed at any given moment, and that, therefore, must be the average of the two speeds, due to the running of the inner and outer road-wheel. Although it is not easy, without suitable drawings, to make clear to the general reader how this arrangement works, the following experiment will help him, at any rate, to understand the function of this important mechanism. Jack up the road-driving wheels to clear the ground, place the change-speed lever in the neutral notch, then turn by hand one of the road-wheels n (Fig. 19), and the other wheel m will revolve in the opposite direction[2] at the same speed, the average speed being zero. Again, let one of the wheels, say n, be fixed, and the bevel wheel d be turned, it will be found that the other road-wheel m will revolve at twice the speed of d,[3] or the speed of d is an average

---

[1] The only practical **alternative arrangement** to avoid the use of a **differential gear** that has been used is to run the road-wheels loose on the axle and drive through ratchets, as is done in many carrier tricycles; but there are so many serious objections to this principle that it is not likely to be revived for motor purposes.

[2] This should help the reader to understand a matter that is very puzzling to some people, namely, the **running** of one of the road-wheels backwards when the foot-brake is applied. If one of the **road-wheels** is, through the condition of the road and tyres, capable of slipping on the road surface whilst the other more or less holds tight, then, when the motion of the wheel d is arrested by the application of the brake, the road will be, as it were, driving one of the road-wheels in the right direction, and the other one will be reversed,

[3] The box T revolving with the bevel wheel d carries with it the two (or more) bevel pinions (called epicyclic, owing to their movement around the axis of motion) e and f, which, being in mesh with the stationary pinion h, cause the pinion g, and the axle i, to which it is fixed (A being also fixed to axle j), to revolve at twice the speed of d, the pinion g being carried round once by e and f, and driven once by being in mesh with h.

of the speeds of m and $n,$ as before. and so, if in turning a corner n revolved at 70 a minute and m at 80, d would be running at the mean or average of 75.

The differential gear shown in Fig. 19, which we have explained, is called the bevel-wheel type, but there is another arrangement used on some cars **called the face-gear** type, in which the same effect is obtained by having two spur wheels on the shafts, with spur pinions gearing into them. Each type has some advantages over the other, but on the whole the balance appears to be in favour of the former. The differential gear in a live-axle type of car is the most important part of the machinery next to the engine (and no part gives more trouble to the novice, who is apt to neglect it), as it is continuously at work when the car is being driven. Every differential case should have an overflow plug-hole closed with a plug, to indicate the proper level of the oil.

Another of the most important parts of a transmission gear is the connection between the fly-wheel and gear-box called—

95. **The Clutch,** as at any moment, when a car is running, the safety of the vehicle, indeed, the safety of the occupants, may be jeopardised by its faulty action; for, when in working order, a push on the pedal instantly disconnects the engine from the transmission gear, and the car can be stopped by an application of the brakes; but should the clutch seize at a critical moment, this release cannot be made without a deal of trouble, and it is easy to imagine what might happen. Fortunately, this is a mishap which rarely occ urs, indeed, should never occur, if the clutch is skilfully designed and constructed, and care is taken to keep it in an efficient working condition. In the development of the car much ingenuity has been displayed in devising friction clutches of **various types,** the following being those commonly used, given in the order in which they are favoured by makers: (1) **The cone;** (2) the **disc** or plate; (3) the **expanding**. Only quite a few cars are fitted with the last-mentioned type, which has the disadvantage of holding tighter the faster the clutch runs, due to centrifugal force, thus retarding withdrawal or

declutching; this type also consists of many pieces, and it is expensive to make. (2) **The disc or plate** clutch, which is one of the latest types, may be arranged with a single plate, as in the 12-14 H.P. De Dion and the 6 **H.P.** Rover car, or it may be fitted with some four or five plates (it is then usually called a **plate** or **multiple plate clutch),** or with forty or fifty very thin discs, when it is called a **multiple disc clutch.** These clutches run in a bath of oil, so that there is no danger of them becoming dry and the plates seizing when a suitable oil is used. A special and ingenious form of this type was introduced by Professor Hele Shaw, the steel plates being stamped with vee corrugations, which greatly increase their holding power. The **chief advantages** claimed for **disc clutches** are (a) they can he adjusted to take up the load gradually; (b) the amount of pressure required to declutch is small; (c) the surface is very large in proportion to the power transmitted; (d) the wear is so small that it does not upset the adjustment. On the other hand, they have **disadvantages**, for, although they are so efficient when in proper order, care must be taken not to use an oil that is too thick, or dragging irregular working may result. Further, they are not so easily taken out without disturbing the gear-box as cone clutches are, and they are more expensive.

The remaining type, number (1) the **cone** clutch, which is most used, is more fully explained in the following Article.

96. **Cone Clutches.—The** most popular, the cheapest, and most commonly used clutch, and in a way the most simple, is the cone clutch, a type that has done good service ever since automobiles came into use, and one that answers well for powers up to about 18 or 20 horse; so we will give our attention to this type and describe three typical examples.

In the **ordinary cone clutch** there is a recess formed in the rear side of the fly-wheel **F** (Fig. 20), and this recess is bored out conical, tapering with the largest diameter outside. The coned fly-wheel is usually bolted to the tail of the crank-shaft **CS**, which is flanged for that purpose as shown. The leather-faced cone **C** is mounted on the end of the shaft (**P**) to be driven, the hub **N** of the cone sliding backwards and forwards

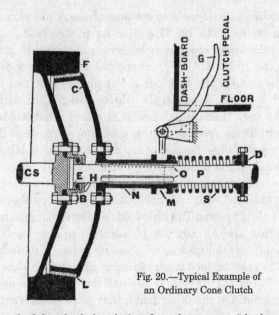

Fig. 20.—Typical Example of
an Ordinary Cone Clutch

on the end of the shaft, but being forced to turn with the shaft
by feathers or keys **O**, or else by having the end of the shaft
squared[1] and the hole in the hub to correspond (as at **D**, Fig.
21). The cone is slid on its shaft by means of a fork (which
forms the lower end of the clutch pedal **G**), working in the
deeply grooved collar **M**; the strong helical spring[1] **S**, with its
back end abutting against the collar **D**, presses the cone home
into the recess in the fly-wheel, setting up sufficient friction
between the conical surfaces to transmit the turning effort of
the engine to the driven shaft **P**. Thus the clutch is normally
kept in engagement, the driver pressing forward the pedal **G**,
and keeping his foot on it as long as he wants to keep the cone
out, so that he can, when stopping the car, throw his change-
speed gears into neutral position, and then let in the clutch

---

[1] The squared driving parts require to be kept properly lubricated to enable them to slide easily, so that the declutching pressure may be regulated to a nicety. The feathers, as in Fig. 20, make perhaps a better job.
This type of spring is most commonly used, but sometimes two or more springs
carried on studs parallel to the shaft are used instead.

without driving anything but the short length of shaft, called the clutch shaft, between the gear-box and clutch.

The cone **C** is usually covered or **faced with leather**[1] to give a good grip and make its engagement smooth; and the leather is often **backed by springs**, so that when the cone is gradually let into the recess the leather facing is at first pressed against the tapered bore, and the friction is just sufficient to start the car gradually. And the springs are compressed into their recesses on the cone's face when the clutch is allowed to go fully into engagement.

The exact angle of the tapered parts is of great importance, because if the taper is too small the cone will seize fast as it is let in, starting the car with a sudden jerk.[2]

In most clutches one of the shafts telescopes into the other, fitting into a bronze bush, which serves as a bearing, and keeps the cone and recess in alignment; and the principal defect of some of the clutches used on cheap machines is the friction due to the end thrust of the helical spring on the clutch shaft; but, as arranged in Fig. 20, this **thrust is balanced** by the use of a ball-thrust bearing **B,** arranged so that when the clutch is in, the thrust causes an equal and opposite pull on the tail end of the crank-shaft, and the two parts of the clutch revolving together with the ball-bearing; but when the spring is compressed by the pedal to declutch, the ball-bearing comes into action, the ball race **E** being fixed to the end of the shaft P, and the

---

[1] The **leather** is usually **riveted** to the conical surface of the male part of the clutch by **copper rivets**. These are sometimes first screwed into the cone and hammered down, till the heads are about J inch below the surface of the leather, the holes in the latter having been previously countersunk. When the riveting is completed, a light cut should be taken off the leather in a lathe, so that its surface is truly conical and the right taper. The **leather** ultimately **wears down** to the rivets, and when this occurs the clutch is apt to become very fierce, owing to the **rivet heads seizing** the metal of the clutch; they then require hammering down till they are well below the surface again.

There appears to be a growing tendency to dispense with a facing, and run the clutch with bare iron contact in oils, forming what is called a metal-to-metal clutch.

[2] For particulars of the way in which this taper is dealt with by the designer and of the allowable working loads on the leather face, &c., refer to the author's "Machine Design Construction and Drawing," p. 109.

MOTORS AND MOTORING

other race supported by the housing **H** bolted to the flange of the crankshaft **CS**.

97. The Reversed Cone Clutch.—This arrangement, which appears to be coming popular, also has the advantage that when the clutch is engaged there is **no end thrust** on any of the bearings. It will be seen that in this clutch the internal cone C (Fig. 21) works in a conical casting E[1] bolted to the fly-wheel F, and the taper has its smallest diameter to the rear (the reverse of the previous arrangement). The helical spring S is placed between the cone and the wheel, and the former moves away from the latter when let in. The sleeve, with the deeply-grooved collar M, into which the fork of the pedal works, is bushed with bronze and works on the tail end P of the crank-shaft CS, upon whose collar A the fly-wheel F is bolted, the ball-bearing B reducing the friction due to the thrust when the clutch spring is compressed by the pedal.

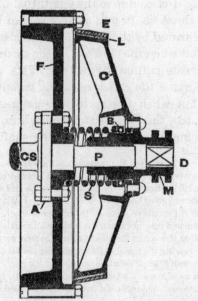

Fig. 21.—The Reversed or Inverted Cone Clutch

[1] This ring is usually bolted on in two halves, which makes the clutch easy to get at, but adds to the cost of the clutch.

The figure shows what a very short clutch lengthways this arrangement makes, but the spring is not easy to get at, and the push-pedal gear for it cannot be so easily arranged as with the ordinary type.

98. The Panhard Clutch.—We have explained two forms of conical clutch in which expedients have been employed to avoid friction due to the end thrust of the helical spring, and may now describe how the difficulty has been ingeniously overcome in the Panhard clutch, which is diagrammatically shown in Fig. 22. It will be seen that in this arrangement the recessed or dished fly-wheel F is bolted on to the tail of the crank-shaft CS, which is flanged at A for that purpose. Through the rim of the fly-wheel, pins PP are fastened, the projecting parts passing through holes in the flange of the

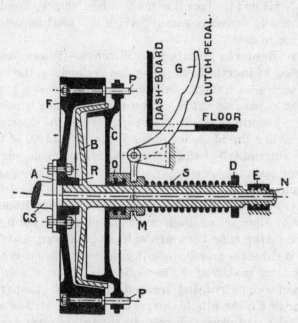

Fig. 22.—The Panhard Conical Clutch.

inner cone C to enable the fly-wheel to drive the latter. The outer cone B is attached to the hollow clutch shaft N,[1] so that

---

[1] This clutch shaft is usually coupled to the change-gear shaft N (Fig 18) by a

when the clutch is engaged, the helical spring S presses the grooved collar M against the cone C, forcing it into cone B, and in so doing creating friction enough between the two conical surfaces to enable the car to be driven through the clutch. The reaction at the rear end of the spring is exerted by the adjustable collar-nut D, so that the opposite forces are completely balanced, without any thrust being thrown on the crank-shaft or gear- box. This balance, it should be explained, is disturbed when the pedal G is pressed to disengage the clutch; an additional pressure is then exerted on the collar[1] D, thrusting the shaft N to the right, but a thrust block E is arranged to receive that. There is also a thrust bearing at O to transmit the thrust of the spring to the cone C during declutching. It will be noticed that the cone end of the clutch shaft N fits into the boss R of the fly-wheel, thereby keeping the shafts in perfect alignment, which is a most important condition to satisfy.

98A. **Remarks relating to Clutches.**—To keep down the effect of **inertia** in clutching and declutching, the **rim** (and parts near it) of the internal cone of clutches is made as light as possible. Often an **aluminium** casting is bolted to a steel-centre sleeve. In some cars, such as the Canstatt-Daimler and the Mercedes Simplex, the withdrawal of the clutch automatically reduces the speed of the engine, whilst in many cases the act of applying the foot- brake disengages the clutch.

99. **Fierce Clutches.**—Clutches may cause trouble, either by slipping too much or by not **slipping enough; in the latter case they are said to be fierce,** and the cause is either the presence of gritty dirt on the leather or the spring being too strong. If due to dirt, the leather should be **washed** with **petrol,** and **dressed** with a small quantity of **castor or Collan oil;** this makes and keeps the leather soft and pliable, and allows the necessary slip to take place should

---

sleeve, inside of which is a distance piece, so that, by opening the coupling sleeve and removing the distance piece, the clutch and shaft can be removed.

[1] This collar is screwed on and is used to regulate the strength of the spring S.

the clutch be accidentally allowed to too suddenly engage. If this treatment does not improve matters, and the clutch takes up its work too, rapidly, causing the car to plunge forward, subjecting the whole vehicle to abnormal strains, instead of gradually moving off, as it should do, then the compression of the spring must be relieved by unscrewing the adjusting nut (D in Fig. 22) to increase its length.

Fierceness is also caused by renewing the leather facing; the remedy is, apply the clutch gently until the leather wears down and becomes fairly smooth.

On the other hand, slip may be due to too much oil getting **on** to the **leather face;** this may be remedied by applying a little petrol to clean the surplus oil from off the leather, or a little **Fuller's earth,** chalk, or lime may be applied, in either case withdrawing the clutch and holding it fully out of engagement to give access to the leather. But slip may also be due to the **leather** being **burnt,**[1] or to the spring being too weak; if the latter be the cause, the spring must be further compressed by screwing up the adjusting nut. The clutch should be so adjusted that it is just on the point of slipping when the car is exerting its full power in mounting a hill on its lowest speed; this may often mean a good deal of strain on the ankle for a long run, and the temptation to ease the spring is great, but it should be remembered that slip means loss of power.

A little patient attention to these matters will enable the driver, by a give-and-take correction, to put the clutch in proper working order.

100. **Gear Changing.—In the case of cars fitted** with the ordinary or **Panhard gear, one of the most** delicate operations the driver has frequently to perform is *gear changing,* for if this is not done with sufficient skill and care the teeth of the wheels are apt to be seriously damaged and the car abnormally strained. We have seen that in

---

[1] Continual neglect of the leather causes it to become quite dry and hard; this greatly reduces the resistance or value of the friction between the leather and the metal, resulting in slip, which, if allowed to continue, causes the generation of sufficient heat to char or burn out the leather.

changing from one gear to another, the teeth of the wheels which are in mesh have to be disengaged and those of others put into mesh by a sliding movement; now, obviously, for this to be done sweetly the spaces must be just opposite the teeth they are to engage, but should they not thus coincide, a clumsy attempt to engage them may result in much grinding, if not broken teeth.[1]

Certain precautions must be taken in gear changing; for example, let us suppose that a car is in motion on fairly level ground, with, say, the second speed gear in, and it is decided to change up to the third speed, the clutch pedal should be pressed down to disengage the clutch and allow the car and gear to continue running by its momentum, then with a pull on the speed-lever the second speed wheels are disengaged, and an attempt made to put into mesh the teeth of the third speed wheels; this must not be done until the delicate sense of touch has conveyed a message that spaces and teeth coincide, when a sharp pull or jerk will engage the wheels. Now, in running on the level or on a down grade, this operation need not be performed hurriedly,[2] indeed, it is best done gently; but in putting in a lower gear uphill, not a moment is to be lost, otherwise the car rapidly slows, and if time is lost in the change, the load on the engine suddenly becomes greater

---

[1] This gear is without question the weak link in the ordinary car; that it is a barbarous device, although a convenient one, no one doubts, and its ultimate disuse as at present arranged can be safely predicted; although they have been much improved by bevelling the tooth-faces and increasing the pitch, it is not so easy to indicate upon what lines further improvements will be made. There are already in use gears that can be easily and safely changed, the teeth being always in mesh, the tightening of a band-brake bringing a particular gear into use; they are of the epicyclic type, somewhat complicated, and are to be found on the cars by Duryea, Wilson-Pilcher, Lanchester, &c.

[2] Many drivers do not give themselves time enough to complete the change, for although the pull on the gear lever to disengage should be simultaneous with the application of pressure to the clutch pedal, the pull over to engage should not be hurried, as the clutch shaft (or driving shaft) should slow down to the same peripheral speed as the driven shaft before moving the lever forward to engage the wheels. Many cars are fitted with a clutch stop, which takes the form of a leather pad, against which the rotating clutch presses when it is withdrawn. The object of this device is to check the speed of the clutch shaft when changing up from one speed to a higher, also to bring the clutch shaft to rest when the road wheels are stationary. This stop should never be used in changing down.

when the wheels get into mesh, often requiring a little relief by slightly disengaging the clutch, allowing a little slipping to keep the engine running above the speed at which it is apt to stop. There is always the danger, when changing speed in mounting a hill, of missing the gear altogether, the car then quickly commencing to run back. In fact, not a few most serious acci dents have happened in this way. This being so, we will carefully indicate what should be done in negotiating a hill which requires a change of gear. Now, as soon as the car gets on rising ground, the throttle should be opened to allow the engine to exert its full power on the gear it is running with (which will probably be its highest one), then, immediately before withdrawing the clutch, be careful to so control the engine that it does not race during the moment or two required for changing the gear, and on the clutch being disengaged the speed-lever is promptly moved over to the required notch,[1] corresponding to the second or first speed, as the case may be, and when this has been done the clutch should be gently let in, allowing slip to occur, until the engine takes up the full load. Briefly, a gear should be put in at the moment the two wheels that are to be placed in mesh are running at the same circumferential speed.

101. **The Gate-Change,** or selective form of change speed gear-box, was first introduced on the Mercedes car. With this arrangement, by an ingenious system of striker rods, each actuating its own separate gear, the driver can operate any one of the required gears without having to first "go through," or put into operation, any of the intermediate gears, as is done with gears of the Panhard or **"run- through"** or "straight-through" type, with which, to get through from the first speed to fourth, it is necessary to run through the second and third gears.

The term **"selective"** is used in connection with the gate-change, because the driver selects his gear and operates that and that only; whilst the term "gate-change" was aptly applied, because on the first pattern the gear-lever operated

---

[1] A deal of practice is required to do this with certainty in the dark or without looking.

in a double quadrant with an opening or gate connecting the two. **Thus the lever** has two parallel and separate slots in its quadrant in which to work, with an opening between; and in some cases there is a third slot for the reverse, also with an opening between. When the **lever** is thrown **forward** to the end of the first slot in the double quadrant, the **first forward gear** is put into mesh; when pulled back, the second gear. When pushed to the centre, and then moved laterally outwards through the gate, the second slot is entered; then the third gear is meshed by pulling back the lever again, and the fourth or top gear by pushing it forwards. Of course, different makers who have adopted this mechanism have varied the arrangement in a number of ways, but the principle remains unaltered.

The principal advantages claimed for the gate-change are: (a) It is impossible to engage two gears at the same time;[1] (b) the shafts in the gear-box can be made shorter and therefore stiffer; (c) the gears can be changed with greater certainty at night.[2] But there are many engineers who doubt whether these advantages are of sufficient importance to compensate for the disadvantages due to the more complicated form and extra cost in manufacture, and they find it not so simple in use as the older form; in fact, they consider that the importance of the claims so generally advanced in favour of the gate-change are very much overrated.

102. **Brakes**.—Every car must by law be fitted with at least *two* brakes, but now all cars have three, one at each driving-wheel, and one somewhere forward of the Cardan shaft on live-axle cars, or somewhere on the counter or differential shaft on chain-driven cars, and it is almost the universal practice to make one of these (generally the latter) a foot-brake, in some cases arranged to withdraw the clutch as the brake is applied, and in some cases to also throttle the mixture. The **foot-brake** generally consists of a contracting

---

[1] This occasionally happened years ago with badly designed and neglected gears of the straight-through type.

[2] On some cars with the straight-through quadrants the first speed forward, neutral, and reverse notches are so close together that even in daytime the returning of the lever to its neutral position is difficult.

band. working upon a drum keyed on the countershaft. Many cars have a steel band with brass or even cast-iron fillets, but the **locomotive type** is gaining favour, particularly on the more expensive cars. In this type a pair of semicircular cast-iron shoes are placed on either side of the steel drum, and they are usually caused to press against it by the action of a right and left hand screw shackled at top and bottom With this arrangement the shoes can be machined a perfect fit on the drum, and can be easily replaced when they are worn out. The other brakes are fitted on the hubs of the **road-wheels**, and worked by a side **hand-lever: these brakes** should on no account be made to disengage the clutch when they are used, as the **engine** itself can be **made to act** in cases of emergency as an **auxiliary brake**, if the clutch remains engaged, as we shall see later. Cars used to be fitted with **band-brakes** on the road-wheels, as shown in Fig. 18, but most makers have abandoned these in favour of some form of **expanding brake** acting on the inner surface of a ring or annular flange.[1] combination of the two kinds is sometimes used on road-wheel drums, as in the small Rovers. It is imperatively necessary that all car brakes should be so constructed that they are **equally effective** whether the car be moving **forward or backward**, for upon the perfect working of the brakes depends the safety of the car and its occupants. The practice of using **cables** for operating brakes is one that **can**not be defended except on the score of cheapness, as they are rarely worked over guide **pulleys** of sufficient diameter, so that the excessive bending permanently **injures them**. Further, being exposed, they suffer from internal **rusting** (which can rarely be seen from outside), and this sooner or

---

[1] In chain drives this is usually a particular form of sprocket ring, enclosing the brake, the form nearly always adopted being that of two semi-circular shoes, whose outside curvature corresponds to the inner periphery of the drum in which they work and which are forced out against it by the action of a lozenge-shaped cam operated by suitable levers. These shoes are anchored to a plate, which forms their dust-cover and is often a flattened extension of the radius rods, the drum carrying the chain sprocket on its outside surface. With such arrangements it is practicable to better protect the rubbing surfaces from dirt, which reduces their efficiency and increases the wear and tear, but such brakes are less get-at-able and more difficult to examine.

later causes them to snap when loaded, perhaps at a critical moment.

A car sometimes stops on a hill, which for some reason or other it can't climb; the tendency then is for the effect of gravity on the weight of the car to gradually make the engine run backwards and allow the vehicle to descend the hill; of course, the instant this happens the **sprag**[1] should be lowered (if the car is fitted with one), and if this holds before the car gets on too much way all is well, but it is easy to see that, so long as the clutch is in, the friction and compression in the cylinder retard the motion of the car (the **engine acting as a brake**), and the withdrawal of the clutch cuts out this resistance, often with a resulting increase in the velocity of the car before the hand, or what is usually called the **emergency, brake** can be put on (refer to Art. 104), although the foot-brake be at once applied. This must not be confused with what is done when a car is running forward, and its speed is suddenly arrested by an application of a brake; the foot-brake is then generally used, the clutch being withdrawn by the same pedal (on some) instantly disconnects the clutch shaft from the engine, which then runs unloaded. This arrangement gives the driver wonderful control over the car, as its stoppage is not dependent upon his power to suddenly bring up his engine to a standstill. Of course, the beauty of the system is that when the car is temporarily stopped the engine continues running, so that a restart can be instantly made by letting in the clutch. Indeed, it is not easy for those who have not driven a car to understand what perfect control the driver has over it; for instance, it was proved by brake tests, carried out by the Automobile Club of America, that over 70 feet were required to pull up a

---

[1] Since brakes have been made so reliable and powerful, sprags have somewhat gone out of fashion. The principal objection to them is that thoughtless drivers are apt to do much damage by failing to put them out of action before reversing, and there is the further objection that a sprag is apt to induce a careless driver to neglect his hand-brakes. With the most perfectly arranged sprag a good deal of presence of mind is required to put it in action before the car begins to slip back; as to the old-fashioned ground type, it is very easy to jump it when time is lost in restarting on a stiff hill.

A 250 horsepower Vanderbilt car. (Courtesy of the Library of Congress)

A Brouhot car in Paris, 1910.

Alice Ramsey, the first woman to drive across the USA
from coast to coast.

Henry Fournier on the 'Mors' machine, with which he won the Paris–Bordeaux and Paris–Berlin races and beat the Vanderbilt record for one kilometre.

Camille Jenatzy, 1903 winner of the Gordon Bennett Cup, in a Mercedes. Jenatzy broke the land speed record three times and was the first man to travel at over 100 km/h.
(Courtesy of suckindiesel)

The king and queen of Italy in a motor car. (Courtesy of the Library of Congress)

The Lohner-Porsche Mixte Hybrid in 1900, a vehicle that could run on both petrol and electricity. It required 1.8 tonnes of batteries.

Louis Chevrolet, American racer ad founder of the
Chevrolet Motor Car Company, in a Buick designed by
himself, around 1900. (Courtesy of Ian Macky)

Cars lining up for the start of the famous New York–
Paris race in 1908. (Courtesy of the Library of Congress)

This vehicle is both a car and a motor boat, an early
attempt at an amphibious vehicle from the early
nineteenth century.

four-in-hand coach running at about sixteen miles per hour, whilst a Panhard car running at the same speed was brought to a standstill in 25 ft. 4 ins. For calculations relating to break power refer to Art. 107 and Appendix II.

103. **Testing the Rear or Hub Brakes.**— These brakes, which to comply with the law must be powerful enough to lock the wheels, should be periodically subjected to a proper test. To do this, jack up both back wheels, and advance the side- brake lever gradually, notch by notch, in the quadrant, and pull each wheel round by hand to see if the pull-rods or cables are acting evenly and properly. Of course, the wheels should both lock at the same moment against efforts to move them in either direction, and if they fail to do this they must be adjusted, for any fault in the adjustment may mean failure to efficiently stop the car or hold it on a hill in ascending when the engine stops; moreover, side-slip may occur when the brakes are applied. The adjustment of these brakes is much facilitated if they are fitted with a balancing or compensating arrangement—as they are on most good cars-to equalise the tension in the pull-rods.

104. **Use of Pedal-Brake** *v.* **Side-Brakes in Traffic.**— Before a driver can intelligently use the brakes with regard to the amount of wear and tear caused by their action, and possible injury to some parts of the mechanism of the car, he should endeavour to understand that the hub rear-brakes operated by the side-lever (sometimes called the emergency brakes) can be used with the least amount of straining actions upon important parts, as the brake drums or flanges are fixed on the road- wheels. On the other hand, the pedal-brake, as we have seen, is usually placed somewhere forward of the Cardan shaft, which causes the retarding influence to be transmitted through such important parts as the Cardan or universal joints, the driving bevel pinion and wheel, the differential, the bevel wheels on the ends of the divided live-axle, and finally through the connections between the road-wheels and the axle ends. Further, the **pedal-brake** (or differential brake, as it is sometimes called) is geared up, as its drum revolves faster than the road-wheels, making

it much more powerful and more easy to apply—that is, it requires the exertion of less pressure. But in driving in traffic the constant alternations between the application of the foot-brake and the clutch cause a good deal of wear at the parts we have mentioned, particularly the bolts and bolt holes of the Cardan joints. Of course, the wear and the possibility of injury are greatly increased when the brake is suddenly applied. Although it is true that these parts, indeed, all the parts of the transmission gear, are in the best cars designed to withstand such shocks, yet the freedom from excessive wear and consequent noise, indeed, the life of the parts, very much depends upon making as little use of the foot- brake as possible. In other words, in traffic-driving, if we are to consider the car, the lever-brakes should be used, and the pedal one held in reserve as an emergency brake.[1] Of course, the objection to this practice is that most drivers find that both hands have quite enough to do in traffic in controlling the steering-wheel and manipulating the throttle, without having to lean over to push or pull the side-lever brake, which might cause a momentary swerve of the steering-wheel.

This is a vexed question, and it would obviously appear from the above discussion that on the whole it would be best to couple up the pedal to the hub brakes and the side-lever to the differential brakes; but probably most engineers would prefer to have the emergency brake as directly connected to the road-wheels as possible, to reduce the possibility of the failure of any part of the brake system, when a sudden application occurs, to a minimum.

105. **Use of the Engine as a Brake.**—The closing of the throttle of any properly constructed engine will cause the engine to act as a brake and the car to slow down. To accelerate the slowing down the clutch may be withdrawn and the gear changed to the second speed, and the clutch let in very gently, when the car will slowly come to a standstill;

---

[1] One of the objections to this arrangement is that in descending a long hill the foot, if continuously pressing the pedal, would become fatigued, but a spring catch could easily be arranged to hold the pedal in the on position for long descents. Most experienced drivers are careful to alternately use the pedal- and side-brakes on long descents to prevent overheating.

excepting when descending somewhat steep Kills, when it will probably be necessary to apply side- brakes to keep the car in hand, the foot-brake being held in reserve to deal with emergencies to stop the car if it suddenly becomes necessary to do so, or to further slow down in order to take a very sharp corner. In mounting a hill it sometimes happens that the descent on the other side is one of great severity; in such a case the car should be got on to its first speed and throttled down just before it passes over the crest, so that it can be held in hand by the engine and brake at will as it descends. In many cases it happens that the brakes are not wanted at all; indeed, that the engine may be required to be driven slightly. So soon as the driver has mastered the art of using the engine in this way, if he can only keep his head, **in the event of the brakes failing** from any cause in descending a hill, he will have a certain means of avoiding serious danger and damages.

106. **Points of a Good Brake.**—The conditions which a good brake should satisfy are the following:—

(1) The maximum force required to work it by foot or hand to be one that can be applied without undue exertion.

(2) The movement of pedal or lever to apply the full power of the brake not to be more than can be conveniently made by the driver.

(3) The bands or blocks to be suspended or arranged in such a way that they are only in contact with the brake, pulley, ring, or flange when the brake js applied,[1] being well clear all round at other times.

(4) Absence of *fierceness* in the action of the brake.[2]

(5) The side-brakes should both equally hold.

---

[1] A common source of trouble in the way of noise, wear, and loss of power is the rubbing of brake-bands or blocks, due to want of adjustment or faulty construction. When these make a screeching noise a little castor oil should be applied (instead of the ordinary lubricating oil) to clutches that are designed to work with lubricated rubbing surfaces.

[2] The true function of a brake is to retard a wheel, not lock it; should it do the latter, then the tyres must skid, and the most expensive part of the car (the tyres) is seriously worn and injured, instead of a little wear occurring in the strap and ring, which can be easily replaced. Of course the brakes must be made strong enough to lock the wheels.

(6) Both brakes should be equally effective in holding a car, either when it is going forwards or backwards. Briefly, the rules to be observed in regard to brakes are : Keep them clean and properly adjusted. Use the throttle in preference to the brake. Use the hand-brake for **sudden stoppages**, and the foot-brake for **gentle retardation**.

No part of the car requires more intelligent care in its manipulation and is deserving of more attention than the brake, if it is to be worked when necessary for all it is worth with effect and without abnormal injury to the tyres. It works with the greatest effect when the tyres, due to its application, are just on the **point of skidding;**[1] for when skidding occurs the rubber is eroded, and the friction between ground and tyre is very muc h decreased instead of becoming greater, as most people would expect.

107. **Brake Power.**—It can be shown that under ordinary running conditions the minimum **distance required to pull** up a car by the brakes is directly proportional to the square of the speed, and may be taken[2] to be **equal in feet to the square of the speed in miles per hour divided by 10**. Thus—

If S = 10 miles per hour, the approximate distance =

$$\frac{10^2}{10} = \frac{100}{10} = 10 \text{ ft.}$$

---

[1] The old-fashioned spoon-type brake, acting directly upon the tread of the tyre, was abandoned on account of its low efficiency and the manner in which it used to wear out the cover of the tyre.

[2] The maximum coefficient of friction between tyres of driving-wheel and road that can be relied upon may be taken to=μ= 0.6; and the centre of gravity of the loaded car, whose weight is W, may be taken to be 0-4 the wheel base from the back axle. Then the weight on the back wheels will be 0.6W. And the greatest resistance of the driving-wheels to skidding R = 0.6 Wμ = 0.6W x 0.6 = 0.36W. But the moving energy of the car= $\frac{WV^2}{2g}$, —and 1 mile per hour= $\frac{1728 \times 3}{60 \times 60}$ = 1.44 ft. per second. Hence energy E for 1 mile per hour= $\frac{WV^2}{2g}$ = $\frac{W \times 1.442}{2 \times 32.2}$ = 0.03219W ft. lbs. But this energy is dissipated in overcoming friction, and it will equal the product of II and the distance the car travels before it comes to rest. Let L = minimum distance the car can be stopped in; then, assuming that the maximum value of R is maintained, R x L = S2 x 0.03219W./ But R=036 or 0.36W or 0.36WL= S2x0.3337W, That is, L = $\frac{S^2 \times 0.03219}{0.36}$ = S2 x 0.0894, or, say $\frac{S2}{10}$ approximately Hence L, the approximate minimum feet the car can be stopped in = $\frac{\text{Speed in miles per hour squared}}{10}$. Refer Appendix II.

If S = 20 miles per hour, the approximate distance =
$$\frac{20^2}{10} = \frac{400}{10} = 40 \text{ ft.}$$
If S = 40 miles per hour, the approximate distance =s
$$\frac{40^2}{10} = \frac{1600}{10} = 160 \text{ ft.}$$

108. **Ball-Bearings.**—Readers who are old enough to have ridden a bicycle before the introduction of ball-bearings, and have had riding experience with both kinds, will be in a position to estimate the marked advantage ball-bearings have over ordinary ones, so far as frictional resistance is concerned, and with cars this difference is just as striking; indeed, few things appear to be more perfect than the running of car wheels, mounted on well-adjusted ball-bearings. But the ball-bearing has an advantage over the plain bearing only so long as the hard steel balls remain perfect in form and uniform in size, and no longer; for should a ball break or flake there is always the probability that a portion or portions of the ball may get across or become jammed in the ball races, scoring them or the axle, or both, whilst in some cases the axles have been held tight and fractured by the sudden strain. Frequently ball-bearings are allowed to run far too long without attention and lubrication, with the result that when they are inspected some of the balls are found to have worn sharp or rough, and perhaps to have grooved the races upon which they run. Renewing the latter is, of course, an expensive matter; it is much more economical to replace the *whole* of the balls as soon as there is any appreciable sign of wear, even if a single ball is faulty, as a new one would have to be exactly the same size as the others, and few people are capable of gauging the size with sufficient accuracy. Obviously, if one of the balls happens to be a shade larger than the others, it will, each time it reaches the bottom of its race, support the whole weight, and sooner or later will break. To be on the safe side these bearings should be examined about every 1000 miles, and the **balls renewed** about every 5000 miles. In placing balls in their races, care must be taken not to get them too crowded; indeed, if there is any doubt as to whether a certain number can be got in, it is better to put in

one less, and be sure that they are not jammed together when the cone is screwed up.

Any kind of dirt, particularly gritty dust, is such a bearing's worst enemy, and must be carefully excluded. This is done by sealing the bearings with **dust-caps**, rings or washers of leather or felt between the housing and the shaft.

If absolutely pure rolling motion could be relied on, and the materials were inelastic and perfect in form, no **lubricant** would be required; but, due to the elasticity of the materials, and the races being concave, some **friction must always occur** in the most skilfully designed and adjusted bearings, to say nothing of the effect of faulty adjustment, **spinning** of the balls, and unavoidable **slippage**. Now on the whole the best **lubricant is motor grease**, with which the races are invariably filled from time to time. It provides a film of the stuff always being present between the various points of contact, and it will last for a considerable time without renewal.

Ball-bearings can only be expected to run efficiently and to be durable when they have been carefully designed with regard to both the load and speed at which the bearing runs, particularly the latter, for the permissible load on any given bearing rapidly decreases with the speed; the ratio of crushing pressure to working pressure being very high in all good bearings; ranging from about 120 at 50 revolutions per minute to over 700 at 2000 revolutions.

For further information, and illustrations of ball- and roller-bearings, refer to the author's book on "Machine Design," &c., page 277.

109. **The Tyres.**—We may now give some attention to the vexed question of the tyres. Should they be solid or pneumatic? is a question, like so many others relating to motor vehicles, that cannot be answered definitely without qualifications. The principal factors which have to be considered in making a decision are the maximum speed the car is to run at, the character of the roads the car is to run on (*i.e.*, is the car required for town or touring purposes?), comfort, reliability, the weight of the vehicle, and the size and flexibility of its

springs. Those who have had long experience with pneumatic tyres, particularly if they have run them after they have given unmistakable signs of depreciation, would willingly sacrifice a little comfort, if they could secure immunity from tyre troubles by adopting solids; but even with the solid rubber tyres we have not perfect reliability, as, under exceptional circumstances, the fixing cement is apt to get heated enough by road friction to melt, and allow the tyres to creep slightly on the rims, the cement accumulating at some parts of the latter to an extent sufficient to gradually force the tyres from them, causing, at the same time, an abrasive action between the tyres and rims, the tendency of the tyres to leave the rims being increased by the centrifugal force, when running at a high speed. Moreover, the use of solid tyres necessitates the use of springs of greater flexibility; and provision must be made for a greater vertical movement between the frame and axles, which means, in most chain-driven cars, a varying tightness of the chains, and in gear-driven ones a greater variation in the uniformity of transmission, due to the greater obliquity[1] of the propeller shaft. But, notwithstanding these drawbacks, there are many who pin their faith to solid tyres, particularly on electric cars for town use, as the roads are generally fairly good, and the speed rarely exceeds some sixteen miles per hour. An additional advantage may be mentioned, and that is, there is not quite so much skidding with solid tyres as with pneumatic ones. So, for those who never wish to exceed a most moderate speed with the minimum of tyre troubles, particularly if they are not too exacting where their ease in riding is concerned, solid tyres, fitted to a light but strong car, *built for their use*, would be a wise selection. On the other hand, it is not easy for any one who has once enjoyed the luxury of driving in a good car, suitably fitted with pneumatic tyres, to revert to solid ones, indeed, the temptation to run the risk of trouble and take his

---

[1] When the universal joints of the propeller shaft (as arranged on some cars) come into action, they cause, or tend to cause, a difference in the uniformity of running of the clutch shaft and driving-wheel axle; that is to say, if the former was running with uniformity, the latter would be moving with slight variations of angular velocity for each turn of the propeller shaft.

chance seems almost irresistible; but we must be careful not in any way to exaggerate the disadvantages of pneumatic tyres, for, in addition to their wonderful resilience, they run, when properly inflated, with less resistance thanolids, nd if they are, in the first instance, of suitable size[1] and of good quality (as they would be if supplied by any of the famous makers), and proper care is taken of them when in use,[2] also when they are stored, or on the wheels of a laid-up car,[3] they may be expected to run some 4000 to 5000 miles before they require retreading (solids, if of the best make, run over twice the distance and cost about half as much); of course, the first serious trouble may be due to the inner tubes commencing to perish; if so, these can be easily and comparatively inexpensively replaced. Every driver of a touring car should be able to repair a puncture, and to lace a leather sleeve gaiter or shoe over the outer cover of a tyre and around the felloe of the wheel should a cover burst on the road. Needless to say, tyres which have suffered from bursts should be returned to their makers at the earliest opportunity, so that the cover may be properly repaired and vulcanised.[4] It is a great mistake to run a car with soft tyres, as many are tempted to do, either by the easy running or to avoid the trouble of pumping up; it

---

[1] There is a tendency on the part of many makers to keep down the size and weight of pneumatic tyres to such an extent that, from the first, they are overloaded. If in doubt as to the size, it is always wiser to err on the right side, and use a tyre of ample size and strength; in fact, the largest tyre that can be conveniently fitted to the wheel.

[2] Refer to footnote on Brakes.

[3] Rubber commences to deteriorate if exposed to a strong light or high temperatures, or if brought in contact with rust, grease, or most of the acids; further, the canvas fabric rapidly rots when exposed to damp; so spare tyres should be protected from the light and stored in a dry place, the temperature of which does not exceed some 75° F. Although tyres which have been in use are not so much affected by heat and light as new ones, care should be taken to protect them if the car is laid up for any time, and to remember that they can only be kept in good condition by washing the mud and dirt off them after every run. In removing the cover from the rim of the wheel the paint is sure to be more or less injured, and if such exposed parts are not painted again, when an opportunity occurs, with some air-drying enamel, rust will accumulate and injure the tyre.

[4] Handy, portable, and inexpensive vulcanisers are now made, and handy drivers soon, under the free tuition of the makers, are able to neatly execute little tyre repairs with much saving of time and money.

means **excessive wear and rapid depreciation. They should be inflated until they** are just on the point of bulging at the tread under the full load; this is a better guide than a pressure gauge, as gauges, unless they are fairly large ones, properly calibrated, are not always to be relied upon, and after the covers have become worn a given pressure[1] has a different effect upon them.

Of course, the pressure necessary to properly inflate a tyre much **depends upon the size** of the tyre for the load it has to support. Formerly, cars were more often met with that were under-tyred, and therefore had to be pumped up to a pressure that severely strained the fabric, on one hand, and robbed the tyre of a great deal of resilience on the other. But now it is more generally understood that the truest economy is to use tyres which are relatively large for the load, and run them at reduced pressures. The leading tyre-makers give suitable pressures for given loads and tyres in their literature, which can be relied upon as a guide.

When **cars are garaged** or stabled for **several weeks** they should be jacked up and the **tyres deflated**, so that the wheels are clear of the ground, and the fabric liners of the tyres are not continuously under stress; but if the car is in frequent use, it is not necessary to deflate the tyres. An occasional wipe with a damp sponge will keep them in condition if they are not exposed to heat and sunlight, as previously explained. The covers, inner tubes, and rims require periodical examination for any of the defects that have been referred to. **Abnormal wear** on the front tyres always occurs when the **front wheels are not in alignment** with the rear ones that is to say, when their horizontal diameters are not parallel for the position they are in when the car is running forward in a straight line. Any want of such alignment means a combined rolling and sliding, or grinding action, as the wheel passes over the ground. A similar action occurs when, through some defect in the design of the steering gear, or through some straining action, the front wheels do not come

---

[1] The pressure per square inch varies from about 35 lbs. in the tyres of the lightest cars to about 80 in those of the heaviest.

to the proper angles which they should make with the front axle when turning a comer. These angles are only equal when the car is running in a straight line, but when turning a corner the near-side wheel should be running in a sharper curve than the off-side one for correct running, therefore the gear must guide it into a position, making a smaller angle with the axle than the off-side one does. A very simple and familiar expedient, due to Ackermann, enables the designer to arrange his steering gear to do this; but it is often in the actual construction of the car that such adjustments are apt to be made without sufficient care, although, of course, in the works of the best makers, both at home and abroad so great is the care taken that such parts are little short of perfect when the car is turned out; but it should be added that too often neglect in keeping the various pin joints of the gear **properly lubricated** leads to the development of such an amount of back-lash that the front wheels freely wobble when the car is running, causing serious injury to the tyres.

110. **Self-Sealing Tubes.**—Many expedients have from time to time been used by manufacturers to make the inner tubes of rubber tyres self-sealing, so as to prevent deflation occurring due to punctures, and probably the most perfect puncture-proof one that has yet been produced is the Sealomatic. It is lined with a patented material, with another lining of a sticky plastic material made by a secret process and it is certainly puncture-proof, but these tubes have the disadvantage of being expensive heavier than the plain ones, and somewhat less resilient. However there are many who willingly purchase immunity from puncture troubles at this price.

111. **Metal-Studded Tyres** give a better grip on some road surfaces, and when a slip occurs, due to sudden clutching or braking, there is less erosive action, but probably more injurious straining action, on the rubber; and often such action causes some of the studs to be stripped off, and severely strains the machinery of the car, but the tendency to side-slip is reduced, both at the driving and front wheels.

On the other hand, the steel studs soon become polished,

and act almost like skates on snow or ice, and on stone setts are not satisfactory. It is usual to assume that fitting a tyre with studs shortens its life by about a tenth, and that the speed of the car is somewhat reduced for a given consumption of fuel, or, in other words, there is a falling off in mileage per gallon of petrol, and this is the price that is paid for more effective steering and a certain amount of immunity from side-slip.

112. Detachable Non-Skid Bands.—The remarks relating to metal-studded tyres in the previous Article equally apply to these, which are rapidly going out of fashion, but it should be added that they are most injurious to the tyres to which they are fitted, materially shortening their life. Any kind of studded tread acts more injuriously on the road surface than a plain tread, particularly at high speed, and when there is an appreciable amount of slip, and during sudden clutching and braking.

113. New Tyres on Front _v._ on Back Wheels.—The many serious accidents due to the bursting of front tyres seem to suggest the wisdom of first using new tyres on the front wheels and running them some 2000 or 3000 miles before changing them to the back wheels. The fabric should then be in a sound condition and the rubber tread worn nearly half through, but in that condition they are equal to good service, and, so far as the author is aware, this practice, whenever adopted, has been satisfactory.

113A. Stepney Wheels and Detachable Rims.— The Stepney wheel has been aptly termed the "Motorist's life-belt." In the old days a punctured or burst tyre was often a very serious matter and always a cause of delay, but since the spare or Stepney wheel came into general use a car can be got under way a few minutes after a tyre becomes deflated. Further, some motorists find it a convenience to have the Stepney shod with steel studs, so that it can be used in wet weather as a non-skid. Recently this wheel has been improved so that it can be fitted to the car in much less time than hitherto. But during the past year or two much attention has been given to the production of **detachable**

rims, and doubtless ere long it will be quite the exception if a car is not fitted with them, as the very obvious and valuable advantage of being able to quickly unfix a damaged type en its **detachable** rim, and replace it by the spare one, is well worth paying something extra for.

114. **Road-Wheels.**—The designer cannot give too much attention to the road-wheels. These are made of either oak or steel, the latter known as **wire wheels**; the former (known as **artillery wheels**) being now almost exclusively used, as they wear very well, have a better appearance than the others of the bicycle type, and are more easily cleaned. But it can be proved that motor-car wheels, to have a margin of safety equal to that which the wheels of horse-drawn vehicles have, must be many times stronger; in fact, they cannot be too strong for our purpose, as the very lives of motorists depend upon the wheels being able to safely withstand the tremendous strain set up by turning a corner at high speed, or by any obstruction that tends to dish them at a time when they are transmitting considerable power.[1] This is one of the reasons why motor-car wheels are kept down in size, although it is common knowledge that the larger the wheels the less power required to drive a given carriage, owing to the smaller amount of rolling and axle friction. There are other reasons why large wheels are not used, for they greatly increase the cost of both wheels and tyres, and make access to the seats more difficult, whilst they raise the centre of gravity of the vehicle, reducing its stability in turning corners. On the other hand, they run smoother, lick up less dust, and more easily surmount any obstacle. So again we have a compromise.

115. **Balanced Engines.**—Perfect smoothness of running can only be secured by fitting the car with a well-balanced engine. This would appear to be a very easy matter, as almost every maker of a petrol engine claims that it is perfectly balanced whether it be a single-cylinder one, a

---

[1] The principal straining actions which are taken into account in designing a road-wheel are : (a) Those due to the load it carries; (b) those due to the drive it transmits; (c) those due to the centrifugal force of the car in turning a corner, which is by far the greatest; (d) those due to the impact that may occur in the wheel striking the kerb, due to a side-slip.

two-cylinder, three-cylinder, or whatever number of cylinders it may have. In fact, when balancing is thus referred to, a very loose interpretation of the word is, or should be, intended. **The balancing** of a reciprocating engine might appear at first to represent the very simple problem which in the **single-cylinder engine** is usually solved by forming weights on the crank arms (as shown in Fig. 1) to balance the revolving and partly balance the reciprocating masses; but after this has been done (without going into refinements that would be of interest to an engineering student, but could scarcely be followed by the general reader), there remain in the petrol engine *unbalanced* **inertia forces**, caused by the moving parts, which produce a vertical hammering action. Now, if instead of a single-cylinder engine we consider a **two-cylinder engine**, with cranks at 1800,[1] and reciprocating masses equal, there are certain forces and couples which cannot be balanced, and they result in a tilting effect which tends to rock the engine in a fore and aft direction, and cause serious vibration. But with **three-cylinders**, with equal masses at the crank radius, and the cranks at 120°, the engine can be arranged to run with a more uniform turning action, and, with the vertical hammering action practically eliminated, a distinct advantage over the two-cylinder one; but, so far as the rocking action (due to certain unbalanced couples[2]) is concerned, this engine has little or no advantage over the two-cylinder one of the same power. Now, by adding another cylinder, we get a **four-cylinder engine**, which gives the designer a much better chance of approximating to a true balance, for with cranks at 180° apart, the usual arrangement in motor-car engines, a perfect fore and aft

---

[1] A two-cylinder engine with the cranks arranged in this way gives the best balance, but the torque or turning moment is more uniform when the cranks are together, this arrangement giving a torque which ii equivalent to one explosion stroke per revolution; whilst when the cranks are at 180° or opposite, there is a variation of turning moment which ii equivalent to that due to a double-acting single-cylinder engine which misses two driving strokes every other stroke.

[2] To keep down the disturbing effect of these couples (the primary and secondary) the cylinders should be placed as near together as practicable. These matters are fully treated in Professor Dalby's and Professor Sharp's works on the Balancing of Engines.

balance is possible; but the vertical hammering effect can only be imperfectly dealt with, in fact, with no more success than in a two-cylinder engine. Notwithstanding this, it cannot be denied that four-cylinder engines are produced which, when run at the speed they were designed to work at, are hard to beat for smoothness of running. But those who have paid attention to these matters will know that to attain the highest possible condition of balance in **an engine five or six cylinders** are necessary. Even with the required number of cylinders, the exercise of consummate skill in designing the balancing system is necessary to produce an engine that will run without vibration; indeed, a wealth of mechanical genius has been lavished on the evolution of the highest form of petrol engine, and some elegant expedients have been devised in solving balancing problems.[1] So it will be seen that the balancing of engines is a subject on which the man in the street is not likely to be very well informed, in fact, is most likely to be easily misled.

LUBRICATION

116. **Introduction.**—No car can be efficiently run without trouble occurring, or even a breakdown, unless it has been constructed in such a way that all the wearing parts can be easily and properly lubricated. No driver can hope to run his car without trouble, unless he has made a business of mastering the arrangements made for lubricating its various working parts and understanding the maker's instructions relating to them; indeed, he should never take a car out without first being sure that everything connected with its lubrication is in order, for, obviously, it is too late to commence to pay attention to such matters when he hears ominous sounds emanating from bearings or rubbing surfaces that plainly tell him they are on the point of galling or **seizing for want of proper lubrication**. New engines in particular require plenty of the best oil, as they are more apt to give

---

[1] One of the most interesting of which is to be found in the Lanchester engine, and another in Gorban-Brille engine.

trouble until all their bearings have rubbed down to their work. Much ingenuity has been displayed in designing the in- numerable forms of lubricators and lubricating devices in common use on cars for securing a regular feed to the various bearing surfaces, with the result that they not only vary with the car, but with different parts of the same car. We shall see that there has, during the past two or three years, been a welcome and much-needed amount of attention given to lubricating systems, and a few of the best cars are now so perfectly fitted that they are as nearly fool-proof as they are likely to be made, until a new solution of the whole problem of car lubrication is discovered; but we have with us, and must expect to have running for many years, a great number of cars that are fitted with what may now be considered more or less old-fashioned arrangements, and these must therefore receive attention in due course.

The most perfect way to lubricate a bearing is to immerse it in an **oil-bath**, and the more nearly this ideal arrangement (which is rarely practicable) is approached, the more satisfactory the result.

The methods adopted to lubricate the many important parts of a petrol motor car, at first sight appear to be very varied, but a careful examination will show that they may all be divided into three principal classes or systems, namely, **gravity-feed, splash or spray**, and **forced-feed.** More than one of these systems are used on some cars, as we shall see when we explain them and the expedients that are employed to lubricate some of the minor parts.

When the feed is controlled by hand, beginners usually err on the side of using far too much oil;[1] but this is a fault on the right side, and with any given car only experience with close observation will teach its driver how to judiciously use an expensive material, and keep his mount in the pink of running condition. After a time the temptation with some to take liberties with the car is great, and they may even run

---

[1] About two and a half to three gallons per thousand miles appears to be a fair allowance for a good-sized car. Of course, the whole of the lubricating oil supplied to the engine is not actually used, as a large percentage is drawn off as spent.

it a whole day without attending to its lubrication, but such a liberty as this cannot be taken every day without at least serious depreciation occurring.

117. **Gravity-Feed.**—The oldest system, in which the lubricant is carried in a tank on the dash-board, from which it is conveyed by pipes to the engine and the other parts where it is required; the flow of the oil being regulated by cocks on the pipes just below the tank, or by conical valves inside the tank, which are raised or lowered by eccentric levers or other arrangements on top of the tank. As only oils of low viscosity and setting point can be efficiently used with this arrangement, owing to the length and small bore of some of the pipes, we shall see that some makers place the oil-tank under the bonnet in front of the dash-board, where the oil is kept sufficiently fluid by the heat of the engine to flow through such small pipes or leads under working conditions.

118. **Splash or Spray Lubrication.**—In this system, which is largely used, the important engine bearings are lubricated by partly filling the crank chamber with a cylinder[1] oil to such a height as to allow the big ends of the connecting rods to dip a little (about $\frac{1}{4}$ inch) into it, and in so doing lubricate the crank-pins each time they come into their lowest position; this causes a deal of **splashing**, which is utilised to lubricate the crankshaft bearings, the gudgeon pin, and lastly the piston,[1] by oil thrown on the wall of the cylinder.

The oil is **introduced into the crank chamber** in either of the three following ways:—

(a) By a **De Dion hand-pump**,[2] a charge of oil, usually

---

[1] The practice of supplying oil to the crank chamber in doses, and trusting to it being splashed over the bearings, gudgeon-pin and cylinder wall, is the one that has been very generally adopted in the past, and although rather haphazard it seems to work well on the whole, particularly for single-cylinder engines; but as the oil has to lubricate the cylinder, it must be of good quality, suitable for cylinder use. Sometimes an additional **drip lubricator feeds** oil to the cylinder-wall near the lowest position of the piston, but, unless this is forced by some means, a thin oil has to he used, and then, for obvious reasons, it is of doubtful utility.

[2] The **hand-pump** fitted to the dash-board, with its three-way cock- one for admission from the oil-tank, and two for delivery to the crank chamber and gear-case (one for each) through short pipes of large bore was first used on the De Dion cars. The objection to this system is the danger of the failure of lubrication if the charge be delayed, and of over-lubrication when a fresh charge is introduced.

due to one stroke of the pump, being injected at such intervals as experience suggests.

(b) **Through a needle valve** by gravity from an oil sight-feed lubricator on the dash-board, the drips being regulated to supply the amount required. But the hole in the valve being small, any difference in the thickness of the oil considerably affects the quantity dripping through.

(c) **Exhaust Gas Pressure** is used to facilitate the distribution of oil by connecting the engine exhaust-pipe by means of a branch pipe to the upper part of the oil-tank, in which a pressure is maintained sufficient to raise a column of oil from the tank through a pipe to the lubricator on the dash-board, whence it is distributed to the crank chamber, gear- case, &c., the gases imparting a slight heat to the oil; among the best-known cars with this system being the Crossley. After a time the oil in the crank chamber becomes vitiated or spent and requires changing,[1] and it is well to do this about every 500 to 700 miles, according to the size of the engine and its special requirements, the smaller ones requiring most frequent attention.

In another arrangement that has been found to work well, the **crank pins** are lubricated by oil, fed **under exhaust** pressure, into **annular channels** fixed to the cranks webs, from which it flows by **centrifugal force** along a pipe on the crank web to a hole in the crank pin; transverse holes in the pin allowing the oil to flow into the brasses. After use the oil falls into the well at the bottom of the crank- case, and a pump, usually of the positive type, returns it to the oil-tank.

119. **Forced-Feed Lubrication** is used on the engines

---

[1] This is done by unscrewing a plug at the bottom of the crank chamber and allowing the oil to escape, the fresh oil being poured into the chamber until the right level is reached through a similar hole in its upper part. It is necessary to occasionally wash out the chamber with paraffin to keep it clean; and, to prevent an excess of oil accumulating in the chamber, an overflow pipe is sometimes fitted, as, should the chamber become too full, oil is apt to find its way into the combustion chamber of the cylinder and to be more or less burnt, causing a bluish smoke to pass out of the exhaust pipe, which is a sure indication of over-lubrication. This may also cause the oil to lodge between the points of the sparking plug, impairing ignition, and perhaps forming gummy deposits or films upon the piston rings and valves.

employed on the Maudslay, Rolls-Royce, Delaunay-Belleville, Armstrong-Whitworth, De Dion, and other well-known cars. In this system the oil is forced through the crank-shaft bearings,[1] into holes running through the crank-shaft webs and crank pins (and in some cases from the latter, through the connecting rods, or through pipes, to the gudgeon pins and to the cylinder walls), from which it falls into the crank chamber, at the bottom of which a well or sump is provided from which the oil is pumped back to the crank-shaft bearings, being filtered or strained as it enters the pump. Thus it is re-used, with the great advantage that it only circulates whilst the engine runs, and ceases when it stops, no turning on or off being required.[2] The most perfect examples of this system (which is referred to below[3]) are arranged on the lines first introduced by Messrs Bellis & Morcom on their high-speed steam engines' Another interesting example of the forced system is the one that was formerly fitted to the Lanchester cars,[1] where the bottom of the oil-tank was made to fit a spindle running longitudinally through it so that the upper

---

[1] A fundamental condition for efficient lubrication is that the oil must be fed or forced into the bearing at or near the slack side. If forced into it on the loaded side it must be done so with a pressure considerably greater than the mean pressure on the bearing. Refer to Mr. B. Tower's experiments.

[2] One pump only is used; it delivers oil to a pipe with branches leading to the various bearings.

[3] In this system, as we have seen, the surface of the oil in the crank chamber is lower than the big ends in their lowest position, and there is a well (or sump) in which, or in connection with which, a small plunger or rotary pump is driven from the crank-shaft or cam-shaft, delivering oil to all the bearings in predetermined quantities in the way we have described. This system, when well carried out, and when the oil is periodically renewed and properly filtered or strained to extract foreign matter, as occurs in such engines as the Rolls-Royce, makes a very perfect but expensive job, causing the rotating parts to float on a film of oil, and reducing friction and wear to a minimum. As an example of the beauty of this system, a Bellis and Morcom engine was run 190,000,000 revolutions without the bearings being touched with a spanner. Refer to the author's "Machine Design," &c., p. 528. In another arrangement (the Clarkson system) the oil flows from the pump through a number of small pipes, which deliver a steady stream of oil upon every bearing of the engine and upon the bottom edge of the piston.

In the arrangement now used a pump in the well of the crank case draws oil through a filter and then discharges it into a copper pipe fitted with branches leading to the main bearings. The pump is driven direct by the crank-shaft by means of toothed wheels.

part of the spindle was in communication with the bulk of the oil, whilst the lower half was opposed to a series of outlets which communicated with the various parts to be lubricated. The spindle, which was rotated by a worm-gear from the half-speed shaft, had a series of pockets or depressions cut in it—one opposite each outlet—so that in rotating these pockets first filled with oil from the tank, and afterwards discharged their contents into the various passages for distribution, under a pressure of about 30 to 35 lbs. per square inch.

With forced lubrication the bearings are always flooded with oil, and the friction and wear are greatly reduced. The principal **disadvantage** of this system when applied to motor-car work (particularly when the engines are small) is that, if too much oil is caused to flow, it may pass into the cylinders and cause the exhaust to smoke, &c. Further, several small pipes are used to convey the oil from the pump to the bearings, and a stoppage in one of these would cause the bearing to run hot, and there is the further disadvantage that the system is costly.

120. **Lubrication of Important Parts.**—Next to the engine, the **change-speed gears** may be considered most important; they are generally run in a fairly thick oil,[1] the gear-case being occasionally partly filled with it after drawing off the spent and dirty oil. The level of the oil need not be much above the lowest wheel rims, as the oil gets well splashed and carried over the working surfaces. Plug-holes in the gear-case are sometimes arranged to test the level of the oil without taking the gear- case cover off; or an oil-gauge on the case is used.

The **differential gear** is one of the most important

---

[1] In the days when the teeth of gear wheels were not so accurately formed and carefully finished as they are now, and when the crank case joints were not so perfect, grease was formerly used for this purpose; but as this was too viscous to flow, the wheels cut for themselves races in the body of the stuff in which they revolved, more or less out of contact with the lubricant, and the grease, becoming banked up, retarded the motion of the sliding parts in changing gear. The same thing occurs with oils that solidify at temperatures that can hardly be considered low. In the best practice the bearings in the gear-case are independently lubricated, either with oil or grease, as the oil in the case becomes charged with metal dust and small chips from the wheels.

parts of the power-transmission system, and want of care in using and lubricating it is probably the cause of more serious trouble than any other part of the machinery. When it is remembered that the **differential is continuously at work**[1] when the car is running, the necessity of efficiently lubricating, not only the bevel wheel and pinion, which take the power off the propeller shaft, but the differential pinions will be understood. Even should the lubricant leak from an ill-fitting box, or through the sleeves on to the road-wheels,[2] it does not follow that it is being over-lubricated. Most gear-cases have an overflow plug-hole, closed with a screw plug, so that the level of the oil may be observed, and after testing this a few times before starting out, it is easy to judge how often to replenish from the dash-board pump, if the case is not supplied by pressure through automatic leads, or is not run in a thin grease.

121. **Gravity Sight-feed Lubricators.**—The lubrication of most of the other important bearings is pretty generally performed by a **gravity sight-feed lubricator,** which should be regulated not so much for a large supply but for a certain and continuous flow In some of these lubricators all the tubes are governed by one tap, which is the only one that requires opening and shutting, the others having been once adjusted for the feed required in each case. Needless to say, the efficiency of this system largely depends upon the tubes being kept clean and free from obstructions.

122. **Ring Lubrication** of the dynamo type, if skilfully carried out, has possibilities which perhaps have not been sufficiently appreciated by the designer of cars. It gives a good approximation to an oil- bath, the bearing being made in such a way that a collar or ring on the shaft loosely fits it,

---

[1] It is often assumed that friction with this gear only occurs when the car is moving round a corner or on a curve; but each time a slight slip of on of the driving-wheels occurs, and whenever the direction of the car Aviates **from** a straight path, due to traffic, there is some movement of the spider wheels, although small in amount, and, as this is continuously going on, whenever this gear is allowed to run dry serious trouble ensues.

[2] Often the end bearings of the axle are fitted with grease boxes, as Often the end" then tends to keep the oil in the casing and the bearings being often used to further prevent leakage.

and, revolving with it, dips into the oil in the well, there being a break in the bearing at its centre to allow of this. Of course, with this arrangement the oil is being constantly lifted from the well by the ring as it revolves, flowing down from its highest position into the bearing, and back into the well again. In a few cars, both of European and American make, the crank-shaft bearings are fitted with these useful devices, and in one or two cases the cam-shaft bearings too; each bearing having a lubricating well, which is from time to time supplied with oil from the **oil sights** on the **dash-board**, or from an oil reservoir by a **De Dion hand-pump**.

The ring oil-wells of the crank-shaft bearings of the Decauville car have openings into the oil-bath in the crank chamber, and the upper parts of the bearings are in open communication with the latter, thereby also receiving oil by the splashing action of the big ends of the connecting rods. The oil in overflowing from the bearings enters centrifugal cups attached to the crank arms, from which it flows by centrifugal force through holes in the crank webs and pins into the big ends, from which it is thrown into the base chamber; thus the oil is constantly circulating between the two oil receptacles and through all the bearings.

122A. **Minor Bearings.—The more out of sight** a bearing may be, or the smaller the amount of motion in it, the more likely it is to be neglected, as, even if it works dry, the feeble squeaking noise it makes is often unheard. This particularly applies to parts which are ordinarily lubricated with the common oil-can, or by **Stauffer grease-cups,** such as the controlling mechanism, the valve-tappets, lever pins, the joints of the steering gear, and the shackle pins of the springs, &c., which require regular attention.

When **grease-cups** or boxes are fitted to some of the minor running bearings, they require screwing up about a quarter of a turn for every 60 to 100 miles run. The advantage of this arrangement is that, should a bearing run hot, the grease melts and flows over the journal.[1]

122B. **Springs.—**Even the leaves of the springs require

---

[1] The part of the shaft or spindle which runs in the bearing.

occasional **greasing**, or they will grind on one another and become noisy. This is done by Jacking up the frame till the leaves of the spring can be separated a little by a screw-driver, when grease is introduced with a knife. Of course, if rust has formed between the leaves, the only thing to do is to take the spring down, clean off the rust, wash in paraffin, and properly grease the leaves before reassembling.

122c. **Effect of Temperature on Lubrication**.—In some systems of lubrication provision is made to prevent the flow of oil being **affected by cold weather**.

By passing through the oil-tank a branch pipe, either from the exhaust[1] pipe or from the pipe through which the circulating water is carried, and regulating the flow of the hot stream; the oil being thus kept warm and its flow fairly constant at all temperatures of the atmosphere. Another expedient is to fix the oil-tank under the bonnet near the cylinders, if there is room, or, failing that, under the floor and near the exhaust pipe, so that heat from the latter may always keep the oil from becoming too thick by falling too much in temperature, and perhaps reaching the **setting point**, when it may have the consistency of grease. On the other hand, care must be taken not to sensibly raise the temperature of the oil, or it will become too thin for lubricating purposes, as we shall directly see.

123. **Lubricating Oils for the Cylinders must** be of a kind specially suitable for use at high temperatures, therefore we are precluded from using ordinary vegetable and animal oils for this purpose, as they partially decompose at high temperatures, liberating fatty acids, and forming pitch.

---

[1] In the James and Browne lubricator, oil is supplied from the tank through sight-feed glasses, by pressure derived from an induced vacuum in the crank chamber. For as the piston reciprocates, a partial vacuum is formed in the crank-case during the up-stroke, and a slight impulsive Pressure during the down-stroke, the latter amounting to about ½ to ¾lb. per sq inch being used in some cases to force the oil from the lubricator into the bearings. Of course, with both arrangements non-return valves are used in the pipes. In this connection it should be explained that broken or worn piston rings are apt to allow an escape of the gases into the crank chamber during the explosion stroke, and this may cause pressure enough to blow out some of the oil through the bearings, unless a relief valve is fitted.

But **mineral oils** stand heat much better, and are, therefore, exclusively used (either pure or compounded) for cylinders of petrol engines, and also, as a matter of fact, for most engine-lubricating purposes.

A peculiarity of all oils is, that as you raise their temperature they become thinner and less viscous, so that a fairly thick oil, at say, 70° F., may become so thin at 212° F. (the boiling-point of water) as to lose over 95 per cent, of its viscosity, and at 400° F. it may be as thin as ordinary paraffin lamp oil, and about as useful as a lubricant, whilst at some higher temperature its boiling-point is reached, and it is converted into gas.[1] So the question that presents itself to the engineer is not so much what the normal condition of a cylinder oil is, but rather what its condition is when heated to the temperature of the cylinder walls, which temperature decides the kind of oil he would order. Now we have seen that somewhere in the cylinder of a petrol engine, during each working stroke, there may be a maximum temperature of some 3600° F., but the temperature of the water- or air-cooled cylinder wall, with which the lubricant is in contact, and which presumably represents the **effective temperature** so far as the oil is concerned, is comparatively a low one, as there is every reason to believe that in **water- cooled cylinders** it does not exceed, or certainly does not much exceed, that of boiling water at atmospheric pressure, namely, 212° F.; so, probably, we shall be on the safe side if we fix it at 250° F. Of course, with cylinders that are only partly jacketed, or inefficiently cooled, this temperature is higher, and in **air-cooled** cylinders higher still; indeed, in most cases it probably varies between fairly wide limits, being

[1] If it be a perfectly pure oil, a vacuum distillate of a crude petroleum with all its impurities oxidised and eliminated before or during distillation, then such a distillate, if untreated with sulphuric acid and soda, or other chemicals, should be capable of being: completely evaporated into gas; but oils refined by the rough and ancient methods in general use invariably leave a gummy deposit, which becomes baked into a char. The presence of acid, may be detected by putting a sample in a glass bottle with a copper wire running down air-tight through the cork. Leave the bottle in a sunny place for two or three weeks, and if verdigris or green rust appears on the copper there is an acid in the oil.

dependent upon the area and kind of gills on the cylinder,
the quantity of air which comes in contact with it in a given
time, the condition of this air, the quality of the explosive
mixture, and the number of explosions per minute. Although
no serious attempts appear to have been made to measure
these temperatures under actual running conditions, the
minimum temperature under the most favourable conditions might safely be taken to exceed the maximum of a
water-cooled cylinder; whilst in some cases where motor
cycles have been run on the low gear up a fairly steep hill,
in the same direction as the wind (the most unfavourable
conditions for cooling), the cylinders have been seen in the
dark to glow with a dull red heat, which is equivalent to a
temperature of some 950° or 1000° F. Of course, no oil could
possibly retain its liquid form at such temperatures and it is
a bit mysterious how engines could pull through such a trial
without something serious happening; but although these
extremely high temperatures may be occasionally reached,
the temperature of the cylinder walls of air-cooled cylinders
probably does not often exceed about 500° F. Now, with these
points before us, it is obvious that, in order to provide for the
reducing effect of heat, the lubricating oil should have the
greatest body, **unctuosity**[1] **or greasiness**, consistent with
a high degree of fluidity at normal temperatures; it should
also have a "**low setting point**,"[2] so that, when the engine
is cold, it will not set in the cylinder, crank chamber, and
oil tubes, The only satisfactory process **at present in use**
for the production of safe mineral oils to satisfy the above
conditions for the higher temperatures appears to be that of
filtering the crude petroleum through animal charcoal at high
temperatures,[3] after the lighter and more volatile fractions
have been removed by distillation, and in so doing eliminating
the tarry matters. This is an expensive process, but the body

[1] A most appropriate word coined by Veitch Wilson.

[2] The setting point (or temperature at which solidification occurs) of heavy mineral oils varies from about 30° to 40° F.; it depends mainly upon the amount of
solid paraffin present in the oil.

[3] The amount of treatment necessary, of course, depends upon the character of the
crude oil, which varies considerably according to its source.

of the oil is not apparently injuriously affected, as it is by the acid and alkali process previously referred to.

124. **Compound Oils.**—It has long been found that highly refined mineral or hydrocarbon oils, enriched by the addition of a small proportion of carefully selected neutral fatty materials (the fatty acid being removed to obviate the action of the acid), of low oxidising tendency, produce a compound oil which combines the superior lubricating properties of the fatty oils with the neutral characteristics of the hydrocarbons.

But such compound oils can only apparently be commercially produced when there is a market for the by-product represented by the free fatty acids of the fatty materials, which are converted into a saponaceous mass by treatment with alkali, and used in the manufacture of soap. The important feature of all satisfactory compound oils that should always he specified is that there should be in them a preponderating proportion of absolutely neutral non-oxidisable hydrocarbon oil.

It might be mentioned that there is a great difference in the various fatty oils in their tendency to oxidise. Thus **Olive oil** sometimes contains over 30 per cent, of free fatty acid, whilst the finest **Sperm** oil only contains some 2 or 3 per cent. **Linseed** has a rapidly drying or oxidising tendency; on the other hand, **Neatsfoot** and **Lard oil** of the finer qualities are slow drying.

It is well known that the rate at which **fatty oils** are **reduced** by heat is much lower than in the case of **pure mineral oils,** and that they are superior to the latter in their efficiency as lubricants and in their lasting powers **when the conditions are favourable. So it** follows that when using pure hydrocarbon oils for cylinder purposes it is necessary to adopt oils of great viscosity at normal temperature in order to secure a sufficient body the working temperature. But it is possible to use a compound oil of unimpeachable character whose normal fluidity is much greater, and in so doing to avoid the trouble due to feeding a thick oil through the small pipes of the lubricating system.

For the reasons given above it is possible for only a very few manufacturers to produce a satisfactory compound oil. So when in doubt as to the origin of a compound oil the motorist would be well advised to stick to a pure mineral oil.

125. **Physical Properties of Lubricating Oils.** — The quality of cylinder oil to stand high temperature is fixed by the flash-point[1] (and its price goes up with it), that which is generally used for motoring purposes having flash- points from 450° to 550° F., varying with the kind of cylinder it is used in. For example, taking one of the best-known brands of compound oils, namely, Price's, their Motorine C is an oil adapted for wholly **water-cooled cylinders** in the largest cars,[2] and its specific gravity at 60° F. is 0-900 to 0-905, flash-point 450° F., setting point 32° F.; their Motorine B is an oil adapted for **air-cooled or partially water-cooled cylinders** in small cars and voiturettes, its specific gravity being 0-890 to 0-895, flash-point 500° F., and setting point 40° F.; and their Motorine A is adapted for air-cooled cylinders of motor cycles,[3] its specific gravity is 0-890 to 0-895, flash-

---

[1] The flash-point is the temperature at which a spirit or oil, when slowly heated in an open vessel, begins to give off a sufficient quantity of inflammable vapour to burn with a momentary flash when a small test flame is brought into contact with the vapour. This open test has many defects, the principal one being that the free access of currents of air to the surface does not permit a uniform accumulation of inflammable vapours, so that with the air in motion the results obtained with the same oil may be entirely different. This defect in the open method led to the invention and construction of apparatus by means of which the oil vapour is produced and tested in a close vessel, which gives a lower but truer value of the flash-point. The best known of these are the Pensky-Marten and Abel's, as improved by Boverton Redwood. The burning point, ignition point, or firing point is the temperature at which the oil takes fire and continues burning. The author has often been astonished by statements made in authoritative quarters that oils with flash-points of about 650°-700° P. were available; although he has had tested mineral oils from practically all the known sources of supply, even the open test failed to come near such high figures. So to settle the question he recently appealed to his friend Veitch Wilson, who very kindly procured from Mr. Mackendrick, of the Anglo-American Oil Co., samples of cylinder oils of the highest flashpoints that he knew of or could offer, and those Veitch Wilson tested.

[2] Most large cars can use thinner oils, because their engines are rarely driven with full throttle, while with lower-powered cars the reverse is more commonly the case.

[3] Light-weight motor cycles run better on Motorine B or C than on Motorine A, which is too heavy for the work.

point 550° F., and setting point 40° F. Table XI., due to Veitch Wilson, gives these values in a more convenient form, also the viscosities or body, at temperatures from 70° to 212° F., &c.

Name of Oil	Specific Gravity at 60° F.	Body for viscosity at				Ratio % of Viscosity at 212° ÷ Viscosity at 70° F.	Flash-Point F.	Setting Point F.
		70° F.	120° F.	180° F.	212° F.			
COMPOUND OILS –								
Price Motorine A	890/895	2750	435	100	65	2.36	550	40
" " B	890/895	2000	340	85	55	2.75	500	40
" " C	900/905	1200	230	60	45	3.75	450	32
" Heavy Gas Engine	905/910	750	150	45	33	4.40	400	30
" Original Gas Engine	905/910	250	65	32	27	10.80	400	28
PURE HYDROCARBON OILS –								
Price's Oleogene D	895/900	1500	250	64	47	3.13	420	40
" " P	905/910	800	150	45	34	4.25	420	10
French Huile D (average) pure mineral	895/900	1500	255	64	43	2.86	420	40
French Huile P (average) pure mineral	905/910	780	140	40	33	4.24	420	5

The above figures given for viscosity denote the time taken in seconds by 1000 grains of oil to flow through a small orifice in the testing apparatus at each temperature, the standard adopted being genuine sperm oil, taken as 100 at 70° F.

High-class cylinder oils are very expensive, their manufacture is in the hands of a very few; but the poor motorist must have the best if he is to be economical and free from trouble in running his car.

Needless to say, the many secondary bearings about a car can be efficiently lubricated by a high- class heavy machinery oil, and there are others fitted with grease-cups, which are usually placed on the commutator shaft, clutch box, pump spindle, &c.; these should be kept well filled and screwed down half a turn about every hundred miles; but it is best to follow the advice of the maker of the car in such matters. Other matters relating to lubrication have been explained in various connections, and are therefore not mentioned in this Article, which could be profitably much extended, if the exigencies of space would permit.

126. **Cleaning and Lubricating the Chains.**— They should be first thoroughly cleaned with paraffin, then soaked in melted refined Russian tallow,[1] care being taken not to allow the tallow to become hotter than is necessary to keep it in the liquid state, as the temper of the chain may be affected. After the chain has been moved about in the melted grease to allow it, the grease, to come in contact with the surfaces of the rollers and rivets, the chain should be hung up and the lubricant allowed to drain into the shallow tin used for the purpose. Plumbago and tallow make an excellent lubricant, but it is very difficult to effectually apply, as the plumbago sinks to the bottom of the vessel as soon as the tallow becomes melted.

127. **On Selecting a Car.**—The great motor car exhibitions never fail to attract numbers of intending purchasers. Not a few of these have formed ideas as to what they want;

---

[1] Apparently there has been very little Russian tallow on the market for fifteen or twenty years, although doubtless there is still plenty of so-called Russian sold. Price's Patent Candle Co. have for many years produced, under the supervision of Veitch Wilson, a substitute, by blending various home and foreign tallows, which very closely reproduces Russian. They also produce a special tallow-wax-graphite compound for chains under the name of "Cirogene." The tallow can be refined by placing it in a pail of boiling water, stirring till it is all melted, when the foreign matter will be precipitated, md a solid block of clean tallow form on the surface when cooled.

they have decided upon the sum of money they will lay out, the form and general arrangement of the body, and perhaps even its colour, the number of cylinders and approximate power of the engine have been settled, whilst the kind of transmission, the ignition, lubricating and cooling systems, and the many other important features their ideal car is to have, have been thought out; but, after a painstaking tour of the stands, the potential motorist will find the nearest approach to his requirements is a compromise, as indeed every car is; but there is generally on any well-known car some particular feature that is more perfect in its way than that on others in the market, and this is often why a certain car is selected in preference to others. Of course, if this feature is a really important one, one that represents higher efficiency, marked accessibility, increased simplicity or greater durability, then the selection may be a very judicious one, but if, on the other hand, it is merely the form, or even the colour and finish of the body, as perhaps it more often is than some purchasers would willingly admit, the least said about the matter the better. Not so very long ago it was far from an easy matter to select a satisfactory English-made car, but fortunately that is not the case now, as cars more perfect in design, materials, workmanship, construction, finish, and durability are not to be found anywhere on the Continent than those which are turned out by our most famous makers. And this can be safely said whilst bearing in mind and duly appreciating the splendid vehicles that have been and are being constructed abroad, more particularly those which owe their development to French, German, Italian, American, Dutch, and Belgian genius. This being the case, an intending purchaser cannot go wrong if he follows the patriotic example of His Majesty the King, and places his requirements in the hands of some well-known British maker. Indeed, probably no sport can become truly national and advanced to the highest degree of perfection without royal patronage.

In providing for the requirements of men of very moderate means, our manufacturers have at last realised that practically a new market is open to them. So long as it was possible to find a sufficient number of customers for powerful and expensive cars they were, with very few exceptions, strangely indifferent to the economic value of small profits and quick returns.[1] The trend of modern design is all in the direction of lighter and quicker-running engines, which is coincident with a rapid falling off in the demand for huge cars of the locomotive type, whose disappearance from our roads will be welcomed by all.

128. Car-Driving.—The principal makers of cars and motor cycles supply their customers with printed particulars of all the important details of their vehicles, and, in addition, very concise driving directions; they also, as a rule, willingly allow purchasers to spend a few days in their works to enable them to become acquainted with the internal economy of the mounts they purchase. This is a privilege that every one should avail himself of, even if he employs a professional driver, as it is only by getting a good grasp of how everything is arranged in a car, and of how the principal adjustments and connections are made, in fact, by learning the function of every detail of the mechanism of his car, that he will in time become independent of a driver's company or assistance, when such is not desired, and be able to detect any attempt to impose where repairs are concerned. A purchaser should always arrange with . the maker for a few lessons in driving and for one or two long runs; he will then be taught the use of the various handles, levers, fittings, and accessories used by the driver in running the car, and will be shown how the speed of the engine can be varied by advancing and retarding the spark, also by varying and throttling the mixture, and by a combination of these. The ignition system will be explained, and he will be shown how the accumulators are tested and the current switched on and off. The lubricating system will be carefully traced out, and he will learn what to do; so that in starting the car everything that requires it will be properly lubricated, whilst the use of the clutch and accelerator (if

---

[1] The author has for many years, in season and out of season, called attention to the folly of so many makers specialising in powerful cars for which, after all, even in a rich country like our own, there can only be a limited demand.

one be fitted) will be made clear, and the action of the cooling system gone into. After the owner has been through all this, he will be taken out for a trial spin on some quiet road, or perhaps in one of the parks early some morning, and he will be able to get a little actual driving practice, at first with the car running on its lowest speed; he will then soon find that there is much to learn before he can with any confidence steer the vehicle, manipulate the clutch, and apply the brake to stop the car with the skill required to avoid sudden strains and shocks. After he has shown some proficiency in these matters, he will be taught how to change the gear from a low one to a higher, and from a high one to a lower, without injuring the teeth of the wheels; he will be warned against trying to reverse the car by changing the gear before it has been brought to a standstill. But all this time he may have been merely doing the fancy work (which can be mastered in a very short time), his instructor controlling the running of the engine by advancing or retarding the spark and regulating the throttle, operations that he will, after the first two or three lessons, soon begin to perform with a fair amount of readiness. Only experience of this kind will enable him to master the art of driving in such a way that he almost instinctively knows what to do the instant any adjustment is required. It is hardly necessary to remark that the qualities necessary to make a good driver are not possessed by every one, but it is simply astonishing to find that so many possess an instinctive aptitude for motoring. They are soon able, without any previous mechanical training to skilfully manipulate their car and intelligent ' diagnose the cause of stoppage, and if they have nerve and presence of mind, they are equipped by nature to enjoy to the full a delightful pastime, for there is a peculiar and indescribable pleasure in feeling that you have at your command an obedient agent that will instantly respond to your slightest command, and, should your car be a fairly powerful one, carry you up the steepest hill with a rush that must be experienced to be appreciated; indeed, the only rational excuse for using a powerful car is to be able to negotiate hills at the legal speed limit, and to rapidly accelerate speed after slowing down or stopping; but this very power is one that is too often abused by unskilful owners and inconsiderate and careless drivers, particularly in the abnormal use of the pedal brake, which, as we have explained,[1] should be used more in the way of an emergency brake, one that should be mainly used when it is necessary to pull the car up very short to avoid an accident, and it can never be effectively used when suddenly applied without the differential gear being somewhat strained, and the tyres in particular suffering.[2] A skilful and careful driver always assumes, on approaching a crossroad, that something is about to move out of it that might come in his way, or in nearing a bend or turn in the road that there is a flock of sheep approaching, or something of the kind blocking the way; he then slows down enough to enable him to pull up the car in time, by instantly but gradually applying the lever-brake. It will be seen that all this really represents organised common sense; it means that a reliable good car can be driven for years with little depreciation, and the annual expenditure of a comparatively small amount on repairs and upkeep, if it is carefully and cleanly kept in running condition; all bolts and nuts liable to work loose being examined, and screwed up when necessary after each trip, due attention being paid to lubrication, and the car itself driven with a sympathetic consideration for its powers of endurance. On the other hand, it means that if the car is roughly used, the teeth of the gear-wheels may be seriously chipped or even partly stripped, many parts severely strained, and the driving tyres practically destroyed in a very few minutes.

It should not be overlooked that in locomotive practice a man has to spend years in qualifying to take charge of an engine, and even then he is not competent to execute repairs, nor is required to do so; and in almost every case, unless a motor-car driver be a trained mechanical engineer, or at least has had some good workshop experience, it is false economy to allow him even to take up brasses and do such

---

[1] Refer to Articles on Brakes.

[2] These matters are fully discussed in the Article on the "Foot-brake the Side-brakes"

jobs, as to perform them satisfactorily no small amount of skill is required. It would not be going too far to say that the least important part of the training of a driver is that which enables him to take charge of the wheel and skilfully steer a car through crowded traffic. The really proficient man is able to detect the slightest thing abnormal about the running of a car, and locate its cause before anything serious occurs. And if his training has been of the right kind, and he takes a pride in his work he will keep his car so that everything about it is in the pink of condition, and screwed up to concert pitch when required for use.

129. **How to Start a Car.**—As some reader may become possessed of a second-hand[1] car, and therefore will not be in so fortunate a position, so far as tuition is concerned, as the owner of a new car, it will be as well to very briefly explain what is usually done in starting the engine and car. But as much information bearing on driving has been given in the Articles on Ignition, Cooling, Gear-changing, Clutches, Brakes, Carburation, and Carburettors, &c., the references to these matters will be very brief. The first thing that may be done is to see that the tanks are filled with enough petrol, lubricating oil, and water for the proposed run, and then make sure that all the working parts are thoroughly lubricated, and that the sight-feed lubricators are adjusted. Next turn on the petrol to supply the carburettor, and flood the latter by moving the float-needle up and down two or three times, fully opening the mixture throttle, push **on** the electric switch, and retard the ignition to prevent back-firing; then place the change-speed lever in the neutral position, and smartly turn the **starting-handle** till the explosions drive the engine, being careful to always exert the effort in **pulling** the handle upwards, and

[1] No one who is not an experienced mechanical engineer should be tempted to buy a second-hand car without the advice of an expert, as the art of the horse-dealer in doctoring a horse is not to be compared with that which is sometimes practised in preparing old-fashioned or even obsolete cars for sale. In many cases, too, modern cars that have been very badly treated, and whose mechanisms are practically worn out, are made to look like new ones, to say nothing of the freaks which are faked. On the other hand, excellent cars can be picked up, sometimes at less than half their original cost, as some owners are never long satisfied with their vehicles and must have a new one at least once a year.

refrain from pushing it downwards, as, should **back-firing** accidentally occur whilst it is being pushed down, it would be violently and suddenly forced upwards, with almost certain **injury to the arm**. Having got into the driver's seat, the clutch- pedal may now be depressed, and the gear lever pulled over till the gear for the first speed[1] is in mesh, and the latch of the lever slips into its notch in the quadrant; advance the spark lever a little, then the clutch may be gently let in to allow the car to gradually accelerate its speed. (Refer to Article 100.) After the car has run about half-a-dozen yards, declutch and quickly, but carefully, change into the second speed, and let in the clutch again. Be careful to release the accelerator (if one is used) so as to prevent the engine racing. Repeat this operation till you get into the highest speed.

The **correct position** of the **ignition and throttle levers** can only be determined by experience, but as a general rule the ignition lever should be advanced to as great an extent as the engine will bear without knocking, and the throttle lever should be manipulated to vary the speed of the engine; in other words, the car should be **"driven on the throttle,"** which is the most satisfactory and economical way of driving.

In taking a hill on top gear, the driver should be careful to **retard the ignition** as the **engine slows down,** so as to prevent knocking. And if the gear has to be changed into a lower one, it must be done in good time, or the car will stop before the change is completed.

After some experience there should be no difficulty in **steering with the left hand,** leaving the right hand free when required to use the side-levers, horn, &c.

In driving over greasy roads care should be taken not to put on the brakes when the **car skids,** as this increases the tendency to **side-slip; the clutch** should be taken out, the accelerator released, and the car should be run as much as possible on the crest of the road. The tyres should be kept well pumped up.

---

[1] Needless to say, the novice should, as we have explained, wait till he is proficient in driving on the lowest speed before he attempts to run his car on a higher one.

In going round corners and in slowing down in descents, the throttle should be used with flexible engines. This is obviously better practice than declutching and using the brakes; the latter should only be put on when necessary.

129A. How to Stop a Car.—Declutch and throw the engine out of gear (by putting the change- speed lever into the neutral notch), in stopping the car. When it is to stand for some time, put on the side-brakes, turn off the switch and the flow of petrol from the tank. Many four- or six-cylinder cars can be started on the switch if, on stopping for a short time, the latter is turned off just before the car is pulled up. The engine will then usually start again on the switch being turned on, and in so doing avoid the necessity for turning the starting-handle.

It is well after a long run to feel the important bearings, to see whether they have become heated, due to faulty lubrication or other causes.

129B. Hints on Cleaning a Car.—The car should be well groomed after a run, particularly those parts which may be splashed with mud; this should be removed with a soft sponge dipped from time to time in water and dabbed on the mud, being careful not to wipe the parts, as the varnish may be scratched. A low-pressure hose should then be used to swill the mud away, after which cloths and soft leathers should be used to dry and polish the parts. If the car is only **dusty,** a large house-painter's brush may be used, followed by a wipe down with a soft chamois leather. After washing the tyres, if any serious cuts or scratches appear on them, wash them out with petrol and then fill with solution. The engine and its connections should be carefully freed from all grease and dirt by using **cloths set apart for this purpose;** these, or any greasy, dirty, cleaning materials should on no account be used on the carriage work. A little paraffin on the cloth very much assists the cleaning of the engine work.

130. Engine Troubles and How to Locate them.— One of the most serious troubles the be ginner has to contend with is the location of the cause of a stoppage, and unless he proceeds in a methodical way he is likely to lose much time in futile efforts to discover the cause of the engine's inaction. Most experienced drivers adopt a sequence of tests that they believe in and have found to work well by long practice. They all **commence by testing the ignition,** as the novice should, and if it is not in order he may proceed to apply the tests in the order suggested in (A) or (B) below, according to whether the car is fitted with accumulators or with high-tension magnetos. **If the ignition is all right** he should next test for compression, and if that is all right he will next test the carburettor and, if that is working well, will proceed to try the **inlet and exhaust valves,** and so on, in something like the order suggested in (C) and (D) below.

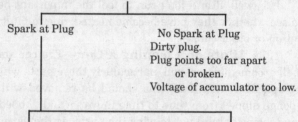

IGNITION NOT IN ORDER (WITH ACCUMULATOR)

Spark at Plug

No Spark at Plug
Dirty plug.
Plug points too far apart
    or broken.
Voltage of accumulator too low.

No Spark at Trembler
Batteries run down.
Tuning disarranged.
Leak in primary circuit,
Trembler blade incorrectly set.
Dirty tremblers.

Spark at Trembler Contacts
If voltage is not high enough, change over
    to reserve batteries.
If voltage is sufficient, seek for following :
Stuck or wrongly set trembler on coil.
Trembler screws loose.
Leakage between plugs and coil.
Secondary wire broken.

(B) IGNITION NOT IN ORDER (WITH HIGH-TENSION MAGNETO)

No Spark at Plug
No contact or broken wire.
Faulty setting of make-and-break.
Contacts of distributor worn down or
    fouled.
Carbon brushes worn.
Faulty insulation of spark plugs and
    wipers, and their connections.
Wires attached to the wrong terminals.

Spark at Plug
Wiring incorrectly connected up.
Timing incorrect.

ENGINE TROUBLES

(*C*) IGNITION ALL RIGHT (NO COMPRESSION)

Seek for Trouble outside Engine
Broken valve-head.
Valve sticking in its guide.
Broken or faulty valve spring.
Cylinder casting cracked.

Seek for Trouble inside Engine
Piston rings broken.
Piston rings gummed to piston body.
Slots or splits of piston rings in line.
Cracked or broken piston-head.
Broken connecting-rod or crank-shaft.
Loose cam or broken spring.

(*D*) IGNITION ALL RIGHT (COMPRESSION ALL RIGHT)

Carburettor all right
Petrol tank empty.
Petrol cock closed or feed-pipe
    clogged.
Timing of ignition wrong.
Broken exhaust-valve stem or
    spring, causing valve to remain
    seated
Perforated or broken inlet pipe.
Water in petrol.
Throttle out of order.

Carburettor not working
Flooded carburettor due to (*a*) punc
tured or too heavy float; (*b*)
needle valve requires grinding.
Not enough petrol admitted to float
    chamber, due to (*a*) badly set
    needle; (*b*) float too light; (*c*)
    nozzle or feed-pipe obstructed.
Broken or worn balance lever.

Cases where the trouble is not confined to one cylinder are nearly always due to either poor carburation, or weak batteries or accumulators. The former gives weak explosions of varying strength, coupled with missed explosions. Weak batteries also give missed explosions, but they are usually of more uniform strength. If the trouble is due to weak batteries, changing over to the reserve set will improve the running, even if the latter is fairly low, as we have seen that both accumulators and batteries pick up more or less after a rest.

130A. **Locating the Faulty Cylinder in a 4-Cylinder Engine.**—The simplest way to locate the cylinder that is not working properly is to cut out the ignition from the cylinders until the faulty one is found; this is usually done by holding down the tremblers. It is customary to number the cylinders from front to rear, No. 1 being the front and No. 4 the rear one. The coils are placed in the same order on the dash from the left to the right. The common order of firing is 1, 3, 4, 2, which should be borne in mind if the defective cylinder is to be detected by the ear.

SUBSTITUTES FOR PETROL

131. **Other Fuels than Petrol.**—The only other fuels that can be employed as substitutes for petrol in internal combustion engines of the motor type are[1] **benzol or benzene**[2] (a spirit distilled from coal-tar) and technical or **denatured alcohol.** Either of these can be used with a little modification of the valves, the carburettor, and the compression, and the former would be a cheaper fuel; but it could not be produced in anything like sufficient quantities, whilst alcohol, the most promising fuel of the future, can be produced in any quantity anywhere.

They both have the advantage of being safer fuels, with the additional advantage, which appeals to every patriotic motorist, that they can be produced in our own country, and make us independent of foreign supply of a fuel whose quality tends to deteriorate, while its price advances,[3] with the danger that in time of war our supply would be partially, if not entirely, cut off, and **famine prices** would be the consequence. But there are other points which can be raised for and against the use of these alternative fuels, which we will proceed to deal with, and we shall see that it is greatly to be desired that the Legislature will make it possible for the almost unlimited store of peat in Ireland, and other parts of the kingdom (to say nothing of our potato-growing capacity),

---

[1] If we exclude at present paraffin (or kerosine).

[2] This is often confused with benzine, one of the heavier distillates of petroleum, and a spirit closely allied to the naphtha group, which, when it began to be substituted for benzene, was given a name as nearly as possible like that of the tar product.

[3] It is not easy to decide whether the steady increase of specific gravity, and consequent decrease of volatility, have their origin in a real shortage in the supply or in purely market manipulations. Be the cause what it may, the effect is not acceptable to the consumer; indeed, if things get much worse, the problem of producing a substitute for petrol will have to be seriously taken in hand. In fact, the recently imposed duty of threepence per gallon, and the extra penny the producers have promptly put on, increasing the price to the consumer by 40 per cent., has already created a renewed and very real interest in the problem.

to be made use of for the production of technical alcohol for industrial purposes.

BENZOL

132. **Notes on Benzol.**—Benzol is derived entirely from the fractional distillation of coal tar, and it is at present principally used in dye-works and for enriching gas. The specific gravity of benzol (C_6H_6) at 60° F. is 0.883. By chemical analysis it is found to consist of 90.07 per cent, of carbon, 8.03 per cent, of hydrogen, 1.56 per cent, of sulphur, and the balance of 0.34 oxygen and loss.

The spirit is generally assumed to consist of 92 per cent, carbon and 8 per cent, hydrogen.

Its **calorific value** is about 18,600 **B.T.U.** per lb., or nearly the same as that of petrol. The following are its **relative boiling - points[1] compared with petrol.**

TABLE XII.—RELATIVE BOILING-POINTS OF PETROL AND BENZOL

Distilling Fractions.	Benzol.	Petrol .
Commenced to distil · · · ·	190°F.	163°F.
10 per cent. below · · · ·	203°F.	189°F.
55 ” ” · · · ·	212°F.	268°F.
90 ” ” · · · ·	228°F.	268°F.
100 ” ” · · · ·	289°F.	350°F.

It will be seen from the above table that the whole of the **benzol distils** at a temperature 61° F. below that needed to vaporise all the petrol; and that there is a smaller range of boiling-points of the benzol (91°) and the petrol (187°) between the temperature at which the first drop distils and that at which the last drop passes over.

One volume of **petrol vapour** requires from **45.5 to 82 volumes of air** to consume it perfectly, but one volume of **benzol vapour** only requires from **36 to 50.5**

---

[1] It is not so well understood as it should be that in selecting motor fuels neither specific gravity nor flash-points are reliable guides, the boiling-point range, which is the commercial standard for benzol (*but not for petrol,* strangely enough), being the only infallible guide to uniformity.

volumes of air. Thus imperfect combustion, due to **errors or carelessness in manipulating the carburettor,** are much less likely to lead to **waste** when the fuel is benzol; but it should be understood that this spirit vaporises less freely than petrol. With benzol an efficient carburettor would probably have to expose larger surfaces of the atomised spirit to the air, and probably either the air or the spirit would have to be warmed; further, with benzol a mixture with 100 per cent, more than the right amount of air is combustible, while petrol is not combustible with more than about 75 per cent, more air.

A disadvantage is that **pure benzol is liable to solidify** at low temperatures. On the other hand, it is a much more homogeneous spirit than petrol.

A tank full of **benzol weighs more** than one full of petrol, in the proportion of their specific gravities;[1] but the energy stored in a given weight of petrol is greater than that of benzol, and that of a given volume less.

As to supply, Mr. Ledoux,[2] in giving evidence before the Fuels Committee of the Motor Union, said he believed that, if the demand for benzol were sufficiently great, 25 to 30 million gallons could be recovered from coke ovens and tar works at about **6d. per gallon** at the works. When he used benzol to run his car, he found that there was a certain amount of **sooting at the valves** after running 50 miles in a hilly district.[3]

The present production appears to be 4 million gallons per annum, and the price to range from 9d. to 1s. per gallon in bulk.

Benzol has another serious drawback in the unwashed state—this is the **smell** or bad odour; but Mr. Ledoux is of opinion that this can be removed and the tendency to **sooting eliminated at the cost** of an extra penny a gallon.

---

[1] The specific gravity of benzol is about 0.870 to 0.885.

[2] The technical director of the Simon-Carves By-Product Coke-Oven Construction and Working Co.

[3] This deposition in the cylinder might be expected having regard to the fact that the proportion of carbon in benzol is so much higher than that present in petrol, as we have seen.

Doubtless the objectionable odour is due to the **sulphur,** and, of course, the highly rectified grades are much freer from this troublesome stuff; but it seems very doubtful whether a spirit, whose exhaust gases will be less offensive than those of petrol, could be produced by treating the raw or crude benzol at the small cost of an extra penny a gallon. But these points, and others, such as the maximum **limit of sulphur** allowable, and the **efficiency of the spirit**—that is to say, the consumption per brake horse-power, very properly are matters that can only be successfully dealt with by taking in hand much expensive experimental work. And the question naturally arises, who is to find the money? **But the insuperable objection** against the general use of benzol is that there is not enough of it, for a ton of coal will only yield ten gallons of tar, and 10 gallons of tar will only yield 0'06 gallons of benzol; therefore it requires 100 tons of coal to yield 6 gallons of benzol. Now it is estimated that the amount of coal consumed in the gas-works of London is about 8,000,000 tons per year, and it is easy to see that if the whole of this coal were employed to produce benzol the yield would only amount to 180,000 gallons.[1] In fact, the coal required to produce the 200,000 tons of spirit (some 50,734,000 gallons), which would be nearly equal to the amount of petrol that was probably used in this country in 1908,[2] would amount to 845,566,600 tons, which is a larger amount than the whole annual output of coal in the United Kingdom.

In a recent paper read by Mr. Readman, D.Sc., giving the results of some experiments on benzol in which he was associated with Sir W. Ramsay, F.R.S., the author said that "the engine, when once started and the inlet air to carburettor hot, worked steadily and well with mixtures containing **equal volumes of benzol and paraffin.** It could be slowed and rapidly accelerated, although it was fair to say with the evolution of some blue smoke. The cooling water

---

[1] For some years the total annual production of benzol in this country has amounted to about 2,500,000 gallons, and it has been principally used in making aniline dyes.

[2] It has been stated that the amount of petrol used in this country in 1808 amounted to 41,807,925, and in Europe 122,760,000 gallons.

became hotter, and so did the waste gases, but to no very serious extent. Curiously enough, with certain proportions of paraffin oil the objectionable odours of the exhaust were much minimised and, were it not for the difficulty of starting when all was cold, he saw no objection to the use of those mixtures, and from the commercial point of view there was much in their favour."

132A. **Comparative Tests with Benzol and Petrol.**— The following table gives the results of some comparative tests with petrol and benzol Mr. Edge had made in the Napier test-shop on a six-cylinder engine, as published in the *Autocar* of 1st June 1907. No adjustment was made to the air-supply or float, nor were the jets altered or changed in any way during the tests with the different fuels. The plugs remained clean throughout the tests. The engine was practically cold at starting each test. But, obviously, the value of the results would have been greatly enhanced if the quantity of fuel used had been measured in each case, particularly the last one.

TABLE XIII.—COMPARATIVE TESTS WITH PETROL AND BENZOL

Distilling Fractions.	Specific Gravity.	Temperature of Testing-room. Fahr.	Average of Three testes B.H.P.
Ordinary petrol	.687	67.1	64.25
„ „	.699	69.8	64.4
„ „	.713	65.3	64.4
„ „	.714	60.8	65.5
„ „	.759	67.1	63.5
Benzol	.873	75.2	64.1[1]

ALCOHOL

133. **Synthetic Alcohol.**—The alcohol group consists of a number of compounds, with similar properties, containing carbon, hydrogen, and oxygen; but the term is popularly used for the particular alcohol which is most widely used and known to chemists as **ethyl alcohol**. This spirit when

---

[1] Exhaust had a sulphurous, pungent smell. Engine started quite easily from cold.

very highly rectified is called **absolute alcohol**, and it is chemically represented by (C_2H_6O). A great many years ago, Berthelot, the famous French chemist, claimed to have produced this spirit synthetically[1] on a laboratory scale, but the author had the honour in 1896 of discovering the late **Dr. J. Macalpine**[2] (for the Alcohol Syndicate), who succeeded in producing for the first time synthetic alcohol in bulk.[3] This pure spirit, efficiently denatured, would probably make an ideal fuel as a substitute for petrol, but, as the carbide of calcium, which was largely used in its manufacture, is certain to remain a comparatively expensive material, we may safely disregard synthetic alcohol for fuel purposes.

134. **Alcohol, its Production and Properties** —It is generally known that alcohol can be produced anywhere, in any quantity, from any **vegetable matter containing sugar or starch**, such as Indian corn, potatoes, beets, sugarcane, fruits, rice, rye wheat, peat and sawdust, &c. Indeed, alcohol may be said to be made out of air and sunshine, for the carbonic acid and water of the air reach the growing plant under the influence of the sun's rays; vigorous plant growth being a cooling process, the solar energy is rendered latent. Then, in the production of alcohol from the vegetable matter, **fermentation** renders the energy stored more available and the **after-distillation** finally yields a concentrated product; and as the mineral and nitrogenous matters can be returned to the land, the latter is not much impoverished. There is the further important advantage that alcohol can always be made in the locality of demand, and therefore it

---

[1] This was an important example of the direct synthesis or building up of a hydrocarbon from its elements.

[2] The discoveries and original work of this brilliant chemist were greatly appreciated by such distinguished authorities as Engel, Dupree, and Sir Boverton Redwood, and it is safe to say that his death represents a serious set-back to the development of more scientific methods of treating liquid hydrocarbons.

[3] This work on the alcohol series as it developed insensibly led up to the splendid work Macalpine did in connection with petroleum distillates, which has been referred to in another place, and which gave the author, who was associated with him for many years as consulting engineer, opportunities of making a serious study of the hydrocarbons as fuels, and gaining much practical experience in connection with them.

would not require, like petrol, transportation from distant parts. On the other hand, the agricultural interests would greatly profit from the vastly increased markets for cereals if the Legislature made it possible to use alcohol for industrial purposes, particularly in engines.

As to the **productiveness of land,** some interesting particulars were put forward by Mr. James Wilson, the United States Secretary of Agriculture, in giving evidence before the Committee on Payne's Free Alcohol Bill. He stated that "**an acre of land** which produces **50 bushels of Indian corn** (nearly 2800 lbs.) will furnish 1960 lbs. of fermentable matter, that is, starch and sugar together; 45 per cent. **(882 lbs.)** of this will be obtained as **absolute alcohol.** A gallon of absolute alcohol weighs 6.8 lbs.; therefore an acre of Indian corn would produce about **130 gallons of absolute alcohol.** Commercial alcohol is about 95 per cent, pure; so that approximately **an acre of Indian corn** producing 50 bushels would make about **140 gallons of commercial alcohol."** Referring to **potatoes,** Mr. Wilson said: "If we assume the average crop of potatoes to be 300 bushels, or **18,000 lbs., per acre,** it would produce **3600 lbs. of fermentable matter.** This would produce **1620 lbs. of absolute alcohol, or 255 gallons of commercial alcohol."** Thus an **acre of potatoes** may produce over **80 per** cent. more **alcohol** than an acre of **corn.** Mr. Wilson believes that by using a grade of potatoes especially for alcohol production, the output could be increased to 500 gallons per acre.

135. **Denatured Alcohol.**—In those countries (France, Germany, and the United States) where the Government allows alcohol to be produced for industrial purposes, the spirit has to be denatured, as it is called—that is, **rendered undrinkable** or non-potable by the addition of a certain amount of **repulsive ingredients** of a combustible character; it can then be sold free of duty. The ingredients or materials generally used at present to denaturise alcohol are crude **wood spirit,**[1] chemically known as **methyl alcohol**

---

[1] Wood naphtha, one of the products of the destructive distillation of woods. It is

(CH₄O), and some one of the **coal-tar preparations** with pyridine bases, such as benzol; roughly in the proportions of 4 parts of the former to 1 part of the latter.

In **Germany** alcohol is denatured by the addition to every 100 litres (26.5 gallons) of alcohol (*a*) *2.5 litres of the* **standard denaturiser,** made of 4 parts of **wood alcohol,** 1 part of pyridin (a nitrogenous base obtained by distilling bone oil or coal-tar) with the addition of 50 grams to each litre of oil of lavender or rosemary; (*b*) *1.25 litres of above standard denaturiser and* 2 litres of benzol with every 100 litres of alcohol.

It is interesting to know that in the year 1903-4 over 26,000,000 gallons were completely denatured in Germany and used for heating, lighting,[1] and manufacturing purposes.

In **France** alcohol is **denatured** by the addition to every 100 litres of ethylic alcohol (90 per cent, rectified) at 15° C. of 10 litres of **methylene**, which itself is composed of 75 parts of methylic alcohol, 25 parts of acetine, 1.5 parts of heavy benzine and a certain quantity of impurities.

136. Advantages claimed for Alcohol as a Fuel.— Its **flash-point** is considerably higher, being 60° C., whilst that of petrol may be taken at anything down to 0° C.or even –10°C.; therefore it **can be used in any climate.** Alcohol is miscible[2] **with water** in all proportions (and in so doing becomes **non-inflammable),** and **does not float** in it like petrol, so therefore it never can be dangerous, as a **blaze** can be **extinguished** by a bucket of **water.** The **water** which is present in all commercial alcohol **assists** in its **decomposition** during **combustion,** and tends to make

---

inflammable, burning with a blue flame, and boils at 66° C. Its calorific value is about 9500 B.T.U., and specific gravity at 0° C. is 0.812.

[1] Great advances have been made (both in Germany and France) in the utilisation of alcohol as a fuel in illuminating lamps. Indeed, hundreds of thousands of beautiful incandescent lamps burning this safe spirit are in use on the Continent, replacing in most cases dangerous paraffin lamps, which are smoky, inefficient, odoriferous, and unhygienic, by ones that are safe, clean, sweet, and bright.

[2] When water is added to alcohol in any quantity, large or small, it mixes thoroughly and permanently, and produces what is called a solution, or a single mixed transparent and homogeneous liquid; the two liquids, water and alcohol, are accordingly said to be **infinitely** soluble in, or **miscible** with, one another.

the latter more rapid. Alcohol is practically **constant in composition,** and the **range** of **explosibility** of its vapour and air is more than **twice as extensive** as that of **petrol vapour** and air, for from 4 per cent, to 13 per cent, of alcohol vapour in air will explode. And, owing to the fact that alcohol **distils completely** in its commercial form over a range of **temperature of 80 to 100° C.** (whilst the range for petrol is 50 to 150° C.), **complete combustion** can more easily be **obtained. During compression** its pressure may be carried to 180 lbs. per sq. inch without sufficient heat being generated to cause **premature ignition,** whilst with petrol the practical limit of this pressure is 90 lbs. per sq. inch. This means that a much **higher thermal efficiency**[1] is possible with alcohol.

Further, the difficulties of **carburettor design** are reduced by the use of such a **homogeneous fuel** with **constant properties.** And the **propagation of flame is less rapid** when this spirit is used with the consequent much more **uniform pressure** throughout the stroke; the indicator diagram bearing a **resemblance** to that of a **steam engine**; and it is due to this that a **long stroke** is so **advantageous** with alcohol, and that the danger of **injurious hammering** is eliminated, and that it **runs more silently.** Mainly owing to the higher thermal efficiency and the **larger charge of fuel** per stroke, due to the higher specific gravity of alcohol, and to the smaller proportion of air, the **maximum** power of an engine is **greater** on alcohol than on petrol.

When an **efficient carburettor** is used with alcohol the cylinders and **valves** do not get **clogged** with the left-over products of combustion. Indeed, alcohol is practically **foolproof,** and its **products of combustion odourless.**

137. **Some Points against the Use of Alcohol.** —A disadvantage, so far as the engine is concerned, is the **higher vaporising point,** as alcohol boils at 78° C. Another point against this fuel is that its **calorific value** is only about

---

[1] Refer to Article 50a.

0.50 to 0.63 that of petrol;[1] but an important set-off against this is as, we have seen, its higher thermal efficiency. Another point which should be mentioned is that it is very **easy to burn an excess of alcohol** without detection, much more so than with petrol.

Now, **pure ethyl alcohol** does not appear to have a **deleterious effect** on any of the **metals** used in motor-car construction, with the **exception** of aluminium, to which alcohol **gives up its oxygen** to form the oxide **alumina** of the metal; but the **exhaust gases** from engines using any kind of alcohol contain a certain amount of **acetic acid**[2] ($C_2H_4O_2$), and if this be in excess its characteristic odour will be noticeable, and the cylinder and exhaust valve may be attacked by the acid if they are not protected by a film of lubricating material; for some tests on the effects of acetic acid, conducted by M. Ernest Sorel in 1902, went to show that to a slight extent petrol acts as a lubricant, whereas, alcohol being a solvent, it assists any oxidising influences that may be affecting the metal.

In burning pure alcohol at about 1500° C., with about seven times its own weight of air, we have theoretically produced water vapour and carbonic acid, thus

$$
\begin{array}{ccccccc}
\text{ethyl alcohol} & & \text{oxygen} & & \text{water vapour} & & \text{carbonic acid.} \\
C_2H_5OH & + & 60 & = & 3H_2O & + & 2CO_2
\end{array}
$$

But in introducing the impurities to denature alcohol, secondary reactions are caused, which with the principal one create such products as acetic acid, formaldehyde, trioxymethylene, sulphuric acid and certain carburetted alcohols; the use of benzol in the denaturant is responsible for the presence of sulphuric acid, but, if thought necessary, the sulphurous[3] **ingredients** can, by double distillation and complete treatment, be almost totally **eliminated** from the

---

[1] Refer to Article 138.

[2] When alcohol is completely vaporised and burnt in air, **aldehyde** (C_2H_4O) is formed, and this compound may become **oxidised to acetic acid**.

[3] We have in sulphur a powerful solvent which may assist to prepare the metallic surfaces to enter into combinations with any other attacking substances; further, it will sulphurate copper, zinc, and iron under the influence of heat.

spirit. So far as the other injurious products are concerned, acetic acid is the most dangerous, and apparently it is only formed at such low temperatures as obtain when starting the engine. But the usual practice is to start alcohol engines on benzol,[1] and when this is done there do not appear to be any fundamental or sound reasons why, with intelligent driving and efficient carburation, specially constructed engines (and in some cases even ordinary petrol engines) should be sensibly affected by these so-called dangerous products.

138. Properties, &c., of Alcohol as a Fuel.—Ethyl alcohol (C_2H_6O) has a **specific gravity** of 0.806 at 0° C. and its **boiling-point** is about 78° C., whilst that of highly purified **wood alcohol** is about 64° C., which accounts for denatured alcohol having a lower boiling-point than pure alcohol. On the other hand, the latent heat of evaporation (the number of heat units required to evaporate a given weight) of the denatured spirit is somewhat higher.

The **calorific value** of 1 lb. of absolute alcohol (chemically pure anhydrous) when complete combustion occurs is 12,600 B.T.U.

The **calorific value of 1** lb. of commercial **denatured alcohol**, containing 10 per cent, of water, is about 10,000 B.T.U.; with 20 per cent, of water it is about 9800 B.T.U.

An explosive mixture can be formed with from 4 to 13 per cent, of alcohol vapour in air.

139. Alcohol Engines, &c.—Primarily in order to increase the demand for agricultural products, great efforts have been made on the Continent to develop the use of alcohol as a source of power, heat, and light; and in Germany this has led to the construction of many engines (and the adaptation of gas and petrol engines) for agricultural and other purposes to run on alcohol. Among the best known of these may be mentioned the Dresdener, the Altmann, the Deutz-Otto, the Swiderski, the Koerting, and the Oberursel, giving our friends in that country many years' start. It is true that much has

---

[1] In Paris a mixture of half alcohol and half benzol is used as the fuel for the motor buses, owing to the high price of petrol. It appears to give fairly satisfactory results.

been done in France since 1901, when the French Minister of Agriculture organised a national competition, followed by an international one in 1902, to provide an opportunity for manufacturers to meet their competitors and compare results.[1] The developments which were reasonably expected to follow this movement were unfortunately delayed owing to a great and sudden increase in the price of alcohol. But if France was somewhat late in taking a hand in this important movement, one of her most brilliant sons, Monsieur Ernest Sorel, has made up for any apparent neglect in the study and testing of alcohol engines by giving to the world the most complete examination of the subject which has yet been printed,[2] a work the author has read with great interest and profit. In America much has been done since the use of alcohol for industrial purposes has been permitted by the U.S. Congress, without the payment of the internal revenue tax levied upon the alcohol in spirituous liquors; and much interesting information was brought out by the Committee of Ways and Means in considering the Payne Free Alcohol Bill. For instance, Mr. L. B. Goebbels, of the Otto Gas-Engine Works, Philadelphia, said "his concern had built a number of 160 H.P. engines for use in **submarine boats** for the United States Navy. The question arose as to the danger of using **petrol,** and a trial was made, which demonstrated that **alcohol** could be used in the motors **without any structural change.** The motor was first **started on petrol,** and after half-an-hour's run the petrol was shut off and alcohol turned on. There was no change then in the amount of power developed, but the full supply valve had to be opened a little more, increasing the consumption from 0.110 to 0.130 gallon per H.P."

Mr. Goebbels also said that "he had examined the interior

---

[1] In anticipation of the threatened injury the new legislation was likely to have on the beetroot industry in many parts of France.

[2] The title of the book is "Carburetting and Combustion in Alcohol Engines." It is largely an account of the original researches made by its author under a commission from the French Minister of Agriculture, and a most admirable translation into English has been made by Prof. Sherman, M. Woodward, and Mr. John Preston of the U.S.A. Published by Wiley & Sons, 12s. 6d. net.

parts of **alcohol engines** that had been in **continuous** use for **three years**, and had found them to be in **good working order."**

The United States Department of Agriculture conducted a series of experiments in the mechanical engineering laboratories of Columbia University in 1906, with alcohol as a fuel, in various types of internal combustion engines in extensive use in America. The engines included the following 4- stroke cycle petrol ones: a 15 H.P. 2-cylinder Nash, a 6 H.P. horizontal International Harvester Co., a 6 H.P. horizontal Weber, a 6 H.P. Fairbanks Morse, a 40 H.P. 4-cylinder American Mercedes Automobile, a 40 H.P. 4-cylinder Pope- Toledo Automobile, a 2 H.P. 2-stroke cycle Mianus marine, and a 6 H.P. horizontal 2-stroke cycle Mietz & Weiss kerosene engine.

Prof. Sherman, M. Woodford, and Mr. John Preston, in their very interesting and lucid translators' introduction to M. Ernest Sorel's fine work, to which we have already referred, have summarised the results of these tests for each of the engines, and remark that "all of them were operated successfully on commercial 94 per cent, grain alcohol; the changes necessary in the adjustments of the fuel-supplying mechanism were in most cases simple and easily made, although a large amount of experimentation was necessary to determine the best arrangements and adjustments, in order to secure the most economical fuel consumption." They also give the **general conclusions** which were drawn as a **result of the investigations,** and the most important of these the author has ventured to briefly summarise as follows:—

SOME CONCLUSIONS RELATING TO ALCOHOL ENGINES

"Any petrol engine of the ordinary type can be run on alcohol fuel without any material change in the construction of the engine. The only **difficulties** likely to be encountered are in **starting** and in **supplying** a sufficient quantity of fuel, a quantity which must be considerably **greater than** the quantity of **petrol** required.

"The **maximum power** of an engine run on alcohol is usually materially **higher than** it is **on petrol.**

"**Alcohol** seems to be especially adapted as a fuel for **air-cooled** automobile **engines**, as the **temperature** of the **cylinder** may rise much **higher** before **auto-ignition** occurs than is possible with petrol.

"The running of the engine on a **load below** its **full power**, or the **poor setting** of the **fuel-supply valve**, makes it easily possible for the **fuel consumption** (either petrol or alcohol) per horse-power hour to be increased to double the best value.

"The **fuel consumption was affected** by the **time of ignition**, by the **speed**, and by the **initial- compression** of the mixture, and when near the **best fuel consumption** the importance of an **early ignition** was shown. So far as tested, the alcohol fuel **consumption** was **better** at **low** than **high speeds;** and **increasing** the **compression from 70 to 125 lbs**. per sq. inch produced only a very **slight improvement** in the **consumption** of the fuel."

140. **The fuel consumption** with any good **small stationary engine** may reasonably be expected under favourable conditions to be as small as 0-7 lb. of petrol (0.118 gallon) or 1-16 lbs. (0.170 gallon), of alcohol per brake horse-power per hour. Based on the high calorific values of 20,200 B.T.U. for petrol and 11,800 for alcohol, these consumptions represent thermal efficiencies of 17.99 and 18.5 per cent, for petrol and alcohol respectively; or, on the basis of the low calorific values of 18,900 and 10,620, the thermal efficiencies for petrol and alcohol become 19.33 and 20.7 per cent, respectively. The preceding very brief remarks on what has been done in developing the alcohol engine in the three great countries referred to will naturally make the motorist pause and wonder why more has not been done in the direction of **perfecting the alcohol engine for automobile purposes,** particularly in **France and Germany.** The explanation is that both these countries number among the

best customers for their motor-car manufacturers, England and other countries where petrol up to now is the only fuel used by the motorist; but the time cannot now be far distant when, due to the ever-**increasing demand** for **petrol**, and its **inelastic supply** (possibly a shrinking one) at anything like **normal densities,** the call for a **substitute** will become irresistible, and will represent a **problem of national importance**. As we have seen, there are only two alternative fuels that are suitable, namely, benzol and alcohol; the quantity of the former that could be produced would, at the best, only satisfy a small fraction of the demand and that, therefore, we shall be compelled to rely upon the latter, and it is safe to predict that an extension of the Cheap Alcohol Act of October 1906, for allowing untaxed alcohol to be used for certain industrial purposes, will be ultimately made.[1]

141. **Safe Fuel for Submarines and other Hazardous Cases.**—Every one will agree that the engines used in submarines (and for **aerial navigation** purposes) should be worked with the safest fuel the chemist can produce, and that the lives of our brave sailor-men should never be imperilled by the use of such highly volatile and dangerous spirits as petrol and benzol (except perhaps in the smallest quantities for starting purposes) when a fuel of such great promise, and almost absolute safety, may be made available.[2] Having regard to all the points as to the danger

[1] The stringent official supervision insisted upon by the excise authorities is largely responsible for the excessive cost of producing alcohol as at present made, but by arranging to automatically run the spirit from the still through a mixing chamber, in which it mingled with the right proportion of denaturant, the cost of official supervision would be considerably reduced; and by using a cheap raw material, such as potatoes or peat, there would probably be no insuperable difficulty in marketing a spirit at a good profit that would compare favourably with petrol at a shilling a gallon. But, of course, the factor of vested interests in distilleries with antiquated plants would have to be dealt with.

[2] A common arrangement for submarines is to use internal combustion engines on the surface, and electric power when submerged; the separate systems involving great weight, with the disadvantages that the speed and radius of action are small, and the drawback due to the slowness in recharging cells when exhausted and to the accumulator dangers. On the other hand, this arrangement gives the advantage of silence and invisibility, there being no splash from the exhaust products. The submerged weight is also constant, and there is ease of engine starting and manoeuvring, whilst there is no possibility of foul air from engine

in using petrol and the safety of alcohol as a fuel that have been touched upon in the preceding pages, it is not easy to understand why the Admiralty have not long ere this made such experiments and tests as would prove the fitness or unfitness of alcohol, or even enriched alcohol, for such highly important service purposes. As we have seen, alcohol is **slower burning than petrol**, and the use of some agent to accelerate the rate of **flame propagation** seems desirable for **high-speed engines**, and it will be instructive to touch upon one of the most promising agents for this purpose known, which is **acetylene**.

142. **Alcohol enriched by Acetylene as a Fuel.**— Experiments have been made by mixing with alcohol vapour a very small proportion of **acetylene**[1] (C_aH_2), formed by the action of watered alcohol upon the **carbide of calcium**, with the object of **enriching and vivifying** it, improving its **ignition**, and causing the alcohol to **burn** with greater **rapidity**. But the success of this promising expedient much depends upon the acetylene being very thoroughly mingled with the explosive mixture. Experimental work in this direction might very well be taken in hand and reliable data of the kind the designer of alcohol engines requires established.

The cost of the **calcium carbide**,[2] small though the

---

leakage when submerged. But there can be no reasonable doubt that if a foreign country perfected some driving machinery that could efficiently supersede the double arrangement, giving greater speed, &c., although with perhaps a little less safety, we should have to follow its lead.

[1] Acetylene is one of the derivatives of coal gas, but it is commonly made by allowing water to act on the carbide of calcium. It contains 92–3 per cent, of carbon and 9.7 per cent, of hydrogen by weight, and when mixed with from 3 to 6′5 per cent, of air it can be exploded with violence, forming water and carbonic oxide. Its calorific value is 21.960 B.T.U. per lb. when burnt in oxygen, and its main heating value when burnt in air is about 1300 B.T.U. per cubic foot. Its specific, gravity is 0.91.

[2] Calcium of carbide is made from limestone and coke by heating lime with powdered carbon in the electric furnace, the reaction being $CaO + 3C = CaC_2 + CO$. It must be kept dry, as it absorbs and is acted upon by the moisture in the atmosphere. One lb. of good commercial calcium of carbide yields about 4.75 cubic feet of acetylene. The heat evolved in the reaction is about 730 B.T.U. The temperature becomes high and the action is very rapid. The price per ton in London is roughly from £12 to £20.

quantity required may be, is an important factor (but not for naval purposes), as the high price which already obtains would probably be at first raised with an increased demand, for it can only be produced economically where there is ample water-power (in such places as Niagara or Foyers) or very cheap coal. Another point that must be kept in view is that **acetylene** forms copper acetylide (a **dangerous fulminate**) when brought in contact with **copper** or its alloys, and a detonation caused by a hammer- blow or impact with a hard body may ignite any explosive in contact with it.[1] But by skilful design and care in working, and the use of suitable materials, there should be **no more danger in using enriched alcohol** as a fuel in submarines in the way described than there is in running a **steam plant in a battleship**.

143. Low-speed High-compression v. Highspeed Low-compression Alcohol Engines.—A perusal of the preceding pages on the use of alcohol as a fuel should make clear that to secure the **highest efficiency** an **alcohol engine** must be designed to run at a **low speed** with **high compression**, say from 250 to 500 revolutions per minute, and a mean pressure of 120 to 180 lbs. per sq. inch respectively. Now this means that the **initial pressure** of the explosion will **greatly exceed** that due to the use of **petrol**, and may amount to from about 550 to 750 lbs. per sq. inch, and with the **longer stroke** required to produce the higher compression and utilise the more slowly falling pressure during the explosion stroke a **heavier cylinder** has to be provided, and a somewhat stronger connecting-rod and crankshaft, with more liberal bearing surfaces. In other words, a **larger and heavier engine** for a given power, and one that requires, if not more skilful attention in working it, certainly more careful inspection day by day, as any loss of compression leads to a marked falling off in the efficiency of the engine.

---

[1] Some years ago a skilled mechanic working under the author struck with a hammer (although cautioned not to do so) a part of the feed apparatus of one of the largest acetylene generators ever made which had got stuck, with the result that a violent explosion occurred, doing much damage.

On the other hand, a **slow-running engine** of this type, with its more **even turning moment** and its greater **flexibility**, would, when used for automobile purposes, require a **smaller** reduction of speed. in the **gearbox**, with a saving in weight. Probably on the whole it would be better adapted to the requirements of industrial vehicles than high-speed cars.

We have seen that the expedient of **enriching alcohol** with **benzol** or **petrol** greatly **accelerates** the rate of **flame propagation** in the cylinder, and in so doing reduces the time required to burn the charge, and, moreover, makes it possible to run the engine at a **higher speed** at a **low compression**; therefore, for speeds of 800 or 900 and upwards, which generally obtain in ordinary motor-car practice, a departure on these lines would lead to the smallest amount of alteration to existing engines and to a promising solution to one phase of the fuel problem. Although in the aggregate much has been done, still more remains to be accomplished, particularly by work on experimental engines, before it will be possible to predict what the ultimate form of the alcohol engine for automobiles will be in its evolution.

144. Final Remarks relating to Alcohol Engines.— We have seen how much can be said for and against the use of alcohol in internal combustion engines, and, before passing on to other matters, the reader may be assisted in balancing his opinion as to the prospects of our future fuel, from the standpoint of our present knowledge, by the following pertinent remarks made by M. Ernest Sorel in the introduction to his learned treatise on "Carburetting and Combustion in Alcohol Engines," to which we have already referred:—

"Much has been said for and against the use of alcohol in motors. Its partisans declare it can be substituted instantly and without any modification for petrol in any engine; that it does not leave any disagreeable odour or smoke. On the other hand, its opponents claim that it forms acid products that corrode the cylinders and suction valves so strongly as to make them adhere to their seats after cooling. Generally speaking, the praises and objections are not well founded; all depends on the circumstances of the use, and the manner of production of the mixture of air and explosion."

CONCLUDING REMARKS

145. In looking over the contents of this little work, the author is forcibly reminded that many matters which could not fail to interest the motor novice have been omitted owing to the want of space. This being so, brief reference to some of the more important omissions may be made in this concluding Article.

One of the qualities of a car which does not generally receive the attention it deserves is **Accessibility**; it is true that much has been done to improve cars in this direction during the past year or two, but, although it is quite the exception to find engines whose valves are not readily accessible, the same thing can scarcely be said for **clutches,** which should always be arranged so that an adjustment is easily made or a new leather fitted; and many other parts, such as **gear-cases, differentials,** &c., should be get-at-able in the sense that they can be got at for inspection or taken out for repairs without dismantling half the car; and, more particularly, in every case those parts which periodically require adjusting, or occasional attention on the road, should be as accessible as possible. In some cars the driving and controlling fittings are not placed so that they can be worked with ease by drivers whose arms and legs are of average length; this is particularly the case with push pedals, which might with advantage be made adjustable (as spinal columns are fairly constant in length), the difference between a tall person and a short one being mainly one of legs. **Reliability** is a quality the importance of which cannot be overrated, and the admirable *reliability trials of the Automobile Club,* which have been held from time to time, arranged so that absolutely every replenishment, adjustment, and cleaning of the cars was done on the road, under official observation in the running time, have enabled the judges to draw up reports that have greatly assisted designers and makers, and have led to a high standard of reliability being reached.

The all-important question of **dust-raising** by motor cars has received a great deal of attention from the Royal Automobile Club, but the problem of running cars on dusty roads at high speeds without creating a nuisance remains unsolved.

But it has been noticed, in a general way, that cars which have a clean underbody without any projections, the lowest parts at the back being higher than those at the front, the bottom forming a taper clearance, raised the least amount of dust at a given speed. It has also been noticed that the amount of dust raised increases with the size of the tyres, other things being the same, and that exhausts impinging on the ground increase the evil; but these are matters that we may know more about sooner or later, and, if some simple means of mitigating what has become a grave nuisance, both to motorists and other users of our roads, can be devised, it will be hailed as a great boon. Of course, whatever can be done in this direction will only partly solve the problem, the real solution of which is the making of waterproof roads,[1] or

---

[1] Many of our highway authorities are public-spirited, and are served by competent executive officers who take a pride in their work, with the result that the roads under their control are kept in perfect condition, bar the dust. But in the streets of our great towns, particularly London, there is a large amount of very heavy traffic, which soon destroys the surface evenness of roads as they are at present constructed, and the evil is greatly increased by the roads being constantly taken up by gas, water, telephone, electric, and hydraulic companies (often as soon as they have been laid, with disastrous effects), with the result that many of them are allowed to get into a shocking condition before being relaid (as has been pointed out in an able article by Mr. Worby Beaumont, C.E., in *The Car*), notwithstanding the enormous amounts that are laid out on them. As every one is aware, wood and asphalt are largely used for town purposes, neither of which is a very satisfactory road material, the former in particular becoming most offensive and unsanitary after it has been in use some time, and both soon become dotted with depressions, due to the material and foundations giving way under heavy traffic. Indeed, much less appears to be done in the way of local mending in our London streets than is done in the country. A huge fortune awaits any one who can invent an ideal road material, one that satisfies all the requirements of motorists and the ordinary user, and can be produced at a price that is not prohibitive.

the protection of their surfaces with a binding waterproof stuff, such as

Westrumite, Tarmac, &c., the cost of which on a large scale would be prohibitive. But if such roads were once made and used only by automobiles, there would be comparatively little depreciation; as it is, on ordinary roads the tyres lick up and disperse the road detritrus (rubbish of attrition), and in so doing accelerate the disintegration of the surface; but, of course, the injury done in this way is slight compared with the hammering effect of horses' feet on the metalling and the grinding effect of the iron-shod wheels of ordinary traffic, which sooner or later destroys the surface, whatever it may be made of. It is not easy to foresee how this road problem is to be ultimately solved, but if motorists continue to increase in number at the present rate, they will ere long be strong enough to influence for the common good those bodies who are responsible for the upkeep of our roads.

146. **Steam Cars** have been greatly improved during the past few years, and when their principal features and points are compared with those of petrol cars, it is not easy at first to understand why the former should be so much neglected by the motorist.[1] But so far as the pleasure car is concerned, although the engine of the steamer is little short of perfection for the purpose, the boiler has inherent disadvantages, which in the opinion of most motorists is not compensated for by the undoubted good features of the other parts of the steamer systems, when compared with the petrol motor. Notwithstanding this, modern steam cars are very fine vehicles, although it is true they did not at one time compare so favourably with the petrol car; boiler[2] troubles were frequently heard of, particularly in cases where boilers which required skilful handling were in the hands of careless and inexperienced drivers. Then, again, fuel consumption was usually excessive, to say nothing about the difficulty of getting a supply of suitable water two or three times on a

---

[1] Refer to Article 2, where it will be seen that the variety of steam cars is small compared with petrol ones.

[2] Makers prefer to call these *steam generators* or, briefly, *generators*.

long run. But all that is a matter of the past, and the modern steam car of the best make can be driven a distance of over a hundred miles without a stop for water or fuel, and with no more attention than is required by the most perfect petrol car, whilst by using the throttle the range of engine power is so great that no change-speed gear is required, and the condensation of steam is so complete that the exhaust is rarely seen. In addition to these good features, the steamer is a splendid hill-climber, and its smooth vibrationless running on a decent road is what many acclaim to be the poetry of motion. Indeed, if, in selecting a car, hill-climbing power and absence of vibration, for some reason or another, are considered the most important features, and a steam car[1] is decided on, a selection could safely be made from the Turner- Miesse or White, which are the two best known. Doubtless, in the time to come, more attention will be paid to the development of the steam motor for commercial vehicles, for which it is more suited, than for pleasure purposes, but, for the nonce, every one knows that, rightly or wrongly, the petrol car is an easy first favourite, and the fundamental fact that it is more economical to burn the fuel in the cylinder of the engine than in a boiler will always be in its favour, notwithstanding its drawbacks and the possibilities of trouble in connection with carburettors and ignition systems.

Briefly, **steam cars** have the following **advantages**: cheapness in first cost, cheaper fuel, absence of gear for change of speed, absence of ignition troubles, pre-ignition and exhaust troubles, &c., high output for short periods, greater speed uphill, complete stillness of car when standing, and starting without turning a crank.

Among the **disadvantages** may be mentioned heavy fuel consumption; boiler troubles; fire must be extinguished, or the car watched during a short stoppage; loss of time, due to re-igniting and getting up pressure; larger number

[1] The late Mons. Serpollet did more than any other engineer to develop the possibilities of the steam car. Indeed, it can be safely said that what he did not know about flash boilers was not worth knowing, and his lamented death at a comparatively early age, it is safe to say, gave the cause of the steam car a serious set-back, from which it may take years to recover.

of adjustments which are not automatic; an owner cannot so easily dispense with the services of a paid driver or mechanician.

Should the day-dreams of some of our advanced thinkers ever eventuate in the creation of a **petrol turbine** of great range of power and moderate weight, or **storage batteries** of great capacity and little weight, suitable for electric vehicles, it is safe to say that a new era in automobilism would rapidly dawn. But, even taking things as they are, it is possible for any man who can afford to keep a dogcart to run a light car and bring a new joy into his life, with little or no additional expense, if he is mechanically inclined, and is not afraid of attending to the car himself.

As might be expected, the evolution of the petrol motor, which has culminated in the production of a compact, obedient, and economical engine, whose high speed makes it possible to develop in a relatively small and light box of machinery a very considerable power, has induced many manufacturers to make use of it in various ways to supersede animal power,[1] whilst it has opened up greater possibilities in **aerial** and **submarine navigation,** to say nothing of the impetus it has given to the sport of boating and yachting. Even in the days when the only power available for mechanically propelling a launch was the steam-engine, with its bulky, smoky boiler, and all the well-known drawbacks inseparable from their use, few could resist the pleasure of a spin up our beautiful river; but when it was found that the **petrol motor** could be efficiently and conveniently used to **propel a boat,** a new phase of motoring appeared, and a departure was made which, when certain drawbacks have been dealt with, is likely to lead to far-reaching developments in the near future.[2] The

[1] As examples of this new departure, the petrol motor mower of Messrs. Green & Sons, the street-cleaning motor, the petrol motor fire-engine, the vacuum cleaner, the locomotive turn-table motor, and the agricultural motor may be mentioned.

[2] The ordinary marine engine, which has been so greatly improved in recent years, seems to be in for a very bad time in the near future for with the steam turbine daily making headway on one hand, and the steady development of the internal combustion engine (with its probable employment on a large scale in some form or other before long) on the other, it will be exceedingly interesting to follow the struggle for supremacy.

various reliability trials, with non-stop runs of twenty hours and more, have proved that the many difficulties and risks of failure incidental to marine motoring are being satisfactorily tackled, and, although the sport has not caught on to the extent that many expected, probably a prosperous future for the motor boat may be safely predicted.

AERO MOTORS

147. The rapid progress which is being made in the science and art of aerial navigation has naturally led many motor engineers and inventors to devote their attention to the production of engines suitable for the propulsion of aerial machines and ships. The conditions such engines have to satisfy are in the main those that designers are familiar with in producing high-class car engines, but, obviously, they are more exacting; particularly is this so in connection with the problem of **balancing** and in **uniformity** of **torque**, also in factors of **reliability, accessibility, safety, efficiency,** and **lightness,** although the last named is not of so much importance if it is to be secured at the expense of one or more of the other features. Indeed, the general problem has already received a very large amount of attention from those who have had great experience in dealing with automobile engines, and therefore, naturally, several of the aero motors which are now on the market, or are about to be put on it, are arranged on lines familiar to all, but in not a few cases with refinements of quite exceptional ingenuity. And much that is new, and perhaps strikingly original, may be expected from the remarkable developments which are taking place, and from the splendid field that is open for the exercise of mechanical genius of a high order.

The following is a—

148. **Brief description of the principal aerial motors** exhibited at Olympia in March 1909.

Dutheil-Chalmers Horizontal Engine.—The cylinders (2, 4, or 6 in number) are opposed, but the pistons of opposite cylinders are connected to separate cranks set at

180° apart. The water-jackets are made of copper, and the inlet valves are of the atmospheric type. This engine is made in two types, namely, *(a)* Has a single-crank shaft between the cylinders; *(b)* Has two crank-shafts, with the cylinders between them.

E.N.V. Aero Motor (used by Mr. Moore Brabazon).— This 8-cylinder V-type engine has its valves arranged side by side, mechanically operated. The cylinders have electrolytically deposited copper water-jackets. Lubrication is effected by a plunger- pump worked off an eccentric on the crank-shaft.

M. Louis Bleriot is having his new and twelfth aeroplane fitted with a 35 H.P. engine of this make.

International Rotary Motor.—The cylinders (which are in the same plane) are opposed and rotate about a crank-shaft, which may be either fixed or allowed to rotate in the opposite direction. Both valves in each cylinder are mechanically operated by a transverse-skew gear-driven cam-shaft. The lubrication is forced, and magneto ignition is arranged by means of a chain drive.

Gnome Rotary Engine.—The cylinders (seven in number) rotate bodily with their crank-shaft chamber about a fixed crank-shaft. All the pistons are coupled to the same crank; the firing order being 1, 3, 5, 7, 2, &c.; the angular intervals being equal without resorting to direct sequence.

Gorbron-Brillie.—This is a modified radial engine in X-form, having eight cylinders, arranged in pairs. In each cylinder are two opposing pistons arranged on the well-known Gorbron-Brillie principle. The cylinders are water-jacketed, the jackets being formed of brass. The engine is fitted with two magnetos and two carburettors, and is provided with forced lubrication.

Green Aero Motor (constructed by Messrs. Aster).— This engine is of the ordinary 4-cylinder vertical type used in cars, but with special features. The cylinders are separate steel castings with copper water-jackets provided with sliding expansion joints. The cam-shaft is driven by screw gearing, and the base-chamber is of aluminium. Another green model is of the V-type, with eight cylinders.

Metallurgique Aero Motor.—Four-cylinder vertical engine, on the lines of the well-known car engines of this make, the cylinders being cast in pairs, and the exhaust valves arranged over the inlet valves. The lubrication is by forced feed, with the high pressure of 90 lbs. per sq. inch, the connecting rods and tappet rods for the valves being hollow.

Miesse Aero Motor.—A radial 8-cylinder engine with vertical **crank**-shaft (two cranks), the horizontal cylinders being arranged in pairs. A fan arranged at the bottom end of the crank-shaft drives air through a casing, which partially encloses the air- cooled cylinders. A single Zenith carburettor feeds all the cylinders, and the ignition is high-tension magneto.

N.E.C. (New Engine Company) two-stroke engine, with four vertical cylinders; a novel feature being their arrangement for internal air-cooling by means of an air-blast directed into the cylinder itself.

Pipe Aero Motor.—The eight cylinders (V- type engine) are enclosed in cowls, through which a stream of air is drawn for cooling by a centrifugal fan mounted on the end of the crank-shaft. The inlet and exhaust valves are combined, and both are mechanically operated by separate push-rods. There is one magneto for the ignition and one carburettor.

Renault Aero Motor.—Eight-cylinder V-type engine, partially enclosed in a casing, and cooled by the draught of a fan mounted on the fly-wheel. The cylinders are cast separately and are ribbed circumferentially in the usual way. The exhaust valves are placed directly above the inlet valves, and both are mechanically operated. Carburation and lubrication are carried out on the same lines as on the famous Renault oar engine.

R.E.P. Aero Motor.—Semi-radial engine with its five cylinders, all arranged above the crank-shaft The Rep engine is made in three models, all fitted with the same size cylinder, having 5, 7, and 10 cylinders. The 10-cylinder engine is virtually two 5-cylinder engines placed end to end; and in the 5- and 7-cylinder engines the cylinders are arranged in two planes, and are fired in the same sequence as in the Gnome engine. Of course, with an even number of cylinders the latter would have to fire in direct sequence, namely, 1, 2, 3, &c., with an even spacing, which would be obviously undesirable. The inlet and exhaust valves are combined.

Simms Aero Motor.—The six cylinders of this V-type engine are cast separately, and are bolted to a base chamber. They are fitted with Philips' auto- mechanical inlet valves, and the crank-shaft and cam-shaft are lubricated under pressure.

Vivinus Aero Motor.—A 4-cylinder vertical engine of the ordinary type. A special feature of the design is the enclosing of the cam-shaft in a separate casing. The most powerful model develops 75 H.P., and, owing to the use of aluminium water- jackets, its weight is less than that of the 60 H.P. model. Mr. Moore Brabazon's flyer was fitted with a 50 H.P. engine of this make.

Wolseley Aero Motor.—V-type engine with eight cylinders fitted with aluminium water-jackets. A gear pump is used for forced-feed lubrication, and the ignition is magneto. The valves are arranged together and are operated from a single cam-shaft.

APPENDIX I

USEFUL TABLES

The following tables, &c., will be found useful in making calculations relating to motors and motoring.

Table XIV.—Conversion of Millimetres into Inches and Fractions

A millimetre = 0.03937 inch $= \dfrac{1}{25}$ inch nearly, or $= \dfrac{2.5}{64}$ inch nearly.

mm.	Inches.	mm.	Inches.	mm.	Inches.	mm.	Inches.	mm.	Inches.
1	$\frac{2.5}{64}$	35	$1\frac{3}{8}$	69	$2\frac{23}{32}$	115	$4\frac{34.5}{64}$	370	$14\frac{9}{16}$
2	$\frac{5}{64}$	36	$1\frac{13}{32}$ f	70	$2\frac{3}{4}$	120	$4\frac{23}{32}$	380	$14\frac{31}{32}$ b
3	$\frac{7.5}{64}$	37	$1\frac{15}{32}$ b	71	$2\frac{25}{32}$ f	125	$4\frac{58.5}{64}$	390	$15\frac{11}{32}$ f
4	$\frac{5}{32}$	38	$1\frac{1}{2}$	72	$2\frac{27}{32}$ b	130	$5\frac{1}{8}$	400	$15\frac{3}{4}$
5	$\frac{12.5}{64}$	39	$1\frac{17}{32}$	73	$2\frac{7}{8}$	135	$5\frac{20.5}{64}$	410	$16\frac{5}{32}$ b
6	$\frac{15}{64}$	40	$1\frac{9}{16}$ f	74	$2\frac{29}{32}$	140	$5\frac{1}{2}$ f	420	$16\frac{17}{32}$
7	$\frac{9}{32}$	41	$1\frac{5}{8}$ b	75	$2\frac{15}{16}$ f	145	$5\frac{11}{16}$	430	$16\frac{15}{16}$ b
8	$\frac{5}{16}$	42	$1\frac{21}{32}$ b	76	3 b	150	$5\frac{29}{32}$	440	$17\frac{5}{16}$ f
9	$\frac{22.5}{64}$	43	$1\frac{11}{16}$	77	$3\frac{1}{32}$	155	$5\frac{50.5}{64}$	450	$17\frac{23}{32}$
10	$\frac{13}{32}$ b	44	$1\frac{23}{32}$ f	78	$3\frac{1}{16}$ f	160	$6\frac{5}{16}$ b	460	$18\frac{1}{8}$ b
11	$\frac{7}{16}$	45	$1\frac{25}{32}$	79	$3\frac{1}{8}$	165	$6\frac{1}{2}$	470	$18\frac{1}{2}$
12	$\frac{15}{32}$	46	$1\frac{13}{16}$	80	$3\frac{5}{32}$	170	$6\frac{11}{16}$	480	$18\frac{29}{32}$ b
13	$\frac{32.5}{64}$	47	$1\frac{27}{32}$	81	$3\frac{3}{16}$	175	$6\frac{565}{64}$	490	$19\frac{9}{32}$ f
14	$\frac{9}{16}$	48	$1\frac{7}{8}$ f	82	$3\frac{7}{32}$ f	180	$7\frac{3}{32}$	500	$19\frac{11}{32}$
15	$\frac{19}{32}$	49	$1\frac{15}{16}$ b	83	$3\frac{9}{32}$ b	185	$7\frac{18.5}{64}$	510	$20\frac{1}{16}$ f
16	$\frac{5}{8}$	50	$1\frac{31}{32}$	84	$3\frac{5}{16}$	190	$7\frac{15}{32}$ f	520	$20\frac{15}{32}$
17	$\frac{21}{32}$ f	51	2 f	85	$3\frac{11}{32}$	195	$7\frac{21}{32}$	530	$20\frac{7}{8}$ b
18	$\frac{23}{32}$ b	52	$2\frac{1}{16}$ b	86	$3\frac{3}{8}$ f	200	$7\frac{7}{8}$	540	$21\frac{1}{4}$ f
19	$\frac{3}{4}$	53	$2\frac{3}{32}$	87	$3\frac{7}{16}$ b	210	$8\frac{9}{32}$ b	550	$21\frac{21}{32}$
20	$\frac{25}{32}$	54	$2\frac{1}{8}$	88	$3\frac{15}{32}$	220	$8\frac{21}{32}$	560	$22\frac{1}{16}$ b
21	$\frac{13}{16}$	55	$2\frac{5}{32}$ f	89	$3\frac{1}{2}$	230	$9\frac{1}{16}$	570	$22\frac{7}{16}$
22	$\frac{7}{8}$ b	56	$2\frac{7}{32}$ b	90	$3\frac{17}{32}$ f	240	$9\frac{7}{16}$ f	580	$22\frac{27}{32}$ b
23	$\frac{29}{32}$	57	$2\frac{1}{4}$	91	$3\frac{19}{32}$ b	250	$9\frac{27}{32}$ b	590	$23\frac{7}{32}$ f
24	$\frac{15}{16}$	58	$2\frac{9}{32}$	92	$3\frac{5}{8}$	260	$10\frac{1}{4}$ b	600	$23\frac{5}{8}$
25	1 b	59	$2\frac{5}{16}$ f	93	$3\frac{21}{32}$	270	$10\frac{5}{8}$	650	$24\frac{19}{32}$
26	$1\frac{1}{32}$	60	$2\frac{3}{8}$ b	94	$3\frac{11}{16}$ f	280	$11\frac{1}{32}$	700	$27\frac{9}{16}$
27	$1\frac{1}{16}$	61	$2\frac{13}{32}$	95	$3\frac{3}{4}$ b	290	$11\frac{13}{32}$	750	$29\frac{17}{32}$
28	$1\frac{3}{32}$ f	62	$2\frac{7}{16}$	96	$3\frac{25}{32}$	300	$11\frac{13}{16}$	800	$31\frac{1}{2}$
29	$1\frac{5}{32}$	63	$2\frac{15}{32}$ f	97	$3\frac{13}{16}$	310	$12\frac{7}{32}$ b	850	$33\frac{15}{32}$ b
30	$1\frac{3}{16}$	64	$2\frac{17}{32}$ b	98	$3\frac{27}{32}$ f	320	$12\frac{19}{32}$	900	$35\frac{7}{16}$
31	$1\frac{7}{32}$	65	$2\frac{9}{16}$	99	$3\frac{29}{32}$ b	330	13	950	$37\frac{13}{32}$
32	$1\frac{1}{4}$ f	66	$2\frac{19}{32}$	100	$3\frac{15}{16}$	340	$13\frac{3}{8}$ f	1000	$39\frac{3}{8}$
33	$1\frac{5}{16}$	67	$2\frac{5}{8}$ f	105	$4\frac{8.5}{64}$	350	$13\frac{25}{32}$		
34	$1\frac{11}{32}$	68	$2\frac{11}{16}$ b	110	$4\frac{11}{32}$	360	$14\frac{3}{16}$ b		

Note.— f means "full"; b means "bare."

The centimetre is a full $\frac{8}{8}$ inch and the metre 3 ft. $3\frac{3}{8}$ inches very nearly. To convert Inches into Millimetres multiply by 25.4.

BRITISH AND METRICAL EQUIVALENTS

TABLE XV.— LENGTH

ENGLISH TO METRICAL	METRICAL TO ENGLISH
1 inch = 25.4 millimetres = 2.54 centimetres	1 millimetre = 0.03937 inch = $\frac{1}{25}$ "
1 foot = 30.4799 centimetres	nearly, or $\frac{2.5}{64}$ " nearly
1 yard = 0.914399 metre	
1 chain = 66 ft. = 20.1168 metres	1 centimetre = 10 mm. = 0.3937 inch
1 mile = 5280 ft. = 80 chains	1 metre = $\begin{cases} 39.37 \text{ inches} \\ 3.280843 \text{ feet} \\ 1.093614 \text{ yards} \end{cases}$
0.62137 mile = 1 kilometre	
	1 kilometre = 1000 metres = 3280.9 feet

TABLE XVI.— SURFACE OR AREA

ENGLISH TO METRICAL	METRICAL TO ENGLISH
1 sq. inch = 6.4516 sq. centimetres	1 sq. centimetre = 0.155 sq. inch
1 sq. foot = 929.03 sq. centimetres	1 sq. metre = 10.7639 sq. feet
= 0.092903 sq. metre	„ = 1.196 sq. yards
1 sq. yard = 0.836126 sq. metre	100 sq. metres = 1 are
1 acre = 0.40468 hectare	1 hectare = 100 ares = 10,000 sq
1 sq. mile = 259 hectares	metres = 2.4711 acres

TABLE XVII.— VOLUME

ENGLISH TO METRICAL	METRICAL TO ENGLISH
1 cu. inch = 16.387 cu. centimetres	1 cu. centimetre = 0.061 cu. inch
1 cu. foot = 0.028317 cu. metres	1 cu. decimetre = 61.024 cu. inches
„ = 28.317 litres	1 litre = 1000 cu. centimetres =
1 cu. yard = 0.764553 cu. metres	1.7598 pints = 0.22 gallon
„ = 764.553 litres	1 litre or cu. decimetre = 61.027052
1 gallon = 4.545963 litres	cu. inches = 0·0353166 cu. feet
„ = 0.1605 cu. feet	1 cu. metre = 35.3148 cu. feet
„ = 277.27 cu. inches	„ =1.307954 cu. yards

1 U.S.A. gallon = 0.83254 Imperial gallon = 231 cu. inches.

USEFUL TABLES

TABLE XVIII.— **WEIGHT**

ENGLISH TO METRICAL	METRICAL TO ENGLISH
1 grain = 0.0648 grams	1 milligram = 0.015 grain
1 pennyweight = 1.5552 grams	1 gram = wt. of cu. centimetre of water at 4° C. = 0.0022046 lbs.
1 dram = 1.772 grams	1 kilo = 2.204622 lbs.
1 ounce (437.5 grains) = 28.35 grams	50.8 kilos = 1 cwt. = 112 lbs.
1 pound (16 oz. or 7000 grains) = 453.5924 grams = 0.4535924 kilos = 445.000 dynes	1 tonne = 1000 kilos = 0.9842 British ton
Pounds per cu. foot × 16.020 = kilos per cu. metre	1016 kilos = 1 British ton = 2240 lbs.
Pounds per cu. yard × 0.5933 = kilos per cu. metre	0.908 tonne = 1 American ton = 2000 lbs.
Tons per cu. yard ×1.329 = tonnes per cu. metre	Kilos per cu. metre × 1.686 = lbs. per cu. yard
1 cu. foot of air at 0° C. and 760 mm. = 0.0809 lb.	Kilos per cu. metre × 0.0624 = lbs. per cu. yard
1 litre air at 0° C. and 760 mm. = 1.2932 grams	Tonnes per cu. metre × 0.752 = tons per cu. yard

1 U.S.A. ton= = 2000 pounds

TABLE XIX.— **PRESSURE**

ENGLISH TO METRICAL	METRICAL TO ENGLISH
1 inch of mercury at 0° C. = 0.34534 kilos per sq. centimetre	Centimetres of mercury × 0.1903 = lbs. per sq. inch
Inches of mercury × 0.4907, or – by 2.0378 = lbs. per sq. inch	Kilos per sq. centimetre × 14.223 = lbs. per sq. inch
1 lb. per sq. inch = centimetre of mercury × 0.193	0.703 kilos per sq. cm. = 1 lb. per sq. foot
1 lb. per sq. inch = kilos per sq. cm. × 14.223	479 dynes per sq. cm. = 1 lb. per sq. foot
Pounds per sq. inch × 0.0703 = kilos per sq. centimetre	Kilos per sq. metre = lbs. per sq. inch × 4.8826
Tons per sq. inch × 1.575 = kilos per sq. millimetre	1 kilo = 981.000 dynes
Tons per sq. foot × 4.883 = kilos per sq. metre	445.000 dynes = 1 lb.
Tons per sq. foot × 10.936 = tonnes per sq. metre	Kilos per sq. millimetre × 0.635 = tons per sq. inch
Tons per sq. yard × 1.215 = tonnes per sq. metre	Kilos per sq. metre × 0.2048 = lbs. per sq. foot
	Tonnes per sq. metre × 0.0914 = tons per sq. foot
	Tonnes per sq. metre × 0.823 = tons per sq. yard

TABLE XX.— **SPEEDS**

ENGLISH TO METRICAL	METRICAL TO ENGLISH
1 mile per hour = 0 463 metres per second	1 kilometre (km.) per hour = 0.9l4 metres per second
1 mile per hour = 27 8 metres per minute	1 kilometre per hour = 54.9 feet per minute
	1 kilometre per hour = 0.624 miles per hour

1 mile per hour = 1.466 feet per second
1 mile per hour=88 feet per minute

TABLE XXI.— **THERMAL UNITS AND WORK**

One pound of water raised 1° from = British thermal unit (B.T.U.), (B.T.U.) British thermal units x 778 = number of foot pounds. Pound-degrees Cent, x 1400.4 = number of foot pounds. One kilogramme of water raised 1° C. = l calorie = 3080.9 foot pounds. No. of calories x 3.968 = No. of British thermal units.

ENGLISH TO METRICAL	METRICAL TO ENGLISH
Foot pounds x 0.1382 = kilogram-metres	Kilogram-metres x 7.233 = foot pounds
Foot tons x 0.323 = tonne-metres	Tonne-metres x 3.088 = foot tons
Horse-power x 1.0139 = force de cheval	Force de cheval x 0.9863=horse power
Heat units x 0.252 = calories	Calories x 3.968 = heat units
Heat units per sq. ft. x 2.713 = calories per sq. metre	Calories per sq. metre x 0.369 = heat units per sq. foot
Pounds per H.P. x 0.477 = kilos per cheval	Kilos per cheval x 2.235 = pounds per H.P.
Square feet per H.P. x 0.0196 = square metre per cheval	Square metre per cheval x 10.913 = square foot per H.P.
Cubic feet per H.P. x0.0279 = cubic metre per cheval	Cubic metre per cheval x 35.806 = cubic feet per H.P.

TABLE XXII.— **AIR, ATMOSPHERIC PRESSURE, &c.**

The standard atmospheric pressure, which is 14.7 lbs. per sq. inch, equivalent to a mercury column of 29-95 inches = 760 mm., is used throughout Europe (and the United States), with the exception of France, Germany, and Austria, where the metric atmosphere of one kilogram per sq. cm., equal to 14.223 lbs. per sq. inch, or a mercury column of 28.96 inches, is used.

Weight of cubic foot of air (14.7 lbs. per sq. inch) at 62° K = 0.076097 lb.= 1.217 ounces = 532.7 grains.

A cubic foot of air at 32° F. weighs 0.08 lbs. and 1 litre at 760 mm.= 1.293 grammes. Note.—1 lb. = 453.59 grammes.

Number of cubic feet of air to the lb. at 62° F. = 13.141.

The co-efficient of cubical expansion of air is 0.002—that is, air expands or contracts 0.002 of its volume for one degree Fahr.

Volume V of 1 lb. of air at 14.7 lbs. per sq. inch, at any given temperature T (F.) and pressure P, can be found as follows :—

$$V = \frac{T+461}{2.7074 \times P} \text{ cubic feet.}$$

Specific heat of air at constant pressure = 0.2375.

,,   ,,   oxygen at constant pressure = 0.2175.

,,   ,,   nitrogen at constant pressure = 0.2438.

,,   ,,   carbon monoxide (CO) at constant pressure = 0.2479.

,,   ,,   carbon dioxide (CO_2) at constant pressure = 0.217.

RESISTANCE DUE TO THE WIND

Let   S = the velocity of the wind in relation to the car in miles per hour.

,,   A = projected end area of the car in square feet.

,,   P = the approximate total pressure or resistance of the wind.[1]

,,   H.P. = the approximate horse-power required to overcome wind resistance.

Then $P = 0.0043S^2A$.

And $H.P. = S^3A \div 87,300$.

Example.—The projected end area of a car is 20 square feet and there is no wind, but the car is running at 20 miles per hour. Find (a) the

---

[1] In deducing the above formula the author has assumed that the resistance per square foot=0.002 V^2, where V is the velocity in feet per second.

approximate total resistance due to the air; (*b*) the approximate horse-power required.

Answer.—(*a*) P = 0.0043 X 20^3 x 20 = 34.4 lbs.

„   (*b*) H.P. = 20^3x 20 ÷ 87,300 = 1.833.

NOTE.—The effective velocity for car resistance is the sum or difference of the velocities of the car and wind. Thus, when a car is running at 20 miles an hour against a head wind of 10 miles an hour the effective velocity is 20 +10 = 30 miles per hour. But if the wind blew from behind, the effective or equivalent velocity S would equal 20-10 = 10 miles per hour.

WEIGHT OF MOTORS IN RELATION TO HORSE-POWER

The weight of automobile engines may be taken to range from 11 to 14 lbs. per brake horse-power, but motors marie for aerial machines are much lighter, the following being the actual weights for a few of the best- known engines.

Name of Engine.	Weight in lbs. per B.H.P.
Gnome	Less than 3
Fait	3
Antoinetto	5
Wright	6
Regnault	7
Metallurgic	8

CITY AND GUILDS OF LONDON INSTITUTE
(INCORPORATED BY ROYAL CHARTER)

DEPARTMENT OF TECHNOLOGY
EXHIBITION ROAD, LONDON, S.W.

74.—MOTOR CAR ENGINEERING

(REVISED SYLLABUS, 1913)

The course of instruction in this subject should occupy at

least three years. Examinations will be held at the end of each year's course.

Students are advised to take a course of instruction in some or all of the subjects included in the first stage of "Practical Mathematics," "Heat Engines," "Machine Construction and Drawing," and "Magnetism and Electricity," of the Board of Education, or their equivalents, before commencing this subject.

Slide rules and tables of logarithms may be used at the Examination. In problems involving calculations, more importance will be attached to method than to arithmetical accuracy.

I. Syllabus:—

GRADE I.

Petrol.—Source, distillation, density, and calorific value. Handling and storage.

Carburation.—The properties of petrol, explosive mixtures, cooling effect of evaporation.

Carburettors.—General principle of the action of a float-fed spray Carburettor and description of the forms in common use. Variable mixture supplied by simple "jet-in-tube" Carburettor, and the principles of the devices in common use attempting to correct this defect. Location of faults in fuel system.

Indicated and Brake Horse-power, compression ratios, heat of compression, difference between adiabatic and isothermal compression. Graphic representation of work, indicator diagrams. Difficulty of measuring indicated horse-power accurately. Brake horse-power and method of measuring same. Mechanical efficiency. Thermal efficiency. Heat losses. Fuel consumption. Calculations involved in connection with the above.

Engines.—General construction of two- and four-stroke Cycle Engines, various forms of engines, valves, and operating mechanisms in common use. Valve timing; lubrication, cooling, practical treatment generally, and locating faults. Such elementary information regarding balancing and torque as will enable the student to understand the advantages of various forms of engines and the principles governing their design.

Gearing.—Angular ratio of trains of gear wheels other than epicyclic gears. Relative torque in shafts, properties of differential gears. Efficiencies of different forms of gearing. Tractive force. Road and wind resistance and gradients. Braking effect. Problems involving simple calculations with the above.

Chassis Parts.—General description of the construction of various types in common use of the following:—Clutches, change speed gears, universal joints, transmission to road driving wheels, brakes, steering gears, circulating pumps, fans, radiators, bearings, lubricators, springs, shackles, torque rods, radius rods, silencers, &c.

Means for operating clutches, speed gears, and brakes. Locating faults in and practical treatment of the above.

Materials of Construction.—Composition, properties, methods of working, and treatment of the materials in common use.

ELECTRIC IGNITION.—*Electrcity.*—Such elementary information regarding electricity and magnetism as will enable the student to form an intelligent idea of the operation of batteries, coils, and magnetos, as used for ignition.

Batteries.—Brief description of primary batteries. Secondary batteries, general construction, charging, and treatment generally. Ohm's law.

Coils and Magnetos.—High and low tension sparks, effect of pressure on the length of spark. Electro-magnetic induction. Construction and theory of working of ignition coils, high and low tension magnetos, operating mechanism, timing ignition. High and low tension distributors.

Sparking Plugs.—Construction, weaknesses, and general treatment.

Wiring.—Various systems in common use. High and low tension distribution.

(*Note.*—Students should be encouraged to use coloured inks or pencils when drawing diagrams of coils, magnetos, and ignition systems, say red for low-tension conductors, blue or green for high, and black for other constructional parts.)

Locating faults in ignition systems.

GRADE II.

Candidates for this Grade must have previously passed the Examination in Grade I.

Candidates will be expected to possess a more advanced knowledge of the subjects mentioned in the syllabus for Grade I., and in addition a knowledge of the following subjects :—

Petrol.—Methods for testing. Other fuels in commercial use on internal combustion motor road vehicles.

Carburation.—Effect of air-petrol ratio on composition of exhaust gases, on rate of combustion, on mean effective pressure and on efficiency.

Carburettors.—Pressure-fed systems. Effects of valve stem leakage, condensation in induction pipe, and throttled petrol supply. Causes of flooding. Brief description of carburettors, other than the float-fed spray kind.

Indicated and Brake Horse-power.—Thermo-dynamic principles of the internal combustion motor. High-speed engine indicators, analysis of diagrams, torque, or crank effort curves from the indicator diagram. Horse-power formulas based on engine dimensions.

Engines.—Calculation of stresses in engine parts, problems on balancing, and the effect of inertia on the torque diagram. Effect of obliquity of the connecting-rod, forced vibration in shafts, design of poppet-valves and cams.

Gearing.—Epicyclic gears. Geometrical properties and construction of various forms of tooth gearing. Side slip.

Efficiency.—The problem of the efficiency of the machine as a whole and in detail, studied quantitatively.

Chassis Parts.—Calculation of stresses in members of transmission. Means for adjustment for wear. Governors, shock absorbers, detachable wheels and rims.

Lubricants.—Properties, flash-point, composition, impurities.

Ignition.—Synchronised ignition, two-point ignition, and effect of nature of spark on ignition.

FINAL EXAMINATION.

Candidates for the Final Examination must hold a certificate in Grade II.

The Examination in this Grade will consist of two parts—a Written Examination and a Drawing Examination—to test the Candidate's knowledge of proportion and his quickness and accuracy in designing.

(I) Written Examination.—In addition to a more advanced knowledge of the matter comprised in to a syllabuses for Grades I. and II., candidates will be expected to possess a knowledge of steam road vehicles, and of the general problems of motor-car engineering. The questions will not necessarily be limited to the subjects specified in the foregoing syllabuses.

(2) Drawing Examination.—Candidates may be asked to design any of the mechanical details in a petrol or steam car; a choice of subjects will be given.

Plain paper or paper ruled in $\frac{1}{8}$-in. squares will be provided by the Institute; all necessary instruments must be provided by the Candidates or the school.

Neat, carefully proportioned hand-sketches are all that is required, and these should contain sufficient detail to enable a draughtsman to prepare working drawings from them. The dimensions of parts should be judged by eye and should not be inserted.

Marks will be awarded for correct proportions.

II. Full Technological Certificate.—For the Full Technological Certificate the Candidate must qualify as stated in Rule 30 of the Programme of the City and Guilds of London Institute. Candidates qualifying under Rule 30 (1) are recommended to pass the Lower Examinations of the Board of Education in the subjects, 6. Machine Construction, and 9. Heat Engines.

TECHNOLOGICAL EXAMINATIONS, 1908

74—MOTOR CAR ENGINEERING

Monday, 27th April, 7 to 10 p.m.

INSTRUCTIONS

The number of the question must be placed before the answer in the worked paper.

The maximum number of marks obtainable is affixed to each question.

The use of scale rules and drawing instruments is allowed.

Three hours allowed for this paper.

Candidates may use slide-rules or tables of logarithms.

ORDINARY GRADE

All Candidates must attempt Question 1,
and not more than six others

1. Draw the outline of the battery, coils, distributor or "commutator" and cylinders of a four-cylinder engine, and show the wiring—preferably with coloured pencils or inks—for ignition for the ordinary form of high-tension battery ignition with four coils. *(40 marks.)*

2. If the engine in question No. 1 is found to be misfiring on one cylinder, how would you systematically set about to find which cylinder is not firing, and then to locate the fault? (*Note.*—Your method of locating the fault should be sufficient to detect any defect which is likely to occur, and you should not merely state how you would prove it to be due to one particular cause.) *(50.)*

3. Sketch diagrammatically two common types of two-cylinder engines, and mention the disadvantages of each with regard to balance, continuity of torque, and adaptability to motor cars. *(40.)*

4. Represent the motion of the crank pin by a circle, and indicate the direction of revolution with an arrow; mark on this circle the dead centres and the positions where the inlet

and exhaust valve should open and close in an Otto cycle or ordinary petrol engine;

or,

If you are not accustomed to this method of setting the valves, state when they should open and close in an engine of 5-in. stroke. *(40.)*

5. Sketch the essential parts of an automatic carburettor— without the float chamber—write the names on the different parts, and explain when the automatic device comes into operation, and why it is necessary. *(40.)*

6. Draw a three-speed and reverse gear-box, with the gears in "neutral," giving a direct drive on top, suitable for a live- axle car. Put a figure on each wheel to indicate that it is for the reverse, 1st, 2nd, or top gear. *(40.)*

7. Show how the cooling of a single-cylinder engine, situated under a bonnet in front of a small car, is effected. Sketch the cylinder jacket, radiator, and pump in their respective positions, and indicate the direction of circulation by arrows. Make a separate sketch of the pump in section. *(40.)*

8. In an ordinary ignition coil, suppose the low-tension or primary winding to be quite separate from the high-tension or secondary winding, how is it that by passing a current through the former you are able to get a current from the latter? *(40.)*

9. Sketch the system of steam and water pipes used on a steam car which condenses its steam and re-uses the water, state where the various pumps and valves are situated, and indicate the complete circuit of steam and water with arrows. *(60.)*

Honours Grade

(Candidates for Honours must have previously passed in the Ordinary Grade)

All Candidates must attempt Question 1, and not more than six others

1. Name some high-tension magneto ignition system with which you are familiar. Show diagrammatically its internal construction and external connections to plugs, &c. Wires

carrying current should be drawn with coloured pencils or inks. *(40 marks.)*

2. If an engine, fitted with the ignition system you have described in question No. 1, is found to be misfiring on one cylinder, how would you systematically set about to find which cylinder is not firing, and then locate the fault. *(Note.—* Your method of locating the fault should be sufficient to detect any defect which is likely to occur, and you should not merely state how you would prove it to be due to one particular cause.) *(50.)*

3. Sketch and describe the action of some two-stroke cycle engine with which you are familiar. *(40.)*

4 Engines sometimes make a noise called "coughing," which is caused by an explosion in the inlet or induction pipe; explain carefully the cause of "coughing and how the mixture in the inlet pipe is able to get fired when the inlet valves are mechanically operated and do not leak. *(40.)*

5. An ordinary "live-axle" car, fitted with 30-in. road-wheels and a four-to-one reduction in the bevil drive with direct drive on top gear, has an engine which gives 15 brake horse-power. Neglecting friction in transmission calculate the tractive force which is available for propelling the vehicle along the road when on the top gear. *(40.)*

6 Describe a good system for lubricating the bearings pistons, and gudgeon pins for a four-cylinder engine; sketch the lubricator and crank case, giving just sufficient detail to indicate clearly how the lubrication of the parts is effected *(40.)*

7. Discuss the relative advantages and disadvantages of low-tension magneto ignition as compared with high-tension magneto. *(40.)*

8. Sketch the burner, the storage tank, and fuel system of a steam car; name the parts, and state whether the fuel is paraffin or petrol. *(50.)*

9. Describe briefly why the armature of an electric motor tends to rotate when a current is supplied to the motor in the ordinary way. *(40.)*

Candidates in Honours must present themselves for the

MOTORS AND MOTORING

Drawing Examination to be held to-morrow, Tuesday, 28th April, from 7 to 10 p.m.

HONOURS GRADE
(DRAWING EXAMINATION)

Tuesday, April 28th, 7 to 10 p.m.

One sheet of drawing paper is supplied to each candidate. Candidates may use ordinary drawing instruments, but sketches only, not scale drawings, are required. The dimensions of parts drawn should be judged by eye, and need not be inserted. Marks will be awarded for correct proportion.

1. Sketch in section an epicyclic gear giving two forward speeds and a reverse, suitable for a small car. *(100 marks.)*

2. Draw two views of a universal joint suitable for the front end of a "cardan" or propeller shaft of a live-axle car. *(100.)*

3. Sketch a multiple disc clutch complete, about half full size, giving separate views of the two kinds of discs used. Enough detail should be given to enable a draughtsman to prepare a working drawing from your sketch. *(100.)*

4. Draw a sparking plug in section, about twice full size and name the insulating materials used. *(80.)*

TECHNOLOGICAL EXAMINATIONS, 1909

74.—MOTOR CAR ENGINEERING

Monday, April 26th, 7 to 10 p.m.

INSTRUCTIONS

The number of the question must be placed before the answer in the worked paper.

The maximum number of marks obtainable is affixed to each question.

The use of slide rules, tables of logarithms and drawing instruments, is allowed.

Such details of calculations should be given as will show the methods employed in obtaining arithmetical results.

Three hours allowed for this paper.

GUILDS EXAMINATION PAPERS

Ordinary Grade

*All candidates must attempt Questions 1 and 2,
and not more than five others*

1. Describe briefly the construction of any small car with which you may be familiar; taking each organ in turn, giving its situation and the type to which it belongs, also noting any special or good features. *(50 marks.)*

2. Supposing the ignition gear in the car described in Question 1 to be in perfect working order but that you cannot get the engine to start, how would you systematically set about to *locate* the fault before attempting to put it right or to alter any adjustments? *(40.)*

3. Sketch, in section, a good design of clutch and fly-wheel, showing the clutch pedal. State briefly what are its good features. *(40.)*

4. What horse-power is required to move a motor delivery van, weighing $\frac{31}{2}$ tons, at 12 miles per hour along a level road, the necessary tractive force to overcome road resistance being 45 lbs. per ton? *(40.)*

5. State precisely what materials are generally used for constructing the following car parts:—Engine cylinders, crank shaft, balls in the ball bearings, core or centre part of magneto armature, ordinary sparking plug points. What is the white metal made of which is commonly used for lining big- end bearings? *(40.)*

6. Answer *either* of the following:—

(*a*) Suppose you have a 3-ampère hour 4-volt accumulator to be recharged, show in a diagram the necessary connections and apparatus for recharging, using any source of current supply you like. State what current you would give, for how long you would charge, and how you would regulate the current.

or;

(*b*) Draw just a line diagram showing the wiring for a non-trembler coil ignition system, for a motor cycle with a 4-volt battery.

If the coil takes 3 ampères, what is its resistance in ohms? *(40.)*

7. Show the construction of a trembler ignition coil by a sketch, taking care to make the connections quite clear, preferably with coloured pencils or inks, stating which terminal has to be connected to the sparking plug and which to the battery, &c. *(50.)*

8. Represent, diagrammatically, a low-tension magneto, and show the connections to a 4-cylinder engine. Show the make and brake mechanism for one of the cylinders, and state the relative speed of the armature to the crank-shaft. *(40.)*

9. Sketch a liquid fuel burner, and show the tank and necessary pipe connections, &c., for a steam car. State the fuel used and how it is forced to the burner. *(40.)*

10. What are the chief necessary electrical parts in an electric carriage? Why are electric cars not more commonly used for country work? *(40.)*

Honours Grade

Candidates for Honours must have previously passed in the Ordinary Grade

All candidates must attempt Questions 1 and 2, and not more than five others

1. Draw up a short catalogue specification of a complete chassis; take the engine, gear-box, and other organs in turn, briefly indicating the good points and selling features which you think you could include at the price. The prices of the parts should not be given, but the specification should conclude with the words:—"Price. ' Chassis only.' £250." *(50 marks.)*

2. Suppose that the engine of the car you have described in Question 1 stops pulling when you are out driving and the car soon comes to rest, how would you systematically set about to ascertain the cause of the trouble? *(40.)*

3. Answer *either* of the following:—

    (*a*) Sketch the apparatus you would use to determine the flash-point of a lubricating oil. State how you would use it and what you would expect the flash-points of two oils to be, one suitable for water-cooled engines and the other for air-cooled engines.

or,

(b) Sketch the apparatus you would use to determine the calorific value of a liquid fuel.

If .008 lbs. of fuel raise 12 lbs. of water from 55° F. to 67° F., calculate the calorific value of this fuel. (40.)

4. Give the name of, or describe, a steel suitable for constructing some part of a motor chassis, mention the part for which this steel is suitable, and describe the treatment to which you would subject it in order to render it serviceable. (40.)

5. An engine being tested with a rope brake round a 2-ft. fly-wheel gives a torque of 92 lbs. feet, e.g., 100 lbs. one end of rope and 8 lbs. the other. If this engine were to be put on a car weighing 1 ton altogether, what is the steepest gradient it could climb on the slow speed, neglecting all friction? A 23- tooth pinion on clutch shaft in gear-box meshes with a 57-tooth wheel on Cardan shaft extension, and the bevel in the back axle has 19 teeth meshing with a crown wheel of 60 teeth; tyres 810 by 90. (50.)

6. What is the difference between isothermal and adiabatic compression? How would you try to obtain each of these? If it were possible in an internal combustion engine to obtain adiabatic or isothermal compression and expansion when required, indicate, on an imaginary indicator diagram, the parts of the curve which you would arrange to have adiabatic and isothermal respectively. (40.)

7. Calculate one of the following:—

(a) The tensile stress in the rim of a cast iron flywheel, 2 ft. diameter, at 2500 revolutions per minute. One cubic inch of cast iron weighing 0.28 lbs.

or,

(b) The maximum tension, in a connecting rod, due to the inertia 'of piston and gudgeon pin weighing 8 lbs. in an engine 5 ins. bore 6 ins. stroke, at 1500 revolutions, neglecting the obliquity of the connecting rod. (40.)

8. Show, diagrammatically, the wiring for ignition for a 2- cylinder engine, cranks at 180°, fitted with two trembler coils and battery. (40.)

9. Sketch the engine of a steam car with which you are familiar, and name the make. (40.)

10. In an electric car, how is the necessary increase in torque obtained for hill-climbing? *(40.)*

Candidates in Honours must present themselves for the Drawing Examination to be held to-morrow, Tuesday, April 27th, 7 to 10 p.m.

HONOURS GRADE

(DRAWING EXAMINATION)

Tuesday, April 27th, 7 to 10 p.m.
One sheet of special drawing paper is supplied to each candidate.

Candidates may use ordinary drawing instruments, but sketches only, not scale drawings, are required. The dimensions of parts drawn should be judged by eye, and need not be inserted. Marks will be awarded for correct proportion.

Only three questions to be attempted.

1. Draw nearly half full size a sectional view of a flywheel with a leather cone clutch, preferably a type in which the spring gives no end thrust on the crank-shaft or gear-box shaft when driving. Show the necessary mechanism for removing the clutch for re-lining and describe briefly how this is carried out. (*60 marks.*)

2. Draw twice full size part of the pitch circle and two involute teeth of an ordinary gear wheel having 30 teeth, 6 diametral pitch, 5-in. diameter pitch circle. Show how the curve is set out and insert the dimensions of one tooth. (*40*)

3. Sketch about quarter full size a well-designed back spring (not of the transverse type). Draw two full-sized views of one of the shackles in position, showing every detail of importance to its efficient use. (*50.*)

4. Draw full size a piston for a double-acting engine used on a steam car and show clearly a satisfactory form of piston ring for same. (*40.*)

THE POLYTECHNIC SCHOOL OF ENGINEERING

309 REGENT STREET, LONDON, W.

ANNUAL EXAMINATION IN MOTOR CAR ENGINEERING

Wednesday, April 7th, 1909, 7 *to* 10 *p.m.*

EXAMINERS:

HENRY J. SPOONER, M.I.Mech.E., A.M.Inst.C.E,. M.Inst.A.E., F.G.S., &c.

AND

W. HIBBERT, A.M.I.E.E., F.C.S., F.I.C., &c.

INSTRUCTIONS

You are not to attempt more than **EIGHT** questions.

Illustrate your answer by hand sketches.

Your answers should be concise and strictly confined to the questions.

All students are to attempt **TWO** of the **FIRST FOUR** questions in the stage of the subject they take.

ORDINARY STAGE

Preliminary Certificates (First or Second Class) will be given to all students who pass this examination. But students who have passed the B. of E. or Poly. Examinations in Heat Engines and Machine Construction and Drawing (either this year or any previous one) will receive the **Full Certificate in the Ordinary Stage**. *Such students must give particulars of these passes (or state whether they are sitting this year in the subjects) below their name on the examination paper.*

1. In a battery ignition system there are two independent circuits. Carefully explain the differences between these.

2 To set a spark some thousands of volts are generally required. How then can a low-tension system produce one?

3. Sketch two forms of commutator and compare their working.

4. Explain exactly the meaning of "advance" and "retard" gear.

5. With what object are petrol motor cylinders water-jacketed? Make a sketch showing a water-cooling system in which a pump is used, and indicate by arrows the direction of flow through all the parts.

6. In a few words explain how petrol is produced about what is (a) the specific gravity of commercial petrol, (b) about what its calorific value?.

7 Why is the explosive mixture in a petrol engine compressed in the cylinder before it is exploded?

Mention three likely causes of faulty compression.

8. Make a sketch of any friction clutch you are acquainted with.

What is the most common cause of (a) slipping, (b) fierceness?

9. Show by a sketch any system of levers &c., you are acquainted with for connecting the push-pedal to the brake.

What important condition must every automobile brake satisfy?

10. Write a brief description of the lubricating system of any car you may acquainted with.

What important condition must every automobile brake satisfy?

11. Why is a heavy cluth casting or flywheel more necessary for a single-cylinder petrol engine than for a four-cylinder one?

Show by freehand diagram how the turning effort or torque between the crank and clutch approximately varies for a complete revolution in a single-cylinder engine.

12. Sketch and explain the action of any form of sliding gear giving a direct drive on top speed.

Why are some cars fitted with the direct drive on a lower gear?

13. A single cylinder petrol engine, running at 1200 revolutions per minute, has a $\frac{31}{2}$" diameter cylinder and a $\frac{41}{2}$" stroke. Assuming that the mean pressure throughout its explosion stroke is 80 lbs. per square inch, what is its indicated horse-power?

If its brake horse-power is eight-tenths the indicated horsepower at this speed, what is its mechanical efficiency?

HONOURS STAGE (Part I)

Only students who passed the C. G. or Poly. Exams, in this subject any previous year are eligible to sit in this Stage. Preliminary Certificates (first or second class) will be given to all students who pass this examination. But students who have been through the Motor Laboratory Course, and who have passed the B. of E. or Poly. Exams, in Heat Engines and Machine Construction and Drawing (either this year or any previous one) will receive the **Full Certificate in the Honours stage, Part I.** *Give particulars on your examination paper of your qualifying passes, &c.*

14. State the faults which lead to back-firing and misfiring.

15. A battery is said to be about half discharged. How would you test this?

16. Give careful sketches of some timing gear.

17. Compare high- and low-tension systems.

18. Make a sketch showing a water-cooling system for a petrol engine in which a pump is used.

Under normal conditions of running about what would you expect the temperature of the inner wall of the cylinder to be? and about what maximum temperature may be reached in the exploded mixture?

19. A car uses on an average one gallon of petrol per 20 miles run in an hour. If all the potential energy of the fuel could be effectively used, without any losses, what horsepower would this consumption correspond to?

About what brake horse-power of the engine is ordinarily got out of the fuel under such running conditions?

20. Explain how you would proceed to determine the

mechanical efficiency of a petrol motor. Be careful to point out any cause of error or want of accuracy in the readings of the indicator that you elect to use. About what value would you expect the mechanical efficiency to have?

21. For a standard car of the best make what materials would you use for (a) the crank-shaft, (b) the frame, (c) the gear wheels, (d) the gear box, (e) the cylinders, (f) the principal bearings? Be careful to specify not only the name of the metal in each case, but the particular quality you would require.

22. In some single-cylinder engines the balancing of the crank and partial balancing of the connecting rod and inertia forces is arranged for by weights on the crank webs produced or extended beyond the crank-shaft. In other cases a balance weight is arranged on the fly-wheel or clutch casting. Which of these two is to be preferred, and why?

23. Assuming that the weight of the reciprocating parts of a single-cylinder petrol engine is 8 lbs. and that the cylinder is 4 inches diameter and the stroke 5 inches, the revolutions per minute being 1200, the initial pressure of the explosive mixture being 200 lbs. per square inch. What would you expect the actual pressure on the crank pin to be at the commencement of an explosion stroke, neglecting the obliquity of the connecting rod?

24. A certain car runs at 30 miles per hour on the top speed, when the engine revolves 1000 times per minute, the diameter of the driving wheels at their tread being 30 inches. Show by a sketch suitable wheels in the gear and differential boxes, being careful to mark on each wheel the number of its teeth.

25. Explain how you would proceed to inspect a petrol motor vehicle, mentioning the parts you would examine in the order of their importance.

What parts in particular would you expect to find defective if the vehicle had been in use some years?

26. What is the primary cause of a smoky exhaust from a petrol engine?

How would you test an engine to determine whether the

fuel has been supplied with a proper quantity of air to ensure complete combustion? About what proportion of partly burnt fuel would you expect to find?

HONOURS STAGE (Part II)

Only students who have passed the Poly. Exams, in Hons. Stage I. in this subject any previous year are eligible to sit in this Stage. Preliminary Certificates (first or second class) will be given to all students who pass this examination. But students who have been through the Motor Laboratory Course, and who have passed in Stage II. the B. of E. or Poly. Exams, in Heat Engines and Machine Construction and Drawing (either this year or any previous one) will receive the **Full Certificate in the Honours Stage, Part II.** *Give particulars on your examination paper of your qualifying passes, &c.*

27. Describe the Lodge system of ignition.

28. The magnetic systems differ in the Simms-Bosch and the Eisemann. State fully what the differences are.

29. Discuss the question of tumbler and non-tumbler coils.

30. A 6-volt battery burns the contact points—why? State fully how you could remedy this fault.

31. Show by sketches typical forms of indicator diagrams when (a) pre-ignition has occurred, (b) when the engine is running light and the spark is retarded.

Mark on each diagram the point in the cycle about where you would expect the actual sparking to occur in the cylinder.

32. Write out a brief specification of the materials that should be used for the principal parts of a high grade standard complete chassis.

33. Make a freehand sketch of a crank effort diagram for a four-cylinder petrol engine, taking inertia and obliquity into account.

34. A single-cylinder petrol engine running on the Otto cycle, diameter of cylinder 4 inches, stroke 5 inches, revolutions 1000 per minute, is fitted with a fly-wheel whose radius of gyration is 8 inches and whose weight is 30 lbs. Assuming that during the explosion stroke the work done in the cylinder

is 400 ft. lbs. and that during the stroke the work done on the piston, whilst the pressure fluctuated above or below the average is 80 ft. lbs., what fluctuation of speed per revolution would occur?

35. Make a sketch design giving leading dimensions of a conical leather-faced clutch to transmit 16 horse-power at 1200 revolutions per minute. Also determine what strength the spring should have.

36. Give the names of two fuels that could be used instead of petrol in the engine, and mention the advantages and disadvantages attending the use of each, and explain what alterations, if any, would have to be made in the engine to efficiently work with each of them.

37. State the advantages of standardising details, and explain the use of *limit gauges.*

What is the difference between *hole basis* and *shaft basis?*

Define the following terms: (1) Tolerance, (2) Allowance (3) Clearance, (4) Force fits, (5) Driving fits, (6) Push fits' (7) Running fits.

What kind of fit would you make: *(a)* the crank pins, *i.e.* between the pins and the big-end brasses; *(b)* between the crank-shaft brasses and the openings in the bedplate of the crank case into which they fit?

Refer to page 290 and following pages for City Guilds Examination Papers for 1910, 1911, *and,* 1914.

APPENDIX II

Page **19. Timing and Setting the Valves.**—The points that have to be attended to in timing the valves have been dealt with in Article 8, p. 19, and an examination of Fig. 23, which has been arranged to give the approximate positions of the crank when the various operations occur in the Otto cycle, should help to make the matter clear.

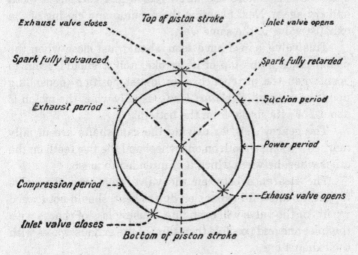

Fig. 23.—Approximate Positions of Crank in Timing Valves and Spark.

It will be seen that the crank path in the figure has been opened out slightly, so that the curves representing the two revolutions of the crank pin are not superimposed.

Timing marks on the fly-wheel (forming the outer member of the clutch) of the engine are made on most engines now. These correspond with similar marks on the crank case when the piston is at the top and bottom of the stroke. Of course if the inlet valve is automatic the timing takes care of itself and has not to be considered; but mechanically operated inlet valves are usually timed to open immediately the piston begins its suction stroke, and, as we have seen, close at some point between the end and about $\frac{1}{5}$ or $\frac{1}{6}$ from the bottom of the compression stroke, depending upon the speed the engine is designed to run at.

To set the two to one gear wheels, turn the engine till the crank is on its top centre, as indicated by the marks on the fly-wheel,[1] and take the cam-shaft wheel and mesh the teeth with the small wheel so that the inlet valve is just on the point of being raised off" its seating. Should the inlet valve open too early, move the large gear-wheel back by a tooth and try again. Next examine the opening and closing of the exhaust valve in the same way.

This valve, as we have seen, should just close when the piston reaches the top of its stroke, and it should begin to open when the piston nears its lowest position (depending upon the amount of *exhaust-lead),* usually when the piston is about $\frac{1}{5}$ or $\frac{1}{6}$ its stroke from the bottom.

The gear-wheels for driving the cam-shafts are usually marked—a single tooth on one wheel and the two teeth on the other wheel between which it is intended to mesh.

The clearance between the valve stem and the valve tappet,[2] to allow for expansion due to heat, should not exceed $\frac{1}{32}$ in., or the valve will open late, causing loss of charge with the inlet one and possible throttling of the exhaust gases with the exhaust one.

AIR REQUIRED FOR COMBUSTION

Pages 69-77.—Dr. Watson, F.R.S.,[3] has found that, using a petrol with C = 85.22 and H = 14.78 per cent., requiring about fifteen times as much air as petrol for complete combustion, only an amount of air equal to fourteen times that of the

---

[1] Should there be no marks on the fly-wheel, the top position of the piston can be located either by a wire passed through the compression-cock or the spark-ing plug-hole. When the latter is at the side of the cylinder the wire is usually weighted at the end which rests on the piston, and is pivoted at a part near its centre (where it passes through the plug-hole) in such a way that the end which projects outside will be in its lowest position when the piston is at the top of its stroke.

[2] In cases where the tappets are not adjustable, the wear may be taken up by a thimble or cap fitted to the tappet, or a thin piece of steel may be brazed on.

[3] Paper on "Thermal and Combustion Efficiency of a Four-cylinder Petrol Motor." *Proceedings, Inst. A.E.,* 1908-9. (Abstd. by kind permission.)

petrol gave practically complete combustion, and he suggests as an explanation that some of the petrol is converted into some other substance of which account is not taken in the exhaust gas analysis. The following table is instructive :—

TABLE XXIII.—EFFECT OF THE RATIO OF AIR TO PETROL, &c., ON THE
PERFORMANCE OF AN ENGINE (WATSON)

Four-cylinder Engine.—Bore, 85 mm.; Stroke, 120 mm.
(Glement-Talbot).

Speed.	I.H.P.	B.H.P.	Lb. for Petrol per 1000 Revolutions.	I.H.P. Hours per lb. of Petrol.	Thermal Efficiency [1]	Mean Effective Pressure M.E.P.	Air / Petrol by weight.
1280	23.1	18.8	.222	1.36	.185	86.1	10.1
1284	24.2	19.9	.192	1.63	.222	90.0	11.6
1287	23.4	19.1	.174	1.74	.237	86.6	12.8
1266	22.3	18.1	.173	1.69	.230	84.1	13.0
1272	22.1	17.8	.159	1.82	.248	82.6	14.1
1260	21.5	17.4	.150	1.89	.257	81.5	15.1
1230	20.6	16.6	.142	1.97	.268	80.0	16.1
1219	20.1	16.2	.136	2.02	.275	78.6	16.9
1021	16.4	13.3	.139	1.92	.261	76.4	17.8
982	14.8	11.8	.134	1.86	.253	71.7	18.6
1023	12.7	9.6	.128	1.61	.219	59.1	19.3
873	10.9	8.3	.127	1.62	.220	59.4	20.3

Dr. Watson remarks that "it will be noticed that the efficiency increases as the mixture gets weaker, up to very nearly the weakest mixture on which the engine will run regularly, In this connection it was observed that with mixtures containing between 17.5 and about 19 lbs. of air to a pound of petrol firing back into the carburettor was liable to occur, while with mixtures either richer or weaker this effect was not observed the reason in one case being that the stronger mixtures burn so quickly that all flame is extinguished when the new charge enters, while in the case of the very weak mixtures the incoming charge is so weak that it

---

[1] Thermal Efficiency. By this term is meant the ratio of the energy corresponding to the I.H.P. to the thermal energy of the fuel consumed.

will not inflame until it is compressed. The spark was in every case so adjusted that the maximum power was developed."

Except for very weak mixtures, when the running of the engine is irregular, the efficiency for any given strength of mixture increases as the speed increases.

Further, at all speeds the efficiency is a maximum for an air to petrol ratio of about 17 by weight.

The completeness of the evaporation of the petrol before entering the cylinder cannot be disregarded, as experiments with very rich mixtures seem to show that the vaporisation of the petrol on the closing of the inlet valve is far from complete. In this connection it should be remembered that the density of the petrol vapour is approximately three times greater than that of the air, while within the limits of the ratio of petrol to air in above Table XXIII.—namely, 10 to *20*—according to Dr. Watson, the maximum variation in the volume of the petrol vapour is always between 1.3 and 3.2 per cent, of the *volume* of the air, even if complete vaporisation occurs before the closing of the inlet valve.

Page 86. **Maximum Brake Horse-Power Rating per Cylinder.**—The Horse-Power Formula Committee of the Institution of Automobile Engineers proposed the following formula in 1911. And it is now regarded as Standard :—

Max. B.H.P. rating per cylinder = 0.464 $(d + s)$ $(d - 1.18)$

where d = diameter of cylinder in inches, s = stroke in inches.

This formula may be considered to give the maximum practicable B.H.P. as determined by a bench test under onerous but still safe conditions for carefully designed and soundly constructed engines of from $2\frac{1}{2}$ in. to 5 in. cylinder diameter and stroke-bore ratio up to 2.5.

AIR FOR COMBUSTION

TABLE XXIV.—MIXTURES OF AIR AND PETROL VAPOUR

Explosion in a Closed Vessel (Boston Experiment).[1]
By the Clerk Method.
Petrol Specific Gravity, 0.680 at 76° F.

Percentage of Petrol Vapour in Mixture (by Volume).	Time of Explosion (Seconds).	Maximum Pressure in lbs. per sq. in. above Atmosphere	0.2 Sec. after Maximum Pressure			
			Area sq. in.	Mean Pressure lbs. per sq. in.	Mean Pressure + Vapour Ratio.	Final Pressure.
1.32	.167	62	1.28	42.7	3240	33
1.41	.117	62	1.42	47.3	3360	35
1.51	.109	64	1.45	48.6	2950	35
1.64	.182	51	1.25	41.7	2540	32
1.79	.109	67	1.53	51.0	2855	36
1.96	.091	73	1.53	51.0	2600	36
2.17	.082	76	1.56	52.0	2391	37
2.44	.060	85	1.63	54.3	2225	36
2.63	.058	85	1.62	54.0	2052	36
2.78	.058	84	1.64	54.7	1970	38
3.03	.066	78	1.60	53.4	1760	37
3.23	.067	83	1.70	56.7	1760	38
3.45	.100	75	1.59	53.0	1536	38
3.85	.117	62	1.42	47.3	1230	35
4.17	.133	55	1.40	46.7	1121	38
4.76	.210	35	1.02	34.0	714	32

NOTE.—THE area in square inches (column 4) signifies the area under the cooling curve from maximum pressure to $\frac{1}{5}$ second after, and the mean pressure in column 5 is taken from this area, as determined by a planometer. The final pressure after $\frac{1}{5}$ second from maximum is given in column 7. The numbers in column 6 give the relative values of the different mixtures. The best mean pressure, measuring the resistance to cooling and best pressure, will be seen to be 47.3 per square inch, giving the number 3360 in column 6, and corresponding to a mixture of 141 per cent, of petrol vapour in the mixture.

Page 117. **Timing the Ignition.**—Approximately, for full advance the spark should occur when the piston is from $\frac{1}{8}$ to $\frac{1}{4}$ below the top of the compression stroke, and for late ignition for safe starting (to reduce to a minimum the danger

---

[1] Refer to Dugald Clerk's "The Gas, Petrol and Oil Engine," p. 152.

of the starting handle being shot backwards) the spark should occur when the piston is about ⅕ down on the power stroke. These two sparking positions (see Fig. 23) should correspond with the end positions of the ignition lever in its quadrant.

Pages 165-170. **Brake Power.**—It will be seen that the rule worked out on page 170 to give the approximate minimum distance a car can be pulled up in agrees very closely with the brake test of the Automobile Club of America, referred to on page 165, in which a Panhard car, running at sixteen miles per hour, was brought to a standstill in 25 ft. 4 ins. Applying our rule, the distance

$$L = \frac{16^2}{10} = \frac{256}{10} = 25.6 \text{ ft. or 25 ft. 7.2 ins.}$$

Again, in Messrs. O'Gorman and New's experiments with a Rolls-Royce car (described in *The Autocar* for 6th March 1907), running at twenty miles per hour, the stopping distance was found to be 38 ft. Applying our rule,

$$L = \frac{20^2}{10} = \frac{400}{10} = 40 \text{ ft.}$$

We have seen that the position of the centre of gravity of the car (page 170) affects the value of R, the retarding force, which we measured for the position of the C.G. that is roughly due to the use of a closed body, where the greater part of the weight comes on the back wheels, but with a two-seater body the centre of gravity may be about a third the wheel base from the front wheels, and with a four-seater body about midway between wheels. With the introduction of front brakes the problem has assumed a more interesting form; and Mr. John V. Pugh, in *The Autocar* for 9th April 1910, examined the cases that ordinarily occur in practice, and explained that the figures he arrived at he was able to approximately verify by some inclined-plane experiments with an actual car.

The following table sets out the results he arrived at:—

TABLE XXV.—EFFECT OF POSITION OF C.G. ON BRAKE POWER FOR FRONT AND REAR BRAKES

The coefficient of friction assumed to be 0.625 and the height of the top of the wheels.

	Limiting Angle of Hill down which Car will not slip.	Retarding Force R of Front Brake.	Load on Front Wheels.	Retarding Force R of Rear Brake.	Load on Rear Wheels.	Total Retarding Force R.	
Neither brake acting	0.0°	.0	.666	.0	.333	.0	Centre of gravity one-third wheel base behind front wheel.
Front brake only	27.0°	.505	.82	.0	.18	.514	
Rear brake only	10.0°	.0	.718	.177	.282	.18	
Both brakes	32.0°	.528	.852	.097	.148	.625	
Neither brake acting	0.0°	.0	.5	.0	.5	.0	Centre of gravity midway between wheels.
Front brake only	20.75°	.379	.610	.0	.390	.379	
Rear brake only	14.75°	.0	.575	.265	.425	.262	
Both brakes	32.0°	.423	.68	.202	.32	.625	
Neither brake acting	0.0°	.0	.333	.0	.666	.0	Centre of gravity two-third behind front wheel.
Front brake only	14.0°	.252	.4	.0	.6	.25	
Rear brake only	19.5°	.0	.432	.355	.568	.355	
Both brakes	32.0°	.319	.512	.306	.488	.625	

NOTE.—By using the values of R in the above Table in the equations in p. 170, the approximate minimum distance L required to pull up a car for the cases dealt with in the Table can be determined.

Vertical Type of Engines.

Name.	No. of Cylinders.	Revolutions.	Weight in lbs.	Horse power.	Lbs. per Horse-power.	Cooling System.
Aster · ·	4	1000	242	51.0	4.7	Water
Bates · ·	4	.....	116	28.8	4.0	,,
Clement ·	6	.....	880	117.5	7.5	,,
,,	4	.....	1100	118.5	9.3	,,
,, ·	4	.....	213	29.0	7.3	,,
Darracq ·	4	1200	550	84.0	6.5	,,
,, ·	4	1500	374	43.1	8.7	,,
Green	8	1100	.....	82.0	.....	,,
,, ·	4	1100	236	60.0	3.9	,,
,, ·	4	1200	160	32.0	5.0	,,
Gregoire ·	4	1000	242	51.0	4.7	,,
,, ·	4	1500	174	26.1	6.6	,,
Metallurgic	4	1600	550	48.5	11.3	,,
,, ·	4	1850	300	32.0	9.4	,,
N.E.C.	4	1500	290	69.6	4.15	Air[1]
Panhard	4	900	836	112.0	7.6	Water
,, ·	4	900	523	90.0	5.8	,,
,, ·	4	900	466	48.5	9.6	,,
Renault ·	4	1300	880	42.5	20.7	,,[2]
,, ·	4	1100	286	38.5	7.4	,,
Vininius	4	1800	280	39.2	7.1	,,
,, ·	4	1600	336	37.5	9.0	,,
,, ·	4	1600	.....	32.5	.....	,,
Wright	4	1200	176	32.5	5.4	,,

---

[1] Two stroke.

[2] Balloon typo.

AERO MOTORS

Diagonal Type of Engines.

Name.	No. of Cylinders.	Revolutions.	Weight in lbs.	Horse power.	Lbs. per Horsepower.	Cooling System.
Antoinette	16	1100	264	134.0	2.0	Water
„	8	1100	209	67.2	3.1	„
„	16	1400	165	64.0	2.6	„
„	8	1400	92	32.0	2.9	„
Anzani	4	1400	308	56.4	5.4	„
„	4	1600	187	30.0	6.2	„
Aeroplane	8	1500	452	59.0	7.6	„
Bronhot	8	1400	308	61.4	5.0	„
Easton Cordage Co.	8	.....	300	74.5	4.0	„
„	8	.....	275	49.6	5.5	„
E.N.V.	8	.....	286	62.0	4.6	„
„	8	.....	440	60.5	7.3	„
„	8	.....	363	60.5	6.0	„
„	8	.....	150	38.5	3.8	„
Gobron-Brillie	8	1400	352	102.0	3.4	„
„	8	1400	330	53.8	6.1	„
J.A.P.	8	1300	303	45.5	6.7	„
„	8	1500	220	38.4	5.7	Air
Mors.	4	1700	213	30.0	7.1	Water
Pipe	8	1950	289	55.0	5.3	Air
Renault.	8	1200	574	58.5	9.8	Water
„	8	1500	550	50.5	10.9	Air[1]
„	8	1800	374	46.2	8.1	„
Simms	6	1000	220	51.1	4.3	Water
Wolseley	8	1350	300	54.0	5.6	„
Horizontal type of engine.						
Darracq	4	.....	242	48.4	5.0	Water
„	2	.....	121	24.2	5.0	„
Dutheil-Chambers	4	1000	792	97.0	8.2	„[2]
„	4	1200	550	75.8	7.3	„
„	4	1000	528	75.2	7.0	„[2]
„	6	1200	385	72.6	5.3	„
„	3	1000	396	56.4	7.0	„[2]
„	4	1200	164	48.4	3.4	„
„	2	1000	220	37.6	5.9	„[2]
„	2	1200	132	24.2	5.5	„

---

[1] Balloon type.
[2] Opposed pistons similar to Gobron-Brlllie pistons, coupled to cranks at each end.

Radial Type of Engines.

Name.	No. of Cylinders.	Revolutions.	Weight in lbs.	Horse power.	Lbs. per Horse-power.	Cooling System.
Anzani . . .	3	1400	231	42.3	5.4	Air
„ . .	3	1500	176	31.6	5.5	„
„ . .	3	1600	145	24.5	5.9	„
„ . .	3	1800	94	15.0	6.2	„
„ . .	3	1800	77	14.0	5.5	„
Buchet · .	6	1800	110	24.0	4.6	„
Clement „ .	7	1100	154	50.0	3.1	Water
Farcot	8	1200	242	64.0	3.7	Air
Miesse . . .	8	1200	245	100.0	2.45	Water
R.E.P . . .	10	1400	216	48.5	4.5	Air
„ . .	7	1400	150	33.5	4.5	„
„ . .	5	1200	115	23.5	4.9	„
Gnome	14	1200	220	123.0	1.8	„
„ . .	7	1200	165	61.5	2.7	„
„ . .	5	1300	132	34.0	3.9	„
International	6	1500	130	66.0	1.9	„
„ . .	4	1500	80	21.5	3.7	„

The remarkable success of the **Gnome rotary engine**, designed by Mr. Laurent-Seguin, and manufactured by the Gauthier Company, is causing many potential aviators to take an interest in its construction. Each of its cylinders, with its radiator fins, is machined out of a solid bar of steel. The cylinders are attached to the crank case by split-locking rings, which are inserted in the grooved ends of the cylinders, where they project a short distance on the inside of the case. The crank shaft, which is hollow and fixed, has a single crank, attached to which is only one connecting rod, with an end big enough to connect by pin joints the remaining connecting rods. The explosive mixture is admitted into the cylinders from the carburettor through the hollow shaft into the crank case and through an automatic inlet valve placed in the head of the piston. The exhaust valves are on the cylinder heads, high tension magneto and storage battery provide double ignition, and a drip-feed lubricator delivers the oil into the centre of the crank case, from which, by centrifugal force, it is .distributed to the bearings and cylinders.

Trend of Aero Engine Design.—There can be little doubt that the pure car type of motor so successfully developed by Germany for aviation purposes will ultimately hold the field, and that the rotating-cylinder motors, and motors radiating from a central crank case (motors of the non-car type) that our good friends in France have specialised in and we have largely used, will be superseded probably before the war is ended. Indeed, the trend of design and production both in England and France is apparently in the direction of using almost exclusively motors of the car type, which at present are so well represented in this country by the highly efficient 12-cylinder (vee form) Rolls-Royce, the 12-cylinder Green, and the 12- cylinder Sunbeam, the varying requirements being met by using engines with cylinders ranging in numbers from six to twelve.

Page 167–187. **Use of Auxiliary Air Valve in Fuel Pipe.**—There is much to recommend the use of an air valve in the induction pipe between the engine and the throttle valve, Bowden-fitted for control by hand, so that when coasting down hill, and at other suitable times when the throttle valve is closed and the engine is acting as a brake, air may be admitted to the cylinder to prevent oil being drawn up between the piston and cylinder walls during suction strokes. For, obviously, the presence of such oil in the combustion chamber part of the cylinders is not only unnecessarily wasteful, but it causes, as soon as the explosions commence again, dense, visible, and obnoxious smoke to be emitted into the atmosphere, with possible carbonisation in the cylinder.

There is the additional advantage that such auxiliary air in passing through the cylinders cleanses and scavenges them.

The editor of *The Auto,* in the issue of 12th March 1910, gives particulars of the running of a car with a 4-cylinder 30 h.-p. engine, fitted in the way described, with which nearly 3000 miles were run on a gallon of lubricating oil, and he properly suggests that not a little of the remarkable economy was due to the expedient employed, and this can

TABLE XXVII. *Pages 184 to 203.*—PARTICULARS OF LUBRICATING SYSTEMS, COMPILED FROM MR. R. K. MORCOM'S PAPER ON FORCED LUBRICATION, READ BEFORE THE INSTITUTE OF AUTOMOBILE ENGINEERS, 11TH MAY 1910.

Name of Car and H.P.	Austin, 15	Crossley, 15.6	Cadillac, 30	Daimler, 15	Lanchester, 28	Napier, 45	Panhard, 18.30
Lubrication System	Forced	Forced	Splash	Semi-mechanical	Forced	Forced	Panhard patent
Type and Size of Pump	Vane	Gears, two 1¼" wide	Plunger, double-acting, 1 g.p.m.	Gear, 1½ g.p.m.	Gear, two ⅞" wheels, 2" long, 12 teeth in each	Gear, 80 g.p.h. at 600 r.p.m.	Panhard patent, very small
Size of Suction and Delivery	$\frac{1}{4}$ "	$\frac{5}{16}$ "	$\frac{1}{4}$ "	$\frac{2}{3}$ " delivery	Suction 4-¼" holes, delivery one hole, 2-⅛" and 1-7/16" bore	....	$\frac{2}{5}$ "
Sight Feed or Pressure Gauge	Gauge	....	Sight feed	....	Tell-tale	Pressure gauge	....
Particulars of Filterz	Inside reservoir	Gauze filter in pump	Oil does not pass through pump	Gauze in base chamber and chilled plate in pump	Over bottom of pump	Gauze cylinder	Gauze filter on return vent to oil tank
Relief Valve and Working Pressure	Adjustable, 2-5 lbs. sq. in.	Adjustable, 10 lbs. sq. In.	....	....	40 lbs. sq. in.	Automatic and adjustable, 10 lbs. sq. in.	Automatic
Speed of Engine and of Pump Pump Drive	E. 900, P 700	E. up to 2600, P ⅞ E.	E. 1500, P. 750	E. 1400, P. 1000	E. 2000, P. 4000	E. 1200, P. 600	E. 900, P. 450
Pump Drive	Spiral gear	Direct off cam-shaft	Off magneto shaft	Spiral gears from eccentric shaft	Gear wheels from crank shaft	Skew gear off cam-shaft	Off end of exhaust cam-shaft
Position of Pump	Central outside reservoir	Front corner over ½ time wheel	Near-side engine	In engine base chamber	Bottom of crank chamber	Back end along side sump	Between fly-wheel and crank case
Oil Reservoir	Separate reservoir	Sump	Oil tank	Sump	Engine base	Sump	Oil tank
Oil { Flash Point	213° F.	Price's H.	Winter, Vacuum A; Summer, " B	....	....	620° F.	....
Oil { Viscosity	367.6 at 15.6° C.	Price's H.	Winter, " A; Summer, " B; 750 m.p.g.	....	....	....	....
Oil { Consumption	....	500-800 m.p.g.	A special trial gave 3000 m.p.g.	....	....	....	....

Name of Car and H.P.	Renault, 14-20	Rover, 15	Rolls-Royce, 40-50	Sheffield Simplex, 45 Semi-mechanical	Talbot, 12,15,20, 25, and 35 Mechanical	Vauxhall, 20	Wolseley, various
Lubrication System	Gravity	Gravity	Forced			Forced	Forced
Type and Size of Pump	Centrifugal ...	Vane, 1 quart p.m.	Gear	Gear, 6 g.p.m.	Plunger, 15 m.p.m. dia.	Plunger, $\frac{3}{4}$" dia. $\frac{1}{2}$" stroke	Gear ...
Size of Suction and Delivery	$\frac{1}{2}$"	$\frac{3}{13}$"	$\frac{1}{2}$"	$\frac{1}{4}$"	10mm.	$\frac{1}{4}$"	$\frac{2}{5}$"
Sight Feed or Pressure Gauge	Sight feed	Sight feed	Pressure gauge	Pressure gauge	Both	Pressure gauge	Pressure gauge
Particulars of Filterz	In center of radiator	30 mesh gauze in sump	Lowest point of sump	Gauze in mouth of sump	Detachable gauze	$3\frac{1}{2}$" dia. gauze surrounding suction value	Copper gauze in sump
Relief Valve and Working Pressure	...	...	Automatic, can be set to required press.; 15 lbs. sq. in.	4 lbs. sq. in.	...	Automatic and adjustable, 10 lbs. sq. in.	5-20 lbs. sq. in., depending on speed
Speed of Engine and of Pump	E. 1100, P. 550	E. 1000, P. 500	E. 1000, P. 500	E. 1000, P. 600	E. 1100, P. 550	E. 1000, P. 500	E. —, P. crank shaft speed
Pump Drive	Off cam-shaft	Beval gear	Skew gears	By spiral gears from cam shaft	From cam-shaft	Eccentric on cam-shaft	Spiral gear off cam-shaft
Position of Pump	In crank chamber	Below front end crankchamber	Lower portion of crank chamber	Low down on crank chamber	In sump	Rear end of camshaft	Side of engine
Oil Reservoir	Sump	Sump	Sump	Sump	Sump	Sump	Sump
Oil { Flash Point	...	...	500° F	250° F	620° F.	Price's motorine 420° F. C.	...
Oil { Viscosity	...	...	1130 secs. at 120° F	...	...	Price's motorine 175 at 140° F. C.	...
Consumption	500 m.p.g.	600 m.p.g.	1000 m.p.g.	2000 m.p.g.	...	2000 m.p.	600 to 1400 m.p.g.

better be appreciated by referring to Table xxviii., Appendix II., where it will be seen that about a gallon of oil for every 1000 miles run represents at present ordinary good practice.

CITY GUILDS TECHNOLOGICAL EXAMINATIONS, 1910

ORDINARY GRADE
Monday, 18th April, 7 to 10 p.m.
All Candidates must attempt Questions 1 and 2, and not more than five others

1. If you had an ordinary chassis, fitted with a 4-cylinder vertical engine under a bonnet and a bevel-driven live axle, to tune up for the road, how would you determine the following points:—

(a) Whether all the mechanically operated poppet valves are seating;

(b) Whether the sparking plugs or valve caps leak;

(c) Whether the porcelains of any of the sparking plugs are cracked;

(d) Whether the cooling water is circulating;

(e) Whether the clutch is slipping;

(f) Whether the engine is getting sufficient lubrication;

(g) Whether some evident loss of pulling power is due to the engine, or is due to friction in some other portion of the chassis.

Do not give remedies for above defects. (42 marks.)

2 Explain, with sketches, how the spark advance and retard are obtained in a 4-cylinder vertical engine—(a) with an ignition system consisting of accumulator and four trembler coils; (b) with some well-known high-tension magneto. Explain how, with each of the above systems of ignition, you would ascertain exactly when in the cycle of operations the spark takes place in each cylinder for any one position of the advance spark lever. Neglect the period of the vibration of the tremblers, &c. (42.)

3. State briefly all the advantages and disadvantages of two similar vertical engines of equal power, the one being a

4- and the other a 6-cylinder. Give a concise reason for each statement. (*42.*)

4. Describe, with sketches, any method with which you may be familiar for measuring the brake horse-power of a petrol engine. Assume certain figures as if you had obtained them experimentally, and show your calculations for obtaining the horse-power therefrom. (*48.*)

5. Sketch one of the well-known and extensively used carburettors, without the float chamber. Name the make, describe its action and any good features it may possess. (*42.*)

6. The gear-box of the chassis described in Question 1 gives a straight through or "direct drive "on the top gear, but has two pairs of spur wheels transmitting the drive on the first speed. Sketch the arrangement roughly, and determine the ratio of engine revolutions to road-wheel revolutions on the first speed when a spur wheel A on the clutch shaft drives a wheel B on the lay shaft, and C on the latter drives D on the foot-brake shaft. D transmits the power through the propeller shaft to the bevel pinion E, which drives the large bevel F on the back axle. The wheels A, B, C, D, E, and F have 24, 36, 18, 42, 14, and 55 teeth respectively. (*42.*)

7. If when recharging an ignition accumulator you cause the current to pass through an ammeter to the positive terminal, and through a second ammeter after it leaves the negative, will both these meters show the same current? If so, how does the accumulator become charged? In a four-volt accumulator the positive of one cell is connected or bridged to the negative of the other cell. If this bridge is brought to zero potential by being connected to the gaspipe or "earthed," state what the voltage of the other two terminals will be, regarding "earth" as zero. (*42*)

8. Sketch a good make of sparking plug, name the materials of which it is constructed, and state how it may become ineffective in working. (*42.*)

9. Sketch in detail any automatic device used on a steam car either for regulating the boiler water or the supply of fuel. (*42.*)

MOTORS AND MOTORING

HONOURS GRADE (PART I.)

Monday, 18th April, 7 to 10 p.m.
*All Candidates must attempt Questions 1 and 2, and not
more than five others*

1. If you had an ordinary chassis, fitted with a 4-cylinder
vertical engine under a bonnet and a bevel-driven live axle, to
tune up for the road, how would you determine the following
points:—

> (a) Whether all the mechanically operated poppet
> valves are seating;
> (b) Whether the sparking plugs or valve caps leak;
> (c) Whether the porcelains of any of the sparking
> plugs are cracked;
> (d) Whether the cooling water is circulating;
> (e) Whether the clutch is slipping;
> (f) Whether the engine is getting sufficient lubrication:
> (g) Whether some evident loss of pulling power is due
> to the engine, or is due to friction in some other
> portion of the chassis.

Do not give remedies for above defects. (42 marks.)

2. Consider each of the defects in Question 1, except (b),
(f), and the engine in (g), in turn, and give the likely causes for
these defects showing themselves after the chassis has once
been in order. *(42.)*

3. Suppose two samples of petrol have the same density
and calorific value, how would you proceed, without actually
using them for running an engine, to ascertain which is likely
to be more serviceable for motor work? *(42.)*

4. Describe, with sketches, the trough and sump system of
engine lubrication, with a pump for feeding the troughs. *(42.)*

5. In an ordinary 4-cylinder vertical engine the forces
belonging to the fundamental or first period vibration are
balanced. Explain the chief inertia forces which are not
balanced, and sketch diagrammatically a design of engine
which is practically free from this defect, giving sufficient
explanation to indicate just how the defect had been eliminated. *(42.)*

6. An epicyclic gear consists of a sun wheel A, with 24

232

teeth, meshing with a planet wheel B, with 16 teeth, and in which B meshes with a large internally toothed wheel C. Calculate the number of teeth in the wheel C. Assume C is held stationary, calculate how many revolutions the planet case or arm carrying the planet spindle will make while A is revolved once. (*42.*)

7. Suppose each cell of an ordinary 4-volt accumulator contains two positive and three negative plates, each 6 ins. by 4 ins. What charging current would you give it, and for how long? Make a diagram showing the wiring of this accumulator to the two side lamps and a tail lamp, each containing a 4-volt Osram lamp consuming one ampere and giving 4 candle power, and all controlled by one switch on the dashboard. How long ought this battery to be able to keep the lamps alight? (*42.*)

8. Sketch, in section, a high-tension magneto so as to show the relative positions of the various parts; name the make. Show in a diagram the internal connections to all the electrical portions of the magneto and the external connections to a 6-cylinder vertical engine to fire in a correct order. Number the cylinders and distributor and name the other parts. (*48.*)

9. Discuss the relative advantages and disadvantages of slide valves, piston valves, and poppet valves in steam-engines for motor road vehicles. (*42.*)

10. Describe, with sketches, the construction of the commutator of an electric motor. Why is the iron armature core built up with laminated plates? Illustrate, with a sketch, what would take place if a solid core were used. (*42.*)

Honours Grade

(Part II.—Drawing Examination.)

Tuesday, 19th April, 7 to 10 p.m.
One sheet of special drawing paper is supplied to each candidate.

Candidates may use ordinary drawing instruments, but sketches only, not scale drawings, are required. The dimensions of parts drawn should be judged by eye, and need not be inserted. Marks will be awarded for correct proportion.

Only three questions to be attempted.

1. Draw two views of a centrifugal water-circulating pump. *(50 marks.)*

2. Design and draw an ordinary exhaust valve cam to give a valve lift of 3/8 in., the distance of the highest portion of the cam to be 1 in. from the centre of the cam-shaft—the valve to commence lifting when the crank-pin is 40 degs. from the outward dead centre, and to close 5 degs. after the crank-pin has passed the inner dead centre. *(50.)*

3. Sketch the lines of some well-known car with four-seater body, with glass screen and cape-cart hood up, but without lamps. Name the make. The drawing should be about 8 ins long. *(35.)*

4. Draw an external foot-brake, preferably of the locomotive type, suitable for an ordinary live-axle car where the foot-brake is situated just behind the gear-box. *(50.)*

CITY GUILDS EXAMINATION (ORDINARY GRADE), 1911.

*Candidates must attempt Questions 1 and 2
and not more than five others.*

1. Show a complete wiring diagram for an ordinary four-cylinder vertical engine fitted with duplicate ignition (battery and H.T. magneto). If possible, use different coloured pencils or inks for wires carrying high and low tension currents. *(48 marks.)*

2. A single-cylinder car with the engine under the body has about 7 ft. of H.T. lead from the plug to the coil on the dash. If the insulation of this wire *gradually* perishes, what are the first symptoms you expect? Describe how, when these symptoms are observed, you would proceed to locate the fault exactly, and prove it to be due to a leak in the H.T. wire and nothing else. What other defects would give similar symptoms? *(42.)*

3. Given a new 4-volt ignition accumulator or lead secondary battery (without any printed instructions) to fill

with acid and charge for use, state what acid you would use, how you would dilute it, and to what density. If you find there are two negative plates and one positive plate, each measuring 5 ins. by 4 ins., in each cell, what charging current would you give, and for how long? (*42.*)

4. Sketch carefully a section of a well-designed cheap piston, showing rings, gudgeon, small end of connecting-rod and bush. Indicate with arrows the materials of which the parts are constructed. (*42.*)

5. A car fitted with live axle and two universal joints in the propeller drive has a torque rod 4 ft. long to prevent the axle-case from rotating; the car weighs 1 ton, and is climbing a hill of 1 in 7. Calculate the force (due to gradient only, neglecting road resistance, &c.) which the forward end of the torque rod exerts on its support. Tyres 810 by 90 (25'4 mm. = 1 in.), (*42.*)

Draw a modern locomotive type foot-brake suitable for the car described in question 5. Show method of adjustment and means for preventing rubbing and rattling. (*42.*)

7. Represent the motion of the crank-pin by a circle about 3 ins. diameter, and indicate the direction of rotation with an arrow. Mark on this circle, for an ordinary four-stroke cycle engine, the dead centres and the positions of the crank-pin when the inlet and exhaust valves should open and close, and when the magneto spark should occur for fully advanced and retarded ignition. Give the angle in degrees of each point from the nearest dead centre. (*42.*)

8. Carefully draw two curves indicating the relation between pressure and volume when the engine piston is on its compression stroke. One curve should show the rise in pressure when the engine is pulled over compression very slowly by hand (isothermal compression); the second curve should represent the result of sudden compression (adiabatic). Insert a few figures of pressures and volumes if possible. (*42.*)

Sketch two kinds of boilers in use on steam motor road vehicles. Give the working pressures and blow-off pressures and approximate diameters and lengths of boiler tubes in each case. Name a manufacturer of each type. (*42.*)

MOTORS AND MOTORING

Honours Grade (Part I.), 1911

*All candidates must attempt Questions 1 and 2 and
not more than five-others,*

1. Show diagrammatically all the electrical connections
for a duplicate ignition (battery and H.T. magneto), for a
four- cylinder horizontal engine. A plan of the engine should
be roughly represented to show the crank shaft and cylinders.
Nos. 1 and 3 should be on one side of the crank shaft, and Nos.
2 and 4 on the other. If possible, use different coloured pencils
or inks for wires carrying high and low tension currents. *(42
marks.)*

2. A single-cylinder car with the engine under the body
has about 7 ft. of H.T. lead from the plug to the coil on the
dash. If the insulation of this wire *gradually* perishes, what
are the first symptoms you expect? Describe how, when
these symptoms are observed, you would proceed to locate
the fault exactly, and prove it to be due to a leak in the H.T.
wire and nothing else. What other defects would give similar
symptoms? *(42.)*

3. What is the chief fault of a simple "jet-in-tube" carburettor used for motor-car work? Sketch diagrammatically
three carburettors (without float chambers) in common use,
with different devices for overcoming or correcting this fault.
One of these examples should have no moving parts sensitive
to the suction of the engine. *(42.)*

4. Calculate the B.H.P. actually developed by the engine
of a small racing car under the following conditions. The car
is climbing a gradient of 1 in 22 on its second speed (the third
being direct drive) at 40 miles per hour, against a head wind
of 20 miles per hour and a road resistance of 40 lbs. per ton.
Weight of car, 25 cwt. Wind resistance on whole car at 20
miles per hour on a calm day, 15 lbs. *(48.)*

5. Draw a typical full-load indicator diagram about 3
ins. long for a single-cylinder engine, 4-in. bore, 6-in. stroke,
running at 1000 revolutions. Assume whatever figures are
necessary as if you had obtained them by measurement, and
calculate the indicated horse-power. Explain, with assistance

of sketches, how you would obtain a torque diagram or crank effort curve therefrom. (*42.*)

6. Calculate *one* of the following:—

(*a*) A $\frac{1}{2}$ in. diameter sample test-piece cut from a $1\frac{1}{4}$-in. diameter round cardan shaft is found to break with a torque or twisting moment of 1000 lb. ins. Using the formula:—Breaking torque T = $\frac{\pi\,d^3\,f}{16}$ where f = the breaking shearing stress of the material in lbs. per square inch, what torque would cause the cardan shaft to fracture?

or,

(*b*) It is found by experiment that the sudden application of the brakes will bring a certain car (on which the brakes are not very good) to rest in 15 ft. when travelling at 10 miles per hour. Show, by numerical example, how you would proceed to deduce the probable stopping distance at some higher speed. (*42.*)

7. With the aid of clear sketches show the working of some system of mechanical lubrication suitable for a four- cylinder vertical engine in which an oil pump is used. (*42.*)

8. Show by a sketch how the reversing of some steam car with which you are amiliar is effected. Narae the make. (*42.*)

9. Describe briefly the battery you would use in an electric brougham or similar electric carriage, giving the total weight of battery, its output, the number of cells, and the size and number of plates in each cell. (*42.*)

HONOURS GRADE (PART II), 1911

(DRAWING EXAMINATION)

One sheet of special drawing paper is supplied to each candidate.

Candidates may use ordinary drawing instruments, but sketches only, not scale drawings, are required. The dimensions of parts drawn should be judged by eye, and need not be inserted. Marks will be awarded for correct proportion.

Only three questions to be attempted.

1. Draw the box, shafts, gears, operating mechanism and

bearings in position for an ordinary gate change three-speed box, giving a direct drive on the top. Shafts, 4-in. centres; scale, about half full size. *(50 marks.)*

2. Plot a curve showing the position of the piston for any angular position of the crank-pin, using the following scales:— Stroke of piston 3 ins., represented as ordinates, and positions of crank-pin, 6 ins. = 360°, as abscissae (horizontally), *(a)* For an infinitely long connecting-rod, *(b)* for a 6-in. connecting-rod. Plot both curves on the same diagram, *(c)* as a dotted line. *J 6-in. rod has been chosen to demonstrate the effect of a short connecting-rod on the motion of the piston. (50.)*

3. Draw a sectional view of a steering gear and box at the base of the column, showing methods of adjustment for wear. *(50.)*

4. Show, about half full size, a section taken right through one cylinder and base chamber of a four-cylinder vertical engine, 3-in. bore and 5-in. stroke, with opposite valves. *(35.)*

CITY GUILDS EXAMINATION

(GRADE I.), *April* 1914.

Not more than seven questions to be attempted.

1. On gradually opening the throttle of a carburettor the engine without load is observed to accelerate at first, with further opening to remain steady, then to slow down, almost stopping, and afterwards to accelerate rapidly and race. The carburettor is one of the jet-in-tube type fitted with a constant compensation jet, without extra air. What are the causes of the trouble, and how can the defects be remedied?

or,

It is noticed that an engine starts up quite readily, runs steadily under light load, but under full load fires rather irregularly and appears to be very sluggish generally. Assuming that the trouble is in the ignition, how would you proceed to locate the fault, and what part would you expect to find defective? *(48 marks.)*

2. Give your experience of fitting and tuning-up any carburettor of standard make, or of your own invention. *(42.)*

3. Describe with sketches a form of friction drive suitable to a small car. Point out the defects and advantages of the system. *(42.)*

4. What is horse-power? Describe some method of measuring horse-power which you have employed or seen employed, giving such hints and information as would assist a beginner. *(42.)*

5. Explain the need of lag and lead in the opening and closing of valves, and show why, and in what way, the valve setting for a touring-car engine should differ from that of an engine designed for racing. Give typical valve diagrams. *(42.)*

6. Make an arrangement sketch of a clutch, showing centering, springing, and declutching arrangements. Do not put in small details; simply indicate the main details. *(42.)*

7. A cylinder 80 m/m by 120 m/m stroke is found to have a compression space of 140 c. cms. How much material

must be removed from the valve covers in order to obtain a compression ratio of five to one? (*42.*)

8. Describe the advance and retard arrangements on any magneto with which you are acquainted and show what effect this arrangement has on the spark. (*42.*)

9. Describe the characteristics of a good plug. (42.)

(GRADE II.), *April* 1914.

Not more than seven questions to be attempted.

1. Upward movements of the price of petrol have brought forward other fuels. Name such fuels and discuss the relative advantages and disadvantages of each. (*42 marks.*)

2. In what way is the analysis of exhaust gas a guide to the character of the mixture delivered to an internal combustion engine?

The exhaust gas analyses of an engine running on petrol are, for different conditions, as follows :—

No.	Percentage of		
	CO_2	O.	CO.
1	10.0	4.0	0.0
2	8.0	0.0	10.0
3	14.0	0.2	0.2
4	10.0	4.0	5.0

What information as to general engine conditions is given by the figures above? (*42.*)

3. Describe briefly any good high speed indicator. Show how indicated horse-power may be obtained. To what extent is such an indicator reliable, and what information, other than that of horse-power, can be obtained by its means?

or,

Explain what is meant by the torque or crank effort diagram of an engine. Show how this may be obtained, and in what way it is modified by the inertia stresses in the reciprocating parts. (*45.*)

4. The following details relating to a car are given:—

Mean engine torque ... ... 80 lbs. ft.
Weight of car ... ... 30 cwt.
Wheel diameter ... ... 910 m/m.
Efficiency of transmission ... . 75 per cent.
Wind resistance ... ... negligible.
Road resistance ... ... 70 lbs. per ton.
Maximum gradient car can ascend . 1 to 4.

Find overall gearing ratio or ratio of engine revolutions to revolutions of road wheels to enable this gradient to be ascended. (45.)

5. With sketches, make clear the action of the differential on the back axle of a car, and show how this is fitted with the bevel drive in the back axle of a live axle car. (42.)

6. What are the essential features of a universal joint for use on the forward end of a propeller shaft? Sketch a good form of such joint. (42.)

7. What material would you specify for use in the following parts:—(1) gudgeon pin bush, (2) side members of frame, (3) crank shaft, (4) main and big end bearings, (5) gear wheel blanks, (6) spring shackle bolts, (7) brackets of intricate shape? (42.)

8. Account for the behaviour of a car on locking the front or rear wheels with the brakes. What precautions are taken to prevent uneven braking on two wheels, and how is the braking of a car affected by the practice of running one studded and one non-studded tyre on the braked wheels? (42.)

9. Describe, with sketches, the construction of a high-tension magneto. Also describe some form of automatic advance, and point out its advantages. (42.)

FINAL GRADE (PART I., WRITTEN), *April* 1914.

Candidates for the Final Examination must hold a certificate in Grade II.

Not more than seven questions to be attempted.

1. To what extent can a V engine be balanced? What is the best angle for the inclination of the cylinder axes to each other? Give your reasons fully. (42 marks.)

2. The relationship between the compression ratio and efficiency of an internal combustion engine is usually given as:—

$$\eta = 1 - (\tfrac{1}{r})^{\gamma - 1}$$

where η = thermal efficiency

r = compression ratio

$y = 1.4$.

Assuming this to be true, what efficiency can be expected with a 5 to 1 compression? How far does this differ from observed results? What explanation is given of this difference? (*42.*)

3. Explain the principle of the constant vacuum carburettor. In what way may the constancy of the mixture be disturbed (*a*) by conditions common to all such carburettors, (*b*) by conditions peculiar to separate types of such carburettors? Show by a sketch the construction of one of these carburettors. (*42.*)

4. How would you obtain the valve opening diagram of a poppet valve engine? What characteristics would be expected in the valve diagram of an engine when (*a*) power, or (*b*) silence was the first consideration? Given the reciprocating weight of valve parts and pressure of spring in maximum and minimum compression, show how to determine for a given speed whether or not the lifter will leave a cam of known contour, *or* give formula; connecting:—weight of reciprocating parts, speed of reciprocation, lift, duration of opening period, spring pressure, and weight of spring. (*48.*)

5. In a gear-box the ratio between top speed (direct) and bottom speed is 4.5 to 1. Arrange two intermediate speeds so that the torque changes are in approximate geometrical progression, taking into account the difference of efficiency of transmission on direct and indirect gears.

Take η (direct) = 85 per cent.

(indirect) = 75 per cent. (*42.*)

6. Indicate the chief types of torque rods and the relative advantages and disadvantages of each. (*42*).

7. What is the relationship between the safe weight of

a laminated carriage spring and the loading to which it is subjected? What effect on the riding of the carriage has friction between the plates of such spring? Describe means of suitably lubricating plates and shackle pins. Specify a spring to deflect 5 ins. under a load of 8 cwt. *(42.)*

8. Give the requirements of a good braking system on a car. What are the objections to the brake on the back of the gear-box? In the case of a 30 cwt. car fitted with such a brake, what will be the probable maximum braking torque in the propeller shaft? Back axle gear ratio 8 to 31. *(42.)*

9. Describe what is thought to take place in the compressed charge of an engine cylinder on ignition, and then show how the combustion may be modified by the character of the spark, type and position of spark plug, and number of firing points. *(42.)*

FINAL GRADE (PART II., DRAWING EXAMINATION), 1914.

One sheet of drawing paper ruled in $\frac{1}{8}$-in. squares is supplied to each candidate.

Candidates may use ordinary drawing instruments, but sketches only, not scale drawings, are required. The dimensions of parts drawn should be judged by eye, and need not be inserted. Marks will be awarded for correct proportion.

Only three questions to be attempted.

1. Draw full size a light cast-iron piston for a cylinder 96 m/m bore by 140 m/m stroke, to run up to 2000 R.P.M. at full load. Indicate clearances of piston in cylinder. *(50 marks.)*

2. Draw half size the forward end anchorage for a combined torque and radius rod in the form of a tube containing the propeller shaft.

Engine Details.

Cylinders	.	.	.	.	.4
Bore	.	.	.	.	.4 ins.
Stroke	.	.	.	.	.6 ins.
Total weight of vehicle	.	.	.	..2 tons	(50.)

3. Draw half size an internal rear wheel brake for a vehicle weighing 2 tons laden. *(50.)*

4. Draw full size a water feed pump and connection suitable to a 30 h.p. steam car. *(50.)*

BRIEF NOTES ON THE TREND OF DESIGN, AS EXEMPLIFIED BY CURRENT PRACTICE.

SIZE OF CARS.

The steady and considerable increase in the number of manufacturers who specialise in cars of moderate power, not far removed from 15 horse-power nominal, is a welcome sign that makers are more alive to the profits which are to be made by providing for the requirements of men of modest means than they have been in the past. Indeed, when the "hundred pound "vehicle appears, a new era of prosperity will dawn. But of course the two most potent factors in bringing down the cost of production are standardisation and a very large annual output of one type and size. In this connection it is interesting to note that one firm alone in the United States turned out 308,213 between August 1914 and July 1915, and claims that it will soon be able to produce 4000 in one day.

ENGINES AND OTHER CHASSIS PARTS.

With the increase in the number of engines of comparatively small bore, there has been a marked increase in the ratio of stroke to diameter in engines up to 100 mm.; indeed, this ratio has in some cases almost reached 2 to 1. The use of chains for driving the cam shafts is steadily increasing.

Cylinders.—The question as to whether the cylinders should be cast separately, in pairs, or *en bloc* is a vexed one, but there is a notable increase in the number of makers adopting the monobloc type (all cylinders in one casting), and this has even been done with six cylinders in two small cars. On the other hand, the Austin car appears to be the only British one in which the four cylinders are cast separately.

Valves.—No part of the car machinery has received more attention in recent practice than the valve gear. Marked improvements all round have been made in the poppet valve arrangements, giving cams of more perfect form, with delicate adjustments of the tappets to secure constant contact. The valves are now generally arranged all on one side of the engine, enclosed by readily removable lids or covers; and the cam shafts (in most cases chain-driven) have in many cases been increased in size to give them increased rigidity.

The success of the Knight (Daimlers) double sleeve valve has led to the introduction of several variations of its type, which have yet to prove their efficiency and durability.

Pistons and Connecting-Rods.—Cast-iron pistons are still used in the majority of British engines, but a few Continental makers favour steel pistons, owing to their lighter weight; the disadvantage of these is the possibility of lubrication troubles.

As, other things being the same, the lighter the weight of the piston and connecting-rod the higher the speed at which the engine can be run, some designers have, by using a higher-grade steel for the connecting-rods and a slightly reduced and better section, appreciably decreased the weight of the rods.

Crankshafts.—To give greater stiffness and to provide for the greater torque due to the higher powers per unit of area of the cylinder which the increased stroke (and in some cases also increased compression) has made possible, a general increase in the size of crank-shafts of the smaller engines has been made. In other cases troubles in the heat treatment of alloy steels have led designers to increase the size of the crank-shaft by $\frac{1}{8}$-in. or more, and to use instead a high-grade carbon steel: this has the additional advantage in most cases of giving increased rigidity, as, other things being the same, the torsional stiffness of a shaft is proportional to the fourth power of its diameter.

Carburettors.—In past years probably no feature of the engine has received more attention from inventors than the carburettor, and although the problem of producing a mixture to economically work the engine to any speed within its range—no matter how the condition of the air may vary due to temperature, humidity, or atmospheric pressure—has been tackled by so many, and the instruments produced by these designers have differed so much in form and arrangement, the wonder is so many of them, widely differing in construction, give such good results. This year there was apparently no novelty about these instruments themselves, many of which could be improved in detail by making the jet or jets more accessible for cleaning purposes, but the problem of reducing the noise made at the air inlet has received a lot of attention, and among the expedients employed should be mentioned— drawing the air through the crank chamber, or through the casings of the poppet valves, and the use of small silencers at the inlets. There is probably some additional advantage in causing the air to flow through the crank chamber in the case of sleeve-valve engines, as it takes with it a slight charge of oil spray, and this assists in lubricating the valves. Formerly it was the fashion for most manufacturers to use carburettors of their own design, but it is now better realised that there are firms specialising in these important instruments who have succeeded in reaching a high pitch of perfection, and not a few manufacturers have this year discarded their own make, and are using such well- known instruments as the Claudet-Hobson, the White and Poppe, or the Polyrhoé multiple jet sort.

Cooling Systems.—The growing tendency to abandon the system of forced or pump circulation in favour of the more simple thermo-syphon system was forcibly brought to light at the Show, there being 72 per cent, of the cars exhibited fitted with the latter system to 28 per cent, fitted with the former system. In years gone by many manufacturers who tried the thermo-syphon did so with pipes that were too small and bends that were too abrupt to allow the small difference in the weights of the rising and falling columns of water to cause a free circulation, with the result that trouble from overheating ensued, but, profiting by experience, the details of this system on most cars leaves little to be desired. It is true that more weight has to be carried when this system is used, but the absence of those worrying troubles which are inherent to forced circulation compensates for this.

Ignition.—The steady improvement of this most vital part of the engine system continues. There is a marked decrease in the number of engines fitted with magnetos giving fixed ignition; either automatic advanced ignition or variable ignition prevailing. The trend of magneto design is apparently in the direction of modifying the machine to enable it to give a spark of approximately equal intensity at all speeds. The dual or accumulator attachment for starting (which is a compromise between the two separate ignition systems the largest engines are usually fitted with) is now used on the majority of engines of moderate size. The low-tension magneto, which was so much used a few years ago, may now be considered obsolete; although it had, when skilfully arranged, much to recommend it. There is a tendency to abandon the skew gear or spur gear drive for the magneto in favour of the silent chain drive, but this necessitates the exercise of a good deal of ingenuity on the part of the designer, if provision is to be made for accurately setting the timing.

Engine Lubrication.—No marked departure from recent practice was noticeable—pump and splash or the trough or splash lubrication, in which a force pump or a gear pump fills with oil small troughs or channels under the big ends, the latter having small projections to pick up oil from the troughs to lubricate the rest of the engines by splash, being the prevalent form; indeed, it was represented on 56 per cent. of the cars. In the most complete form of this system the main bearings of the engines are fed individually by the pump, the latter also keeping the troughs overflowing with oil. An increased number of engines were so fitted. Doubtless the extra cost of the more perfect system, namely, forced lubrication, as used in its most complete form on the Rolls-Royce and other high-grade cars, stands in the way of its more extended use, but, notwithstanding the expense involved, about 40 per cent. of the cars were fitted with this system.

Ball and Roller Bearings.—Recent cars go to show that it may now be considered standard practice for the chassis of all high-class cars to be fitted with bearings of the ball or roller type for all important journals, with the exception of those of the crank shaft. It is true that some few makers run these shafts in ball bearings, but they are quite the exception, and the departure is not being followed; the standard practice for crank shafts being plain bearings, the phosphor-bronze ends being lined with white metal. Both ball and roller bearings are only satisfactory when skilfully designed and constructed and when made of materials of the highest quality. Conical roller bearings, which are now coming somewhat extensively into use for the road wheels, steering boxes, and steering pivots, are capable of taking both the journal load and end thrust, and they can be easily adjusted for wear, but with ball bearings there is no provision for adjustment, and separate rows of balls should always be used to take the thrust (as the cup and ball type cannot be considered satisfactory); thus for such bearings as the road wheels, or the bevel pinion ones, compound bearings are used. But a feature of some of this year's cars is a combination of rollers to take the journal load and ball thrusts to take the end pressure. The ball bearings on cars a few years ago were often very unsatisfactory; for instance, the author found that in a car of one of the most famous Continental makes no provision for end thrust at the bevel pinion was made, with the result that the bevel gear gave endless trouble.

There are a few very famous makers of ball and roller bearings with wide experience, and they supply the bearings to the car manufacturers, who are wise enough not to make these specialities themselves.

Brakes.—As the brakes should be counted among the most vital parts of the chassis, anything which tends to increase their efficiency, reliability, and durability is of great importance. Front wheel brakes made their first appearance at the 1909 show; the following year several well-known cars were fitted with them, but the current cars show that they are falling out of favour, and it is well that this is so, for although when used the whole weight of the vehicle is available to cause resistance at the tread of the road wheels, and when the front brakes only are used there is little tendency to side-slip, there is the outstanding defect that, so soon as the front wheels are gripped tight enough to prevent rotation, they lose their steering power. These points may be quite easily studied by manipulating a toy car on a tilted smooth board. Other things being the same, the durability of a brake (not its power) depends on the width of the rubbing surfaces, and there is a welcome tendency noticeable to increase these widths, thereby increasing the length of time a brake will run before adjustment is required or the shoes require renewing. The drums of the internal type of driving (or propeller) shaft brakes are now invariably made with cooling fins, as these brakes are much more often used than the road wheel brakes; and, rotating at a higher speed than the latter, much heat is generated when they are applied for any length of time, and this sometimes causes them to seize. Of course this may happen with external brakes, but the latter are more easily and more safely cooled by the application of water than internal ones are; so on the whole they are to be preferred. Owing to the higher speed at which the driving-shaft brake runs, much injury can be done to the mechanism between this brake and the road wheels by Brutal or unskilful manipulation, and doubtless this is the reason why there is an increase in the number of firms who are concentrating all the brakes on the rear driving wheels; but as the drums of these brakes are slower moving ones, the presence of oil or grease between the rubbing surfaces causes a greater falling off in their holding power, hence the necessity in such cases to take greater precautions to prevent leakage of the lubricant from the casing of the back axle.

There are still some makers using wire rope for connecting up the brakes to lever or pedal; such ropes always have an abundance of strength when new, but they are liable to become very unreliable owing to internal corrosion, and I should, for such vital parts, welcome their disappearance from motor - car practice.

Clutches.—Clutches of the metal plate type were fitted to about 12 per cent, of the cars exhibited, and the multiple disc type was represented by about 16 per cent. These clutches, when well designed and efficiently lubricated, answer very well, and they are smaller in diameter and lighter than the ordinary cone clutch, even for large powers, which is an advantage for easy gear changing; but they are somewhat more expensive, and if the oil is allowed to become viscous, the declutching becomes sluggish; further, they are not so readily taken apart for cleaning or repairs. So, therefore, it is not astonishing to find that the majority of makers (some 64 per cent.) still pin their faith to the leather- faced clutch, which, when properly designed to take up the thrust of the spring and for the work it has to do, and is fitted with a friction pad for reducing its speed when declutching occurs for *changing up* the gear, is extremely reliable, rarely giving trouble, and it is easily repaired.

Gears.—A conspicuous feature of recent cars of moderate power is the increase in the number fitted with four speeds. Formerly, strangely enough, it was, as a rule, only high-power cars that were so fitted, but, obviously, the luxury of a fourth speed is more needed on the smaller car. With the object of making the gear teeth stronger and less likely to be damaged by unskilful gear changing, several makers during the past year or two have been increasing the pitch of their gears. At first it was thought that this might somewhat increase the noise due to their running, but there is no apparent increase, and the lead thus given is being freely followed. Of course, the increase of pitch only leads to increased durability when the breadth of the teeth is also increased, and some increase in this dimension could well be made with advantage in some cases without appreciably lengthening the gear case, Further, a reduction in the length of the teeth would probably give a quieter gear without any appreciable disadvantage.[1]

For some time now certain motor buses have been running beautifully with chain change-speed gears, and the Maudslay car in the recent show was conspicuous by having its gear-box fitted in this way. Contrary to what might be expected, this departure has not led to any apparent increase in the size of the gear-box. There is no question about the smoothness of running of these gears, and there can be little doubt that, if experience shows the factor of durability to be all right, this example will be widely followed, as designers are rightly doing all in their power to produce silent vehicles.

[1] Refer to author's book on "Machine Design," &c., page 301.

TREND OF DESIGN

It is now quite the exception to find the gear-box of a new machine of any importance not fitted with ball bearings.

Notwithstanding the cost of production, a few makers are still turning out cars with epicyclic gears; of course, the best known example of this type is the Lanchester.

Self-Starters.—For many years designers have been endeavouring to produce some efficient means of starting the engine without having to use the starting handle, which every owner who drives his own car cannot but regard as a bit of drudgery. Hitherto the attempts have not materialised into anything very practicable, and no car has been marketed with such an arrangement, but during the past year two quite novel forms of self-starters have been brought forward, namely, the Cadillac and the Cowey, the former making its first appearance in Europe at the Motor Show of the 1912 cars. The vehicle in question is the 10-30 horse-power four-cylinder car, fitted with the electrical self-starting apparatus as a standard, the starting handle being wholly superseded. The car is equipped with a dynamo which fulfils a threefold purpose, namely, furnishing current for the electric-starting device, current for firing the explosive mixture in the cylinders, also for lighting the car by electricity. The dynamo has an 80-ampere hour battery, and the electrical apparatus of the car is supplemented by the well-known Delco distributor ignition system, with dry cell current. The dynamo is temporarily and automatically transformed into a motor for starting the engine, the current to operate it as a motor being furnished by the storage battery. The driver on taking his seat in the car retards the spark lever and depresses the clutch pedal, thereby automatically engaging a gear of the electric motor with teeth in the fly-wheel of the engine, causing the crank-shaft to turn, and as soon as the charges of mixture commence to explode and the engine rotates by its own power, the driver releases the pressure on the clutch pedal, when the electric motor gear disengages its connection with the fly-wheel and the car is ready to be driven. Then the electric motor again becomes a dynamo or generator, and its energy is used in firing the mixture in the cylinders and in charging automatically ceasing as soon as the full capacity is reached.

The makers claim that the battery's capacity is sufficient to work the starting device and run the engine under full compression as long as twenty minutes, although of course it does not often require to do so longer than a few seconds to perform its ordinary functions.

There can be little doubt that the time is not far distant when mechanical starting will be a feature of every car. Indeed, we have already among the favourably known systems the Adams, S.C.A.T., Sunbeam, Wolseley, and Cantano.

Steering Gears.—No part of the chassis of any car requires more constant attention to keep it in good working order than the steering gear. No part should receive more careful attention in the drawing office and shops than this vital part to secure a simple, reliable, durable, and efficient means of steering the vehicle. On cars where the coned spindle of the swivelling end of the front axle (or its equivalent) are arranged with ball or roller bearings, and the screw or worm is also fitted with ball thrusts—the pin joints of the steering rod and arm being of generous proportions— and all the joints and bearings being well protected, and lubricated at short intervals, the operation of steering is a pleasure, and the car can be run thousands of miles without any appreciable wear. On the other hand, where these conditions are not satisfied, the steering wheel will soon work stiffly, and with back-lash, and the joints of the steering rod and arm become so worn as to cause the front wheels to appreciably wobble: this of course rapidly increases and sets up a grinding action between the tread of the wheels and the road, which rapidly wears the tyres; at the same time these parts become noisy, and they set up a good deal of vibration.

Many of the cars of this year show a welcome improvement in the size of the various joints and in other details, but steering gears generally might with much advantage receive a good deal more attention in the drawing office; indeed, the present types can hardly be regarded as the best possible or as incapable of further improvement.

TREND OF DESIGN

Universal Joints.—In recent years much improvement has been made in the Hooke or Cardan joints, or the variations of them used between the clutch and gear-box and in the propeller shaft; to give these parts the necessary flexibility, indeed a good deal of ingenuity has been displayed in their design, and care is taken to fit them with suitable grease pots for efficient lubrication and covers for their protection from dust and mud. When these pre- cautions are not taken the wear soon becomes very pronounced, with objectionable back-lash and noise.

Such high-speed parts require careful balancing, particularly when fitted with projecting lubricators, otherwise the vibration set up becomes very pronounced; annoying and destructive, these points in some cases have not received the attention they deserve.

Wheels.—Detachable wheels have come into use to such an extent that they may almost now be regarded as standard practice. Most firms now deliver the chassis with five wheels and five tyres. The Artillery or wooden wheel is rapidly giving place to the stronger and more reliable wire wheel; indeed, in cases where front-wheel brakes are used, they become almost a necessity to allow of the steering pivot being placed in a large specially formed hub, so that the pivot axis may be in the centre plane of the wheel.

Worm Drive.—The back-axle drive by worm gearing (first used in the Lanchester car), in place of the well-tried bevel type, has been adopted by one after another manufacturer, and at the Show over 30 per cent, of the British cars were fitted with this noiseless and smooth drive; in fact this departure, from what had become standard practice, was one of the outstanding features of the exhibition. In years gone by the worm gear was considered a very inefficient one, but with the threads of the worm and the teeth of the wheel accurately cut and the highly finished rubbing surfaces practically running in an oil-bath, the considerable thrusts being taken on high-grade ball-bearings, the gear has become one of the most efficient for the purpose of transmitting power through a right angle known to the engineer. Worm gears reach their highest efficiency when the angle of the thread of the worm is inclined at 45° to the axis of the worm wheel, and, according to Mr. Lanchester, the underhung worm gives a slightly increased efficiency over the overhead worm as the power transmitted increases. At first it was assumed that the latter arrangement could not be so completely lubricated, but experience has shown that the wheel lifts up sufficient lubricant from the bottom of the casing for the purpose. A point of some importance is that with the underhung and more popular arrangement the ground clearance is small; further, the engine must be raked; on the other hand, the overhead worm brings the propeller shaft and the top of the worm casing somewhat too high for convenience in fitting the body.

When it is considered that with worm drives we have only *point-contact* between the worm and the wheel (analogous to the contact between a ball and its race), whilst in the bevel drive we have *line-contact* between pinion and wheel (analogous to the contact between a roller and its race), the durability of the high-class worm drive is very remarkable, and it can be understood that, until this was established, makers were very chary of adopting it; but doubtless the successful use of this gear for such heavy vehicles as motor buses has greatly accelerated its general adoption. But it should not be overlooked that when the wear becomes pronounced or the lubrication fails, the falling off in efficiency is very rapid.

Magneto *v.* American Coil Ignition.

The large number of cars we are importing from the United States has caused much attention to be given to the American practice of combined electric starting, ignition and lighting. In the past the main difficulty of the coil and accumulator system of ignition was the trouble of keeping the electrical storage cells charged, but with the new arrangement this does not exist, as each car is fitted with a small dynamo that creates electrical power for lighting and starting up the engine and whose energy is passed into the battery of accumulators which forms part of the electrical outfit (as explained in the article on Self-Starters). In the ordinary running of the car this dynamo is constantly charging the cells, thus they keep in better condition, and are always in a fit state for their duties. The rapid way in which this system is being developed naturally raises the vexed question as to whether the magneto is doomed, but its wonderful reliability as it is at present made in the best practice is perhaps the strongest argument in favour of its retention, and it certainly will not be easily dislodged, but the new system seems particularly well adapted to the comparatively low efficiency and speed of the American engines, as the battery system gives a better spark at low speeds, which makes starting easy and improves the running at slow speeds, with automatic advance. At first sight, the wiring of the battery system appears to be somewhat complicated, if all the lighting and starting wires are included, but the actual ignition system differs very little in wiring from the dual magneto system, and we may certainly expect that, as the American system is developed and improved, such details and arrangements as experience proves to be liable to give trouble will be perfected. On the other hand, no doubt the magneto will be used for years to come in high-priced, high-speed, high-efficiency engines, as it gives a more powerful spark at high speeds.

THE LIGHT CAR.

Since the early part of the year 1914 there has been a great development of the light car, a neatly-built two- or three-seater fitted with a four-cylinder engine of from 8 to 10 h.p.; and a large number of different makes are now on the market ranging in price from about 150 to 250 guineas. It is true that the war requirements have greatly interfered with the production of these handy little vehicles, but there can be little doubt that, as so many people will have to economise after the war, there will be a great demand for them in the time to come. Fortunately, there will then be an enormous number of machine tools suitable for their production available, and it is to be hoped that a strenuous effort will be made to meet our requirements and to stop the dumping of foreign made vehicles on our markets.

INDEX

INDEX

INDEX

INDEX

MOTORS AND MOTORING